HILL STATIONS

OF

INDIA

Gillian Wright is an ardent Indophile who has spent more than a decade in India working for radio and television especially for the BBC. She has a first class degree in Indian languages from London University and has contributed to a number of books on Indian wildlife, history and politics. She is the author of *The Odyssey Illustrated Guide to Sri Lanka* (1993), *Sri Lanka, Our World in Colour* (1998) and has translated two novels from Hindi into English for Penguin Books. She has travelled extensively in the mountain ranges of the subcontinent to collect material for this first ever guide to the hill stations of India.

HILL STATIONS

OF

INDIA

Gillian Wright
Photography by Sarah Lock

Local Colour

A CIP catalogue record for this is available from the British Library

ISBN 962–217–299–7

Editors: Madhulita Mohapatra and Sheela Jhaveri

Map Artwork: Bai Yiliang

Design: Gulmohur Press Pvt. Ltd.

Photography by Sarah Lock. Additional photography: Jyoti Banerjee/R. Fotomedia 98 (above right and below); Pallav Bagla 106 (below); Sujoy Das/R. Fotomedia 79 (above) 122, 126; Ashok Dilwali 3, 32, 51, 59, 66, 67, 79 (below), 82-3, 87, 135, 135, 145, 183, Nigel Hicks 114, Nazima and Earl Kowall 8, 45, 48, 55, 157, 161, 169, 173; Paul Lewis 107, 164; Aditya Patanker 238; Philip's Antiques, Mumbai 40; Toby Sinclair 6, 10, 13, 41, 57, 73, 90, 91, 95, 99 (below), 119, 142; Joanna Van Gruisen 223.
Front cover: Fredrik Arvidsson.
Back cover: Aditya Patanker (top); Ashok Dilwali (bottom).
Printed and bound in Hong Kong

View towards Mount Nanda Kot between Almora and Geshwar

Contents

Christchurch, Shimla

Fernhill Palace Hotel, Ooty, formerly the summer residence of the Maharajah of Mysore

Advertisement for the Rugby Hotel, Matheran

Literary Excerpts

Special Topics

Maps

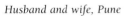

Husband and wife, Pune

Leh in the Zanskar mountains, Ladakh

Moustached gentleman, Kullu

Introduction

In the northern quarter is divine Himalaya,
the lord of the mountains,
reaching from Eastern to Western Ocean,
firm as a rod to measure the earth...

There demigods rest in the shade of the clouds,
which spread like a girdle below the peaks,
but when the rains disturb them
they fly to the sunlit summits....

Kalidas, fifth century AD

For thousands of years Hindus have looked on the Himalayas with wonder and reverence. They are the abode of the gods. There Shiva, the great god of destruction, sat deep in meditation until Parvati, the daughter of the mountains, succeeded in winning his love. Temples to Shiva and Parvati stand high in the mountains and tens of thousands of pilgrims make the arduous ascent to them each year, returning to the plains enriched by religious experience. In the words of the *Skanda Purana*, 'As the sun dries the morning dew, so are the sins of man dissipated at the sight of the Himalayas.'

Centuries of pilgrimage produced temples and hermitages, but no hill stations. The population in the plains had learned to live with the hot weather, and didn't need to escape from it. For most of the year the mountains were left alone to the hill peoples and nomadic herdsmen.

The credit for the invention of the hill station as a summer retreat should be given, not to the British, but to the Mughal emperors. Three of the Great Mughals — Akbar, Jahangir and Shah Jahan — were entranced by Kashmir. Kashmir was on the borders of the empire and strategically important; so it was also sound commonsense to establish a base there. The emperors constructed formal terraced gardens with waterfalls and fountains against the spectacular setting of the Himalayas. It was a landscape which brought out the more poetic side of their characters. Emperor Jahangir, who was quite capable of having his enemies sewn up in asses' skins, wrote:

Kashmir is a garden of eternal spring.... There are running
streams and fountains beyond count. Wherever the eye
reaches, there are verdure and running water. The red rose,
the violet and the narcissus grow of themselves; in the fields
there are all kinds of flowers and all sorts of sweet-scented
herbs — more than can be calculated. In the soul-enchanting
spring, the hills and the plains are filled with blossom;
the gates, the walls, the courts, the roofs are lighted up by the
torches of banquet-adorning tulips.

By the beginning of the 18th century the Mughal Empire was in decline
and the British began to take over more and more Indian territory. They
were unlike any rulers India had ever seen. Many dynasties had come
from outside, but they had all been absorbed into Indian society. The
British, however, were determined to remain British. They did not settle
in India and, to start with at least, obstinately refused to behave in any
way suitable to the climate. They continued to wear tight woollen
jackets and flannel underwear, and their eating habits became even
more excessive than they would have been at home. Huge meals
washed down with quantities of Madeira ensured that many did not live
to see more than the proverbial 'two monsoons'.

The first settlements of the East India Company were at the main
ports of Surat, Bombay (now called Mumbai), Calcutta and Madras. But
whether they lived on the coast or in the later acquired territory inland,
there was one enemy the new rulers of India could not defeat — the
climate. Typhoid, cholera and malaria killed thousands of Britons while
others were debilitated by tropical fatigue. One of the main problems
faced by the British was how to keep the army healthy. In the 1830s
there were 41,000 Europeans in India, 37,000 of them soldiers. By
1859, two years after the Mutiny or First War of Independence, there
were 126,000 Europeans in India, including 85,000 troops. In fact, it
was the soldiers garrisoned in the hill forts who proved that the hills
could be ideal sanatoria for ailing British who could not afford to go
home. During the cholera epidemics of 1817-19, it was noted that they
'remained exempt in a remarkable way and the removal of troops from
an infected district to an elevated station was followed by a speedy
disappearance of the disease from among them.'

British-built bungalows, bearing such names as Dingly Dell *and* Woodlands, *are still inhabited*

Once it was established that the hills were healthier, enterprising officials set off in search of sanatoria. The first hill station house in the first hill station was built by an assistant political officer, Lieutenant Boss, in Shimla (then spelt Simla) in 1819. It was 'a mere cottage of wood and thatch' and Shimla 'a middlingsized village where a faquir is situated to give water to travellers'. Ross's house was the very first step in a revolution in the Anglo-Indian way of life. His mud cottage was soon followed by the first permanent hill station residence, belonging to the hospitable Captain Kennedy. During the next few decades over 80 hill stations were established at altitudes of between 1,230 and 2,460 metres (4,035-8,071 feet). Their construction demonstrated British confidence in their own supreme power. The stations were built on open hilltops, symbolising perhaps the British view of themselves. The expenses of building mountain roads and railways did not deter them because they had vast resources and could rely on local labour and assistance. On the rare occasions this was denied it threatened the very establishment of the hill station.

Such was the case with Darjeeling, which lies in the Himalayas north of Calcutta. The Darjeeling tract had been granted to the British by the Raja of Sikkim in 1836. Lieutenant Colonel G W A Lloyd, in charge of the new hill station, complained that

> there has been a great backwardness on the part of the Lepcha population in the neighbourhood to assist us in any way, and they have uniformly asserted that they were afraid of being punished by the Raja if they did. I have twice requested the Raja to make known to his subjects that they had his permission to work for ... us if they chose.... He has always evaded compliance with my requests.

The failure of the authorities to enlist Indian co-operation led to these irate words in the editorial of the *Hurkuru* newspaper at the beginning of what was meant to be Darjeeling's first season:

> We have distressing accounts from Darjeeling where everything is at a standstill for want of food which is abundant in the plains, but coolies cannot be obtained for love or money to carry it up to the hills. This really is too bad! After all the fine promises of Government which induced individuals to take grants and build houses — which induced the public to

come forward and subscribe a large sum to build a hotel to
find that they have been either deceived or at least neglected
by the Government who induced them ... to come
forward.... Without road to or food at Darjeeling, or coolies
procurable to carry it up from the plains, what is to become of
the 'Bright Spot' which otherwise would be the earthly
paradise to invalids in the hot season?

As the *Hurkuru* put it, Darjeeling was in danger of becoming 'a wreck
in sight of port'. However, the doggedness of the authorities finally
succeeded in snatching success from the jaws of failure.

The new hill settlements began as sanatoria but soon turned into
imitations of that great 19th-century institution, the British resort. They
were compared with Scarborough, Brighton and even the Isle of Wight.
Ootacamund in southern India, like Bath in England, was referred to as
a 'watering place' and had 'Assembly Rooms'. Shimla was later referred
to as 'a watering place gone mad'!

The British resort wasn't just a place to 'take the air' and 'the water'
for health, it was also a very social and often socially elite place. This
was even more true of India, because some hill stations became centres
of government for six months of the year. The Bombay administration
shifted to Pune and Mahabaleshwar, the United Provinces to Nainital.
The Viceroys moved with pomp not to nearby Darjeeling but halfway
across the subcontinent to the most elite of summer homes, Shimla. As
the geographer Spate put it, 'There can be few places in the world
where the upper ten was so literally upper; the Viceroy and the
Commander-in-Chief had naturally the best peaks.'

The British brought with them another European characteristic — the
appreciation of the picturesque. Beautiful landscapes inspired them,
particularly mountain landscapes such as they could never see at home.
When James Tod, the chronicler of Rajasthan, laid eyes on 'the bluff
head of Mount Abu' in 1822 he wrote, 'My heart beat with joy as, with
the Sage of Syracuse, I exclaimed, Eureka.'

Major General E F Burton wrote with almost religious fervour about
modern India's highest mountain, Kanchenjunga:

The great valley living north of Darjeeling was still occupied by
floating, changing cloud masses; and I pitched my eye enough,

as I thought, to see the wished for peaks beyond, when a rift
in the clouds should give the opportunity, at last I happened to
look up very much higher, and, with a feeling of awe and
astonishment, I then saw a dazzling snow peak rise, vast and
majestic, above the mantling clouds, where I should never
have thought of looking of anything of human mould.

This love of the picturesque helped make even the most arduous ascent
to the hills bearable and in the early days these journeys could be
extremely difficult. The indefatigable traveller Fanny Parks described her
climb to Mussoorie in her diary of 1838:

I was to be carried up in a jampan. A jampan is an
armchair, with a top to it, to shelter you from the sun or rain;
four long poles are affixed to it. My two women went up in
dolis, a sort of tray for women, in which one person can sit
native fashion... The different views delighted me; on the
side or the Hills facing Rajpur the trees were stunted, and
there was but little vegetation; on the other side, the northern,
we came upon fine oak and rhododendron trees — such
beautiful rhododendrons! They are forest trees, not shrubs, as
you have them in England. The people gathered the wild
flowers, and filled my lap with them. The jangal pear, in full
blossom, the raspberry bushes and the nettles delighted me; I
could not help sending a man from the plains, who had never
seen a nettle, to gather one; he took hold of it, and,
relinquishing his hold instantly in excessive surprise,
exclaimed, 'It has stung me; It is a scorpion plant'.

The new inhabitants took great delight in the Englishness of the colder
climate, even in the middle of the monsoon when houses leaked and
roads were buried by landslides. Fanny Parks remarked that Mussoorie
was 'just as wet, windy and wretched as England'. Lady Betty Balfour
described a similar season in Ootacamund in 1877, 'The afternoon was
rainy and the road muddy, but such beautiful English rain, such
delicious English mud. Imagine Hertfordshire lanes, Devonshire downs,
Westmorland lakes, Scotch trout streams and Lusitanian views.' Emily
Eden, the quietly humorous sister of the Viceroy, Lord Auckland,
summed it up another way. 'Like meat,' she wrote, 'we keep better here.'
There was a studied attempt to make hill station architecture as English

The High Range Club, Munnar

as the weather. The typical hill station house was constructed in its own compound to make the most of the views in a half-timbered style described most graphically as 'wild west Swiss'. The houses were given such names as Glenthorn, Langdale, Rose Bank and Strawberry Cottage; the hotels were called The Savoy, The Waldorf, The Metropole and The Cecil. The gardens were full of British annuals and shrubs, even if the Indian environment did make some grow to sizes unheard of in England. R Baikie, in his book on the Nilgiris, published in 1857, records that 'one heliotrope in Mr Dawson's garden is 10 feet high and 30 feet in circumference, and a verbena attaining the height of 20 feet, with the branches of a tree.' Setting up house in the early days required a great deal of improvisation. Emily Eden discovered this when she was furnishing the governor-general's residence in Shimla in 1838. In her new house, full of carpenters making curtain rods and rings, she remarked, 'We did not bring half chintz enough from Calcutta, and Simla grows rhododendrons, and pines, and violets, but nothing else — no damask, no glazed cotton for lining — nothing.'

Indian merchants were, however, quick to take advantage of new opportunities in the hills. In the very same year Fanny Parks saw a bazaar at Landour which offered pâté de foie gras, *becasses truffles*, shola hats covered with skin of pelican, champagne, *bareilly couches*, shoes, Chinese books, pickles, long poles for climbing in the mountains, and various incongruous items.

Despite the best efforts of the British, they could not entirely succeed in making a little England of India. An Indianness pervaded even the hill stations. The jungles surrounding them were Indian, and full of dangers alien to English woodlands· 'Taking the air' on the narrow and slippery mountain roads, you not only risked tumbling to your death over the 'cud', as Fanny Parks recorded:

> Mrs M was riding this evening when a leopard seized her
> spaniel, which was not many yards in front of her pony;
> the shouts of the party alarmed the animal and it let the dog drop;
> however, the poor spaniel died of its wounds. Some officers
> laid wait for the leopard, and shot it; I saw it, coming up the
> Hill, fastened on a bamboo, to be stuffed and prepared with
> arsenical soap.

For the huntsman, the hill jungles provided good sport. The technique of hunting to hounds in India was developed in Ootacamund, or Ooty. It still has a fine pack of foxhounds attached to the Ooty Club where the game of snooker was invented. The quarry, however, is jackal, not fox. Today hunts are conducted on horseback, though in the 1830s the hunting was on foot. The participants concealed themselves on the edge of a wood.

> When the sportsmen have taken up their positions, the master
> of the chase sounds his horn, and every dog rushes into the
> wood ... nothing is heard for a few minutes but the dog-boys
> cheering the pack; some hound then strikes upon the scent or
> catches a view, and then begins the stimulating cry of the dogs,
> and every sportsman anxiously looks out for elk, bear or
> jungle sheep.

Hunting was only one of the many 'do-it-yourself' entertainments devised by the summer residents. The entertainment in the hill stations were in fact so successful that many military centres were carefully situated away from the main resorts to lessen the temptations for the troops.

There were countless balls, dinners and picnics. The grassy glen of Annandale in Shimla was a focal point of social life. In May 1851 there was a flower fête which inspired these verses in the *Delhi Sketchbook*, the Indian equivalent of *Punch*:

> The morning was warm, and the sun shining bright,
> And the company teeming with joy and delight!
> The gardens were deck'd in gorgeous array,
> The ladies, like flowers, were blooming and gay;
> The Malees (gardeners) and Dalees were waiting to be
> Beprais'd and bepriz'd by the great committee.
> But alas! that sage council, so careless and free,
> Had forgotten refreshment for their companie,
> Oh! the Annandale Fête! Oh! the Annandale Fête!

The *Sketchbook* advised,

> Now all sage committee men, take my advice,
> When you get up a flower fête, provide something nice;
> Be careful, that whenever Englishmen meet,
> They never depart without something to eat.

Annandale later became a sporting centre with horse races, polo, cricket and soccer. Sir Mortimer Durand inaugurated the annual football tournament in Shimla. The tournament still bears his name, the Durand Cup, and is modern India's most prestigious football trophy.

Shimla was also the home of amateur dramatics in India and its Gaiety Theatre is still sometimes called into use. As early as the 1830s, plays were rehearsed, though not all found an audience, as Emily Eden related:

> Captain N got up a prospectus of six plays for the benefit of the starving people at Agra, and there was a long list of subscribers but then the actors fell out. One man took a fit of low spirits, and another who acted women's parts well would not cut off his moustachios, and another went off to shoot bears near the snowy range.

Practically every hill station had a Mall, restricted to equestrians and pedestrians. The Mall was a place to see and be seen. As almost everybody wanted to be seen it remained unpleasantly crowded during

Ooty: Colonial-style houses on the terraced hillsides (above)
and the Botanical Gardens (below)

the season. The club was a social centre where the British could reaffirm their sense of community. The hill clubs were replicas of those in the plains whose mysterious exclusivity led Indian children to call them *jadoo-ghars* (houses of magic), where they imagined the British performed secret and terrible rites. Some clubs were decidedly eccentric. The Gloom Club of Shimla was 'for bachelors who wished to return hospitality'. Its invitations were black-bordered, its dance programmes were designed in the shape of coffins and decorated with a skull and crossbones and the club itself was festooned with funeral draperies. The church was another institution essential to the community. Victorian Gothic churches were among the first buildings to be constructed, and the mountain graveyards show that, until the end of the 19th century, there were still many deaths from diseases like typhoid and dysentery.

The main church in Ooty, St Stephen's, was consecrated in 1830 by the Bishop of Calcutta. The local citizens were proud of their church and one wrote, 'the foundations have been so deeply laid that we may expect it will last for ages — a monument to the Majesty of God.' Reminding the congregation that they were in an alien land, the Bishop said in his sermon, 'Let us not fail to turn our thoughts to that cheerless moral desert where ignorance is the most appalling, superstitions the foulest and most degrading... in this land of heathen darkness every Christian may be, 'nay more, must be a missionary.'

No doubt many did try to live up to Christian principles, the missionary spirit was decidedly lacking in the holiday atmosphere of the hills. The spirited social life led to any number of emotional entanglements· The hills were the one place in India where there were plenty of European women often with their husbands in the plains. Married or unmarried they were assiduously courted by officers and 'invalids'. Rudyard Kipling described this rumour-laden society in *Plain Tales from the Hills*.

He might well have also been the author of this anonymous rhyme from the *Civil and Military Gazette:*

I had a little husband
Who gave me all his pay.
I left him for Mussoorie

A hundred miles away.
I dragged my little husband's name
Through heaps of social mire,
And joined him in November
As good as you'd desire.

The flirtations were such that one jealous husband was heartily glad of
the Crimean War, 'For now,' he said, 'there will be fewer captains.'

By the turn of the century, the hill stations were not merely
sanatoria, recreation, government and military centres· They were also
major educational centres with schools for British and Eurasian
children. Municipalities were being set up to run the burgeoning
summer settlements, and they encouraged small-scale local industry and
cash-crop agriculture. The hill stations were also becoming more open
to Indians.

From the beginning, the hill station relied on Indian labour, Indian
merchants and Indian farmers for fruits and vegetables. 'Native' bazaars
spread across the lower hillsides. Kipling described the bazaars in
Shimla in his novel *Kim*, albeit somewhat romantically:

> ...a man who knows his way there can defy all the police of
> India's summer capital; so cunningly does verandah
> communicate with verandah, alley-way with alley-way, and
> bolt-hole with bolt-hole. Here live those who minister to the
> wants of the glad city jhampanis who pull the pretty ladies'
> rickshaws by night and gamble till the dawn; grocers, oil-
> sellers, curio-vendors, firewood dealers, priests, pickpockets,
> and native employees of the government; here are discussed
> by courtesans the things which are supposed to be profoundest
> secrets of the India Council; and here gather all the sub-sub-
> sub agents of half the native states.

At the other end of the social scale, the Indian princes had elaborate
establishments in the British hill stations. The Maharaja of Patiala
actually went one step ahead and built his own hill station at Chail
from where he had the satisfaction of looking down at Shimla.

Gradually the wealthy, but not princely, and middle-class Indians
also began to holiday in the hills. Matheran, the hill station nearest to
Mumbai (or Bombay), had become largely a preserve of the Parsi

community by the beginning of the 20th century. There were more Parsi than British hotels. The bi-weekly newspaper, *Matheran Jottings*, and the local sports were also the preserve of this community. In fact the Parsis established themselves in all the hill stations of the Bombay Presidency, and the British found them a particularly attractive community, as the following extract from *Murray's Guide* of 1881 explains:

> The Parsis, so called from their original country Pars, Persia. They migrated to India in the 7th century, and are of larger stature than the other peoples of Bombay. They are fire-worshippers, but endeavour to maintain the purity of all the elements, whence their dead bodies are placed in towers to be devoured by vultures and then dissolved into dust. In this way they fancy that none of the elements are polluted.... Their numbers do not reach 200,000, of which the greater part reside in or near Bombay. They eat meat and drink wine, and many of them wear European clothes. Their women are remarkable for their morality, and, taken as a body, they are the most civilised people in India.

There's a lot to be said, it seems, for drinking and being non-vegetarian.

At the end of the Raj in 1947 many predicted the demise of the hill station. However, Indians have always absorbed new ideas and made them their own, and they entered into the holiday spirit with great enthusiasm. The hill stations are even more popular now than they were during the Raj, and continue to be leading educational centres and even seats of government. The erstwhile summer capital of Shimla has become the state capital of Himachal Pradesh. New hill stations have also sprung up, and Kashmir and Kullu only became popular after Independence. The modern hill station does not try to hide its British origins but is today a thoroughly Indian institution which offers a unique experience to all visitors whether Indian or foreign, Mall-strollers or trekkers.

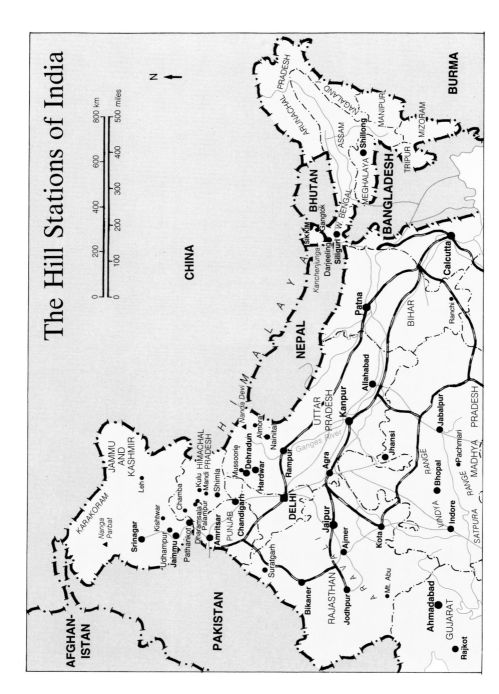

The Hill Stations of India

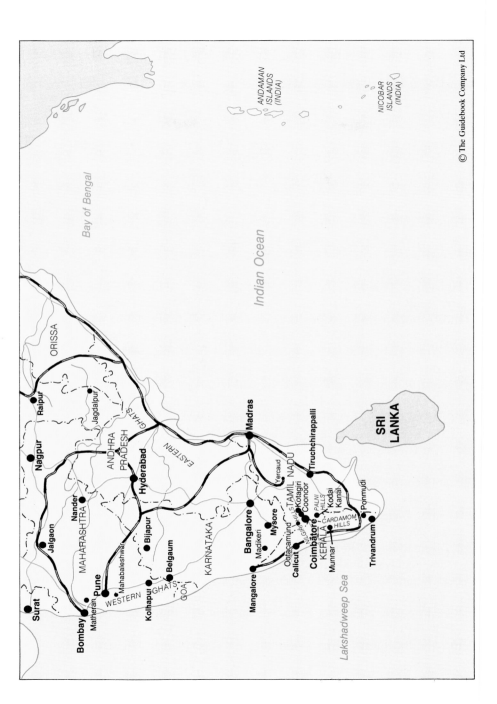

© The Guidebook Company Ltd

The Hills of India

India has seven principal mountain ranges. Among these, pride of place belongs naturally to the Himalayas — the abode of the snows. The Himalayas are the world's youngest and largest east-west mountain chain and stretch some 2,500 kilometres (1,600 miles) in an arc across the top of the Indian subcontinent. This impressive natural frontier encompasses an immense half a million square kilometres (200,000 square miles) and gives India the largest area under snow and glacier outside the polar regions. The mountains were formed between 50 and 60 million years ago. The most recently formed are the lower foothills known as the Shivaliks which consist of sedimentary rock very susceptible to erosion. Beyond the Shivaliks lie the Himachal, the Lesser Himalayas. It is in these ranges that the most celebrated hill stations are found: Shimla, Dalhousie, Mussoorie, Nainital and Darjeeling. Like most northern hill stations they are situated between 1,230 metres and 2,460 metres (4-8,000 feet) and the peaks on which they stand would no doubt have qualified as mountains rather than mere hills were it not for the Himadri, the Great Himalayas, beyond. In the Himadri are Everest and Annapurna, which lie within Nepal, and Kanchenjunga, Nanga Parbat and Nanda Devi, which fall within the boundaries of India. From the Himalayas flow the great rivers of the Punjab, as well as the holiest river of all, the Ganga or Ganges.

The Himalayas are the highest mountain range in the world but the lesser known Aravalli is one of the oldest. Formed over 600 million years ago, its once snow-capped peaks have been reduced to a line of scrub-covered hills running between Delhi and Gujarat to the southwest. In some places they have been completely eroded but they can still boast one hill station, Mount Abu, and one peak, Guru Shikhar, over 1,700 metres (6,000 feet) high.

The Vindyas divide the wide Gangetic plain of the north from peninsular India, the triangular plateau which forms the southern part of the country. They stretch over 1,000 kilometres (627 miles) across the top of the peninsula at an average altitude of 300 metres (974 feet) and form one of the country's main watersheds. There were, however, too few Europeans posted nearby to develop a single hill station.

The Satpuras, another ancient mountain system, run south of, and more or less parallel to, the Vindyas. They have one hill station, Pachmarhi, which is found near the highest point in the range, Dhupgarh at 1,350 metres (4,429 feet). 'Sat' means seven and 'pura' folds, referring to the lines of hills which make up the Satpuras.

More impressive than these are the Sahyadris, the Western and Southern Ghats, which run for 1,600 kilometres (1,000 miles) down the western edge of India to the southernmost tip of the country. The popular hill stations of the former Bombay Presidency are in the Western Ghats. The word 'ghat' itself means pass and here are the passes from the higher peninsula down to the coast. The Sahyadris rise cliff-like on the western, coastal side and catch the heavy monsoon rains. Their more gentle eastern slopes consequently have a much drier climate. The hills become progressively higher towards the south. The highest point is reached in the spectacular Nilgiri Hills, literally 'blue mountains', the site of Ootacamund which stands at the foot of the 2,637-metre- (8,615-foot-) high Dodu Betta Peak.

Beyond the Nilgiris are the southernmost Sahyadris — the Anaimalai or Elephant Hills, the summits of which are said to resemble elephant heads. Also here are the Palni Hills, site of the hill station Kodaikanal, and the Elamalai or Cardamom Hills which are named after their cardamom plantations.

On the opposite side of the peninsula, the Eastern Ghats run southwest from the Mahanadi River until they meet the Nilgiri Hills. These ghats have summits over 1,000 metres (over 3,200 feet), but are devoid of hill stations. To the southeast of them are the Shevaroy Hills and the hill station of Yercaud.

The last great range of India is the Purvachal, or Eastern Mountains, running along the Indo-Burmese border in northeastern India. These remote hills again have no hill station. The great centre for the British in the northeast was Shillong, the capital of British Assam. Shillong lies in the Khasi Hills, which geologically belong more to peninsular India than to Purvachal. Shillong is now the capital of the recently formed state of Meghalaya which means 'abode of the clouds'. Until recent deforestations began changing the climate (see page 124) nearby Cherrapunji was renowned as the wettest place in the world.

Facts for the Traveller

Visas

All foreign visitors to India require a valid visa. A tourist visa, valid for 90 days from the date of entry, can be obtained from any Indian embassy, high commission or consulate. If you intend to leave India and return within a 90-day period, then it is worth applying for a double- or triple-entry visa. An extension for a further 90 days can be given to a tourist visa by the Foreign Regional Registration offices in most large cities. The visa fee varies from nationality to nationality, with British passport holders paying the most. If a visa extends beyond 90 days, an Income Tax Clearance Certificate is required at the time of departure (available from main tax offices).

Health

India demands yellow fever certificates from travellers arriving from Africa, Latin America and Papua New Guinea. Other shots, although not legally required, are advisable. Typhoid, polio and tetanus are important. A gamma globulin injection against hepatitis A immediately before departure is also recommended. Many countries demand that travellers from India have an up-to-date cholera vaccination. A vaccination against rabies is now available, but you must visit the nearest hospital following any bite from a dog or monkey for a further course of shots. Malaria is still widespread in many parts of India. Advice as to which pills to take is constantly being revised and it is best to seek advice from your local travel centre or clinic before departure. Courses must be continued for four to six weeks after you leave India. You may want to put together a basic medical kit in advance of departure; this could usefully include something against diarrhoea, antiseptic cream, lip salve, mosquito repellent and soothing cream for bites, suntan lotion, water purification tablets, if bottled water is not available, and elastoplast. If you do have stomach problems soon after arrival, you are advised to drink lots of fluids (water with a little salt and sugar) and keep to a simple diet for a couple of days to give

Near Thal, Pithoragarh District, Kumaon

your system time to adjust. If the problem should worsen, however, seek medical advice.

There are a few things not to do which will make your stay more comfortable. Never drink tap water (often hotels provide flasks of filtered water and bottled water is available almost everywhere). Avoid salads, even in hotels, and do not eat the street food until you have tested the strength of your stomach.

Time Zone

Despite its size, India has a single time zone. It is 2° hours behind Hong Kong and Singapore, 5° hours ahead of London (GMT), 4° hours ahead of British Summer Time, 10° hours ahead of New York, and 13° hours ahead of San Francisco.

Customs

Visitors are usually asked if they have anything to declare on arrival. An individual should not bring more than US$10,000 in cash without declaring it. Likewise, video equipment, cameras and other high-value items should be declared upon arrival. If the customs officer prepares a Tourist Baggage Re-export Form (TBRE) detailing the items declared and their value, then this form must be shown when departing from India together with the items listed. Exchange receipts must also be shown on departure for currency declared.

India allows the standard bottle of spirits, 200 cigarettes and a small allowance for gift items to be imported free of duty. Indian customs officials are thorough and professional. Usually on the lookout for the smuggler, they rarely trouble the genuine tourist.

On leaving India you may be asked to produce exchange certificates, but this is unlikely unless a declaration was written into your passport on arrival. Traditional souvenirs can be exported without any restriction. Only Rs2,000 worth of gold and up to Rs10,000 worth of ready-made jewellery or precious stones can be exported without a permit. Any object over a hundred years old needs an export certificate from the Director of Antiquities, Archaeological Survey of India, Janpath, New Delhi. India is a signatory of CITES and the export of ivory, animal and snake skins, and products made from them, is forbidden.

CITES certificates can be issued by the Deputy Director of Wildlife Preservation in New Delhi.

Climate and Clothing

Visitors should bear in mind that the day and night temperatures in the hills can vary greatly. During the summer months (May to June) most Himalayan hill stations are pleasantly warm (up to 30°C or 86°F in daytime). The evenings, however, are much cooler and a light sweater is useful during the monsoon, since rains and clouds help to keep temperatures down. An umbrella is therefore also useful. The weather becomes progressively colder until winter (December to February) when temperatures can drop below freezing point, and there is snowfall. March and April, warm months in the plains, are bracing in the hills and woollens are still essential in these months.

The hill stations of central, western and southern India are never as cold. Ootacamund never has snow, although its climate is cooler than that of the hill stations near Mumbai. They offer fresh air but in Mahabaleshwar, for example, summer temperatures rise to above 30°C (86°F) and in winter to 24°C (75°F). The height of the monsoon (June to July) can be just as cool as winter but in these hills neither gum boots, raincoat nor umbrella can protect you from the worst downpours.

Transport

The journey to a hill station will most likely comprise a combination of air, train, bus and rail travel. Apart from Shimla, Darjeeling, Ootacamund and Matheran, no railways will take you all the way to your hill destination, and the last part of your journey will have to be completed by bus or car. The same can be said of airlinks with a few exceptions, notably Kashmir.

INTERNAL FLIGHTS

Indian Airlines has been augmented by new private airlines like Archana Airways, Jagson Airlines, Jet Airways and Sahara India. Domestic flights are bookable with an international flight, and arriving in India with confirmed seats is essential during the high seasons

A Woman's Place

*T*he Sayyid next enters upon the long and difficult subject of a woman's peculiar duties, religious and domestic. These he enumerates as follows:—

1st. She is to pray five times a day, and fast: also to exhort her husband to devotion: always bearing in mind that on the day of resurrection the first question put to a woman will be concerning her prayers; the second, how she performed her duty to her husband.

2nd. To meditate on the sanctity of a wife's duty to her spouse, to obey him in all things, except when the order is contrary to a higher command.

3rd. Never to break, by thought, word, or deed, the laws of modesty, recollecting the tradition, "A woman without shame is a food without salt."

4th. Not to apply for divorce without the best of reasons; also not to fall in love with handsome young men, and lavish upon them the contents of the husband's purse.

5th. To stay at home, except when the husband permits her to go abroad; not to visit even her parents without leave of absence, though those parents might be dying or being carried to their graves. Any woman who quits the house against orders, exposes herself to the curse of Heaven, and to sixty stripes religiously administered; she also loses all right to Nafakeh, or maintenance money.

6th. To devote herself to household affairs, such as cooking (for her mate, not herself), sewing, darning old clothes, spinning, washing, milking cattle, lighting the house, and attending to the furniture and stores. It is very sinful to eat before the husband has fed, and to refuse coarse victuals, because others live more luxuriously. To comb the spouse's hair, to wash his clothes and spread his couch, are, in a religious sense, equal to Haj and Umrah (the different kinds of pilgrimage).

7th. *When at home, to dress as well, and when going out, as plainly as possible. In the house, to apply oil, antimony, henna, and other cosmetics, to keep the person very clean, and by no means to neglect the teeth. At the same time, the virtuous wife must not be extravagant in dress, or torment her husband for Tattah silks, Multani muslins, embroidered slippers, and similar articles of luxury.*

8th. *If wealthy, never to boast of supporting the husband; and if poor, never to be discontented with humble living.*

9th. *Always to receive the husband especially when he returns from abroad, with glad and smiling looks.*

10th. *Never to speak loudly and fiercely to, or even before, the husband; the words Laanat and Phit (curse!) are particularly to be avoided. Never to taunt her spouse with such words as these; "thy teeth are long and thy nose short;" or "thy head is large and the calves of thy legs small;" or "thy face is a black creation of God's!" or "thou art old, weak, and scarely a man!" or "thou art a real beauty, with those grins and exposed teeth!" or "lo! What a fine turban and charming gait!"*

The Sayyid concludes this enumeration of female duties with a pathetic lament that the Ran (wenches) of Sindh are in the habit of utterly neglecting them. Probably, like the great Milton, he was a better author than husband, and generalises from the individual case.

Richard F Burton,
Sindh and the Races That Inhabit the Valleys of the Indus, 1851

(wait–listing is thoroughly unsatisfactory). So book as soon as you know your dates and reconfirm the bookings on arrival. Indian Airlines runs various discount deals including Youth Fares and the Discover India Ticket, bookable with an international ticket. Indian Airlines plies routes to larger towns and cities while Archana Airways and Jagson Airlines fly to Kullu. Be prepared for delays. In the depths of Delhi's winter, its airport is often shrouded by fog in the early morning when many flights leave. Naturally this can have a disastrous effect on the day's scheduling.

TRAINS

Don't expect to buy a ticket and be on the train a few minutes later. Book in advance if possible, and always book in advance for overnight trains. Booking procedures are much easier than they once were now that computerised booking offices have been introduced in many cities. However, for a reserved seat, and you are strongly recommended to get a reserved seat, unless you enjoy travelling rough, you still have to fill in a form with your name, age, sex, address etc. In major cities like Delhi and Mumbai there is also a special tourist quota of reserved seats on many trains, which can be booked the day before departure from the railway's tourist guide. His office will also sell Indrail passes. Travel agencies can help you with rail tickets, although some would rather have you travel by car so they can make a bigger profit. For some hill destinations you can book a through passage — for example Madras to Ooty, or Delhi to Shimla — by certain trains. The higher the class the more comfortable the accommodation, but remember if you want to see the countryside you can do so better from a non-air-conditioned carriage where you can open the windows. On the hill railways, where there are no air-conditioned carriages, try to get a window seat.

HIRED CAR

This is a convenient way to travel if you can afford it. Cars come with drivers. Rates depend upon car type, number of days and distance, with a small fee for the driver's food and lodging, which is often payable daily (plus a good tip for a good driver given directly to him). Cars hired at the hill stations may be more ramshackle than those hired from a reputable city firm in the plains.

Bus

The Indian bus system is one of the most remarkable in the world. You will find buses wherever there is a roughly motorable road, and they will be very well patronised. Bus drivers in the hills are thankfully more cautious than their brethren in the plains, although the state transport buses themselves may appear a little the worse for wear. There are now frequent deluxe services from the plains to most hill stations, which stop at fewer places on the way than normal buses. Some deluxe buses also have air-conditioning, and if you are unlucky, a video on board. When catching buses in the hills be prepared for unpunctuality and a slow journey and take them in your stride.

Money

Foreigners are expected to pay for their airfares and hotel bills in foreign exchange. All hotel bills, where the tariff is over Rs1,200 for a single room, are subject to a 20% luxury tax payable to the Central Government. Many hotels also levy a state luxury tax ranging from seven percent in Maharashtra to 20% in Tamil Nadu. International credit cards are generally accepted throughout the country. Whenever exchanging foreign exchange at a hotel, shop or bank ensure that an encashment certificate is issued. This will be required if purchasing an air ticket in rupees or reconverting the balance of rupees to foreign exchange on departure.

The money denominations are straight forward: 100 paise make one rupee. Coins and smaller notes are vital for tips but scarce. It is easiest to change money at your hotel, where you can ensure notes are not torn and ask for small change. The rate may be less good than that offered by a bank, but for a few paise, you save hours of queuing. Keep your encashment certificates carefully.

Banking

In smaller hotels, especially in the minor hill stations, there may be no facility for changing travellers cheques. However, foreigners are often asked to settle their hotel bills in foreign exchange. The hotel may ask to see an exchange certificate. All major and most minor hill stations have nationalised banks which accept travellers cheques, although they

The Ooty-Coonoor Road

may only accept certain currencies (the US dollar and pound sterling are always acceptable).

TIPPING
The amount of a tip should not be enormous, about Rs5 for good service, and up to Rs100 to a guide for a good day's work, or to a driver who has been efficient and punctual.

Photography

Colour print film is available in most cities, and in many other places, but it is often expensive. All slide film is generally available except for Kodachrome which has not been imported since the Kodak laboratory in Mumbai closed. However, it is best to bring a good supply of film with you — some people suggest twice what you expect to use. Any film left over makes a good and welcome present for someone who has been of help.

Taking photographs without a special permit is strictly forbidden at airports, bridges and railway stations.

Communications

First class hotels may have direct dial facilities from the room for both local and international calls, but in out-of-the-way places it is best to use the hotel operator or local operator to connect local and long-distance calls (be prepared for waits of up to several hours). Many hotels also have fax facilities. Check the markup first (often between 100 and 250 percent) before making extensive use of these. Most towns now have a small manned booth with international and domestic direct dial facilities, easily identifiable by their STD/ISD signage. Many also have fax lines. These are generally much cheaper than hotels and more efficient than the local post office.

Post is rather erratic. Letters and postcards sent by air to Europe or North America take from four to 14 days and parcels follow their own rules. Hotels usually sell stamps, or you can buy them from the local post office.

The Post Office and Mall, Shimla

Kashmir

This state covers three regions with vastly different landscapes, peoples and languages. The low-lying Jammu region has a Hindu majority, including the Dogras who once ruled Kashmir. To the east is the bare, monsoon-less barren landscape of Ladakh, 'Indian Tibet', with its largely Buddhist population. The people of the famous Vale of Kashmir are mainly Muslim, and speak their own Kashmiri language written nowadays in the Persian script. This same Valley which once entranced the Mughals, continues to attract tourists still. In late 1989, a popular movement demanding independence from India and backed by various militant groups badly disrupted life. Frequent curfews and strict security measures helped to ensure that hardly any tourists came to Srinagar and the famous houseboats on its lakes since 1990. Sadly, since about 70 percent of the population of Srinagar was dependent on the tourist industry, they look forward to seeing the visitors come back again.

Srinagar and the Vale of Kashmir

The Vale of Kashmir is an oval plain 140 kilometres (87 miles) long and up to 40 kilometres (25 miles) wide. It is surrounded on all sides by high mountains. Among the highest peaks are Nanga Parbat (8,114 metres or 26,621 feet), Haramukh (5,150 metres or 16,896 feet) and Amarnath (5,280 metres or 17,323 feet) as well as the magnificent Pir Panjal Range with many peaks over 4,570 metres (14,993 feet). The fertile land of the valley, by the Jhelum River and its tributaries, produces crops of rice, maize, an enormous variety of fruit and saffron (*Crocus sativus*) which has been cultivated in Kashmir for over a thousand years.

Kashmir is a land for all seasons. Spring (March to early May) is the season of the flowering fruit trees and meadows; summer (May to August) is the time higher altitude destinations are most accessible; at the beginning of autumn the saffron fields are carpeted with violet-blue flowers and the leaves of the chinar trees begin to turn to gold; in winter (December to March) the snows cover the high meadows and much of the valley for a few weeks.

The expanding city of Srinagar is home to over half a million souls. It stretches along the bank of the Jhelum River, which is spanned by nine old and several other new bridges. Canals intersect the city and link the Jhelum with the spring-fed Dal Lake which is divided by causeways into four parts — Gagribal, Lokutdal, Boddal and Nagin. Part of the Dal Lake is covered by the famous floating gardens made up of reed platforms moored to the lake bed and covered with heaps of weed and mud. These market gardens produce cucumbers, tomatoes and melons.

At the Dal Lake end of town is the main Maulana Azad Road, on which are the Roman Catholic Church and the Golf Club (which has an 18-hole course and accepts temporary members). In the same area are the Tourist Reception Centre and the leading hotels, but it is the canal-crossed old part of the city with its wooden houses, colour and bustle which is most authentically Kashmiri.

BACKGROUND

There have been settlements in the valley since at least 2500 BC. Emperor Ashoka is credited with bringing Buddhism to the area in the third century BC and remains from the Buddhist period are to be seen at Harwan, north of the Shalimar Gardens. As elsewhere in India, Buddhism was eclipsed by Hindu resurgence and it was a Hindu raja, Pravarasena II, who made Srinagar his capital in the sixth century. Islam in its turn overcame Hinduism and the Mughals defeated a Muslim ruler to gain control of the valley.

The celebrated Mughal Gardens were the first hill resorts of Kashmir. Akbar laid out Nasim Bagh; Jahangir laid out Shalimar, Acchabal and Verinag; and Shah Jahan, the builder of the Taj Mahal, founded the Chashma Shahi gardens. After the last great Mughal, Aurangzeb, died in 1707 the Balkanisation of the empire began. Kashmir passed first into the hands of Nadir Shah of Persia and then to the Afghan, Ahmad Shah Durrani. The great Sikh leader Ranjit Singh conquered the valley in 1819 but Sikh rule was brief and after the First Sikh War in 1846 the British assigned the territory to the Dogra maharaja, Gulab Singh of Jammu, whose successors continued to rule until Indian Independence.

For the British, Srinagar was never a true hill station. There was a British Resident but neither he nor any Briton was allowed to own land in the state. Kashmir was also expensive and difficult to reach and attracted only a few summer visitors, many of whom chose to live in houseboats decorated according to English taste.

At Independence, the maharaja, a Hindu ruling a largely Muslim state, opted to join the new state of India after Pathan tribesmen from Pakistan had invaded his territory. Indian troops were called in to drive back the tribesmen and the first Indo-Pakistan war was fought. A ceasefire was called and a Line of Control drawn across the state, dividing it into the Pakistani state of 'Azad Kashmir' and the Indian state of Jammu and Kashmir.

GETTING THERE AND AROUND

Flights from Delhi are either direct or via Amritsar, Chandigarh or Jammu and there are at least two flights a day throughout the year. All are generally heavily booked and reservations should be made as far in advance as possible. Srinagar airport is 14 kilometres (nine miles) from the city, linked by taxis and buses of the Jammu and Kashmir State Road Transport Corporation (J&KSRTC).

The nearest railhead is at present Jammu Tawi, a distance of 305 kilometres (190 miles) away. The line is currently being extended to Udhampur, 224 kilometres (139 miles) away. Trains run to Jammu from Delhi, Calcutta, Pune and even Kanyakumari at the southernmost tip of India.

There is a Tourist Reception Centre at Jammu which gives advice on how best to reach the hills. You can hire or, more reasonably, share taxis to Srinagar. The journey by taxi or J&KSRTC luxury minibuses usually takes eight hours. Other buses can take up to eleven hours.

Those with a strong stomach can take a video coach, travelling direct from Delhi to Srinagar (contact the J&K Tourism Office, Kanishka Shopping Plaza, New Delhi, tel. 332 5373, 332 7400).

Several places on the road between Jammu and Srinagar have been developed with tourist bungalows and restaurants. **Patnitop** is 112 kilometres (70 miles) from Jammu and J&K Tourism run a Tourist Bungalow and Cottage complex. A tourist bungalow has also been built at **Banihal** just before the 2,500-metre-long Jawahar tunnel dives under the Banihal Pass to emerge in the Vale itself, giving the distinct impression of entering another world.

Sunset over Dal Lake

Local Transport

When in Srinagar, travel by *shikara* — shallow, well-cushioned boats which can be hired from any of the ghat steps leading down to the lakes. Rates for some journeys are officially pre-determined, but Kashmiris are inveterate businessmen and it's impossible to eliminate bargaining entirely. Other non-polluting forms of transport are the bicycle and the horse, for hill excursions.

There are taxi stands in the city and again rates for popular routes are fixed. Scooter-rickshaws provide a cheaper alternative. Bus tours run to local sights as well as to other resorts, and tickets can be booked at the Tourist Reception Centre (TRC). Due to current disturbances it is advisable to check with the TRC or your hotel before making a trip.

SIGHTS

JAMMU

Jammu itself is an unprepossessing town, although it has some fine temples, notably the **Raghunath Temple Complex** and the **Ranbireshwar Temple** of Shiva with a 75-metre- (246-foot-) high tower.

There are also collections of exquisite miniature paintings in the local *pahari* (hill) style. One is at the **Dogra Art Gallery** and the other at the **Amar Mahal Palace**, an eccentric building resembling a medieval French chateau. Jammu is also on the route to one of the most important Hindu shrines, the **cave temple of the mother goddess Vaishno Devi**, 60 kilometres (37 miles) to the northwest. Most tourists, however, prefer to head for the hills.

SRINAGAR

The **Shri Pratap Singh Museum** in Lal Mandi has many exhibits related to the state's Buddhist and Hindu past as well as 200-year old textiles and carpets, and fine examples of calligraphy. The museum is closed on Wednesdays.

There are some fine mosques in the old city, although access for non-Muslims and women is limited. On one bank of the Jhelum is the wooden **Shah-i-Hamdan's Mosque**, with a pagoda-style roof. This mosque was first built at the end of the 14th century. On the opposite bank is the fine **Patthar Masjid** (Stone Mosque) built by Nur Jahan, wife of Emperor Jahangir, in 1623. One of the largest mosques in Kashmir is the **Jami Masjid**, another wooden building, which was originally erected in 1385 by Sultan Sikandar Butshika (the 'idol smasher') and subsequently burnt to the ground several times. The mosque has over 300 pillars supporting the roof, each made of a single deodar tree. The present mosque was rebuilt in 1674 by Emperor Aurangzeb.

Rising above the Boulevard is the **Takht-i-Sulaiman Hill** (Solomon's Throne Hill) surmounted by the **Shankaracharya Temple**, believed to have been founded by the Hindu sage of the same name and dedicated to Shiva. From here there is a fine view of the lake and city and you also come face to face with the Srinagar TV tower.

The Boulevard leads around the edge of the lake to the **Mughal Gardens**, which can be reached at a more leisurely pace by *shikara*. The closest garden to the city by road is the **Chashma Shahi** (Royal Spring), named after a stream of clear water emerging from the hillside. The gardens are above the new **City National Park** where an 18-hole golf course is being laid out. The gardens were originally planned according to the instructions of Shah Jahan in 1632, but they have since been enlarged. All the Mughal Gardens are symmetrically arranged

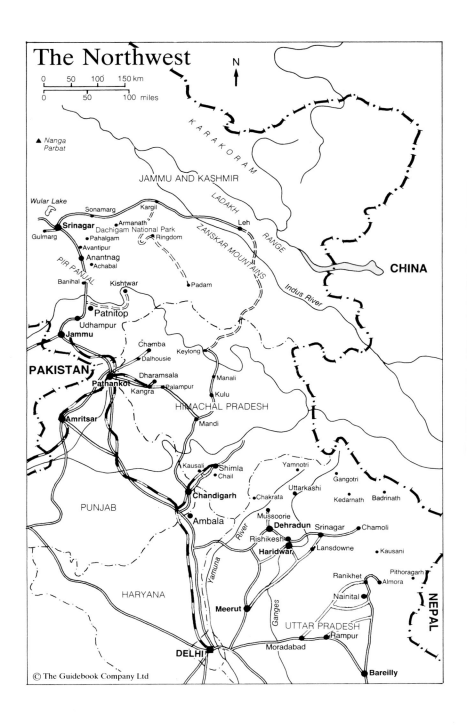

The Northwest

N

| 0 | 50 | 100 | 150 km |
| 0 | 50 | 100 miles |

▲ Nanga Parbat

KARAKORAM

JAMMU AND KASHMIR

LADAKH RANGE

Wular Lake

Sonamarg
Kargil
Leh
Srinagar Armanath
Gulmarg Dachigam National Park
●Pahalgam Ringdom
●Avantipur
Anantnag
●Achabal
Banihal Kishtwar ➤Padam

ZANSKAR MOUNTAINS

PIR PANJAL

Indus River

CHINA

● **Patnitop**
Udhampur
Jammu
Chamba Keylong
●Dalhousie
PAKISTAN
Dharamsala ●Manali
Pathankot ●Palampur
Kangra ●Kulu
HIMACHAL PRADESH
Amritsar Mandi

Kausali ●Shimla Yamnotri
●Chail Gangotri
Uttarkashi
Chandigarh ●Chakrata Kedarnath Badrinath
Mussoorie
PUNJAB **Ambala** **Dehradun** Srinagar ●Chamoli
Rishikesh ●Lansdowne ●Kausani
Haridwar
Ranikhet Pithoragarh
●Almora
HARYANA Nainital ●
Meerut
UTTAR PRADESH
DELHI Moradabad ●Rampur
© The Guidebook Company Ltd **Bareilly**

NEPAL

Carpet seller, Srinagar   *Nishat Bagh created in 1633*

in a series of terraces around a central watercourse. Above the Chashma Shahi are the ruins of Pari Mahal (Fairy Palace) built by Shah Jahan's brilliant son, Dara Shikoh, as a school of astrology and astronomy for his tutor, Akhund Mullah Shah.

Nishat Bagh (Garden of Gladness) on the shores of the lake was laid out in 1633. It looks out over the Pir Panjal and is the largest of all the royal gardens. The probable owner was the elder brother of Nur Jahan. The gardens on either side of the water course are planted with tall chinar trees, which you can see at their best in autumn.

Two kilometres (just over a mile) further on is the **Shalimar Bagh** built for Nur Jahan, 'Light of the World', by her husband the Emperor Jahangir. This garden is the most secluded, reached by a tree-lined canal, and is more refined in detail and proportion than Nishat Bagh. The central black marble pavilion in the *zenana* or ladies' garden is surrounded by water and looks out in four directions. Below, in the **Diwan-i-Am**, the Hall of Public Audience, the emperor used to sit on a black marble throne above the water. Every evening from May to October there is a sound and light show which describes Jahangir's court. As the nearest taxi stand is five kilometres (three miles) away it's best to keep a waiting taxi.

Across the lake from Shalimar Bagh is the shiny white dome of the new **Hazratbal Mosque**. On the way across the lake is the artificial island of **Sona-Lank** (Golden Island) which corresponds to a similar island in the southern part of the lake known as the **Rupa-Lank** (Silver Island). It was believed that gold and silver were buried there. Sona-Lank is now more commonly known as **Char Chinar** (Four Chinars) because of the trees that grow there.

The mosque, built by Akbar in 1586, is next to **Nasim Bagh** which now forms the grounds of an engineering college. The Hazratbal Mosque houses the sacred relic of a hair of the Prophet Mohammad, which is displayed on certain religious occasions. Some years ago it was reported stolen and riots broke out. It was soon recovered and is now very carefully guarded. On the edge of the lake is the **tomb of Sheikh Abdullah**, Lion of Kashmir, who dominated the state's politics until his death in 1982.

To the west of Hazratbal and separated from its neighbouring lake by a causeway is the cleaner and quieter **Nagin Lake**, beyond which rises the hill of **Hari Parbat** on which Emperor Akbar built a fort at the end of the 16th century. It was rebuilt in the 18th and 19th centuries. To enter the fort you have to get permission from the Archaeological Department in Lal Mandi and so most people see it only from the outside. On the western slope of the hill is a **Parvati temple** and on the southern face is the Muslim shrine of **Khwaja Makhdoom Sahib** and the **mosque of the scholar Akhund Mullah Shah**. Close to the outer wall of the fort is an historic Sikh *gurudwara* (temple), **Chatti Padshahi**, which commemorates the visit of Guru Hargobind to Kashmir.

A tomb of interest to Christians is that at **Razabal**. It is believed to be the grave of Yuz Asaf or Jesus Christ who, according to legend, is supposed to have survived the cross and come to Kashmir, identified as the home of the lost tribe of Israel.

SHOPPING

Evidence of Kashmir's prolific and now commercialised handicrafts industry can be seen all over Srinagar. Shops line the Boulevard, Dalgate, Polo View, the Bund, Residency Road and Budshah Chowk. If you don't feel strong enough to bargain, there are two government-run shops which offer quality at fixed prices: the **Government Arts Emporium** on Residency Road and the **Government Central Market** at the Exhibition Grounds.

The most expensive of the famous woollen shawls are the pashmina and the shahtush; the latter is so fine it can be drawn through a signet ring. Jamawar shawls are covered with delicate embroidery. A familiar pattern is the *amchi* or mango design, which was copied by the British in their own country and renamed Paisley. Both shawls and carpets from Kashmir have been prized in Europe for centuries. There is an immense variety of these handknotted carpets on sale. Kashmir tweeds are of good quality and a useful garment is the loose-fitting *pheran* which protects you from the winter cold. Folk art can be seen in the cheerful designs on *namdas*, a type of woollen rug which resembles thick felt. Some shops are stacked full of splendid copper vessels like samovars, some plain and others with raised designs. Lighter to carry are the locally made papier-mâché items, which are beautifully decorated. Kashmiri craftsmen also produce richly carved furniture using locally grown walnut.

MOUNTAIN RESORTS

Pahalgam, Sonamarg and Gulmarg are the three main mountain resorts around Srinagar. They offer a quiet contrast to the city. **Pahalgam** is 96 kilometres (60 miles) east of the city and lies at a height of 2,400 metres (7,874 feet). Some 29 kilometres (18 miles) from Srinagar, the road runs through **Avantipur**, where there are two remarkable ruined temples built by King Avantivarman in the ninth century. The larger is dedicated to Vishnu, and the other to Shiva. The road goes on to **Anantnag**, a town famous for its wooden toys. From where there is a short but worthwhile diversion to the **Mughal Gardens at Acchabal**, 58 kilometres (36 miles) from Srinagar. The gardens were largely the creation of Nur Jahan and lie on the old direct Srinagar-Jammu road. Their main feature is a stream which gushes out of the bottom of the hillside into a reservoir and over a waterfall. There are tourist huts here for overnight halts.

The other Mughal Gardens outside Srinagar (also with overnight accommodation) are the **Verinag Gardens**, 78 kilometres (49 miles) away, which have an octagonal pool and which were the favourite gardens of Jahangir and his consort.

Back on the Pahalgam road is **Martand**, 64 kilometres (40 miles) from Srinagar. It is the site of the grand ruins of a sun temple said to have been built by the warrior king Lalitaditya Mukhtanpida in the seventh century.

Pahalgam itself is little more than a single street on the banks of the Lidder River. The Lidder Valley is full of streams and is surrounded by mountains and glaciers. For hotels here, see page 270.

There are a few pleasant walks here. One leads to **Mamaleswara** an ancient Shiva temple, around a kilometre (half a mile) downstream. Another leads to the **Baisaran meadow** five kilometres (three miles) away and overlooking Pahalgam, and 11 kilometres (seven miles) further on, the **Tulian Lake** (altitude 3,335 metres or 10,942 feet). You can also walk to the village of **Aru**, 11 kilometres (seven miles) upstream. This is the first stage in the trek to the Kolahoi Glacier, for which Pahalgam is the base.

Pahalgam is the most crowded during July and August when thousands of pilgrims converge on the town on their way to the cave shrine of **Amarnath**, a 45-kilometre (28-mile) trek away. Pilgrims cover

Skiing in Gulmarg

the journey in four days. The shrine (at 3,888 metres or 12,755 feet) has a Shivalinga naturally formed of ice.

Sonamarg (Meadow of Gold), 80 kilometres (50 miles) northeast of Srinagar, is surrounded by mountains up to 5,300 metres (17,390 feet) high. The valley here is divided by a tree covered spur of the Thajiwas range. There is a government tourist bungalow and some private accommodation. Sonamarg is on the Ladakh road and is a trekking base, especially useful for those heading to Gangabal Lake. An easier trip for visitors is by pony to the Thajiwas meadow.

The green valley of **Gulmarg** (Meadow of Flowers), at 2,730 metres (8,957 feet), lies 56 kilometres (35 miles) west of Srinagar, and has an excellent view of Nanga Parbat. Among the flowers is an 18-hole golf course laid out to international specifications and which stakes a claim to being the highest in the world. Golf attracts sportspeople in the summer while in the winter (mid-December to mid-April) Gulmarg becomes India's major ski resort. Ski gear can be rented from the government ski shop and there are short courses for beginners. It's a particularly good base for cross-country skiing.

Ladakh

Ladakh's awesome bare granite mountains and the unique culture of its people — Shia Baltis, animist Dards and Buddhist Ladakhis — are the lodestones drawing an increasing number of visitors each year. Ladakh means 'land of several passes' and its plateau, lying between 2,900 and 5,900 metres (9,500 and 19,350 feet) above sea level, is bounded on the north by the Karakoram chain and on the south by the Himalayas. The Indus River bisects this district, which accounts for 70 percent of the total area of Kashmir state, but its climate is so inhospitable that there are on average only six inhabitants to every five square kilometres (two square miles). In summer, temperatures rise to 37°C (98°F) and in winter can drop to -40°C (-40°F). For seven months of the year Leh airport is the region's only link with the outside world. Leh, the capital, is situated on a tributary of the Indus at 3,380 metres (11,090 feet) above sea level. Once a halt on the silk route to China, Leh is now a sparsely populated town whose transformation into a tourist resort has considerably changed the way of life.

GETTING THERE

There are flights to Leh from Delhi, Chandigarh, Jammu and Srinagar, although they are frequently delayed due to bad weather. From mid-June to October there is a bus service from Srinagar to Leh although the 434 kilometre (270 miles) journey via Kargil takes two days while the flight takes 30 minutes. The jeepable road between Manali, in Himachal Pradesh, and Leh can be done in two days but is more comfortable in three to four days. An advantage of the road journey is that it gives one time to acclimatise to the high altitudes besides being an excellent way to view the dramatic Trans-Himalayan scenery.

The green forested slopes of Kashmir are left behind when you cross the Zoji La at 3,500 metres (11,580 feet) or leave the Kullu Valley over the Rohtang Pass at 4,075 metres (13,370 feet). After the Zoji La the road from Srinagar enters the predominantly Muslim town of Kargil, formally an important trade post and now the base for treks down the Suru Valley and into Zanskar. Beyond lies Buddhist Ladakh, with its monasteries or *gompas*, wayside shrines or *chortens* and the capital — Leh. For details of where to stay, see page 270.

SIGHTS

Above the town is the long-deserted **Namgyal Palace** of the rulers of Ladakh and above the palace are the **Leh and Tsemo monasteries**. The Vajrayana sect of Mahayana Buddhism is the main religion of the region, and the *gompas* have for centuries played a central role in Ladakhi society. They are generally situated high on rocky outcrops or hilltops. Many charge small entrance fees and some are only open to the public for limited hours in the early morning or evening.

The nearby **Shey Gompa** is one of the oldest monasteries in Ladakh and was attached to the summer palace of the rulers which now lies in ruins nearby. The **Thikse Gompa**, 19 kilometres (12 miles) from Leh, is a spectacularly situated reddish building with several temples. The **Hemis Gompa**, 30 kilometres (25 miles) from Leh, is the richest monastery, but thefts by tourists and traders in the mid-1970s have made the monks wary and many of the finest works of art are no longer on display. In this monastery is the largest *tankha* (painted temple cloth) in Ladakh which is only unfurled once every 12 years, the next time in 2004. Above the **Spituk Gompa**, eight kilometres (five

Dachigam National Park

The Dachigam National Park, only 21 kilometres (13 miles) from Srinagar, is the home of the hangul or Kashmir stag, one of the world's rarest deer. The 140 square kilometres (54 squares miles) of the park, ranging from 1,700 to 4,000 metres (5,580 to 13,100 feet), also have some 20 other mammal species, as well as 150 species of birds, including the iridescent monal pheasant, the koklas pheasant, the bearded vulture, golden eagle and the colourful western yellow-billed blue magpie.

The park provides half the catchment area for Dal Lake and so its survival is as vital to the inhabitants of Srinagar as it is to the hangul. Maharaja Hari Singh realised this and declared Dachigam his private hunting ground in 1910, moving ten villages (*dachi gam*) within the area to the periphery. Hangul were protected as royal deer by the Maharaja until the confusion of partition when the hangul population was decimated by poachers. Although Dachigam was made a sanctuary in 1951, poaching and destruction of habitat had brought members down to between 140 and 170 by 1970. The persistence of graziers still threatens the deer but poaching has been controlled and there are now over 300 deer in the sanctuary.

The hangul are best seen in the winter when they move into the lower part of the park. Large herds, chiefly of one sex, form and congregate near salt licks where some food is left during the worst of the winter. In spring the herds break up and the males move up the hillsides where they shed their antlers in April. Fawns are born in May and June in the higher pastures. In the autumn the hangul again move downwards and in September the rutting season begins. The stags generally gather in the Numbal where their bellows can be heard over long distances.

Dachigam is divided into two parts. In Upper Dachigam there are flowering alpine meadows, high ridges and the Marsar Lake — source of the Daghwan River. Lower Dachigam consists of grassland, pine forest and woods of Indian horse-chestnut, walnut, poplar, willow, mulberry and chinar. Upper Dachigam is accessible from May to August, while the best game-viewing in Lower Dachigam is from September and through the winter. Birdwatching is especially good from March to May. Visitors should bring strong walking shoes. There is limited accommodation within the park. For reservations, contact the Chief Wildlife Warden at the Tourist Reception Centre in Srinagar.

miles) from Leh on the Srinagar road, is an image of the Hindu goddess Kali whose face is unveiled once a year. One of the most outstanding monasteries is the **Alchi Gompa**, 70 kilometres (44 miles) from Leh, which dates back a thousand years and has some of the finest wall paintings in Ladakh. In the museum at the **Palace of Stok**, 15 kilometres (ten miles) from Leh, there is a collection of 400-year old *tankhas* painted in colours made from crushed precious stones.

FESTIVALS

The *gompas* are famous for their festivals when monks dance out tales of good and evil and wear fantastic masks and costumes. Most temple festivals are held in the winter but the celebrated Hemis festival is held around the end of June and the Thikse Gompa's celebrations are held in either the last half of July or the beginning of August. Archery contests are another feature of these celebrations. The week-long festival of Ladakh held in Leh in the first week of August also has archery contests, traditional dances and the Ladakh Sarai Ladakhi Polo tournament.

RIVER RAFTING

The River Indus has several stretches of river suitable for rafting. They vary from a half-day run for amateurs from Phey to Niemo, or a two-day

Shepherd and child on the Mughal Road

Nubra woman in traditional dress, Ladakh

run, also for amateurs, from Phey to Alchi and Nurla. The Zanskar River offers experienced rafters six-day trips with numerous rapids, starting near Padam. The best season for rafting is August to September and the Tourist Reception Centre at Srinagar will give up-to-date information on the rafting companies. Advance booking of river trips can also be made in Delhi through the Mountain Travel India office (tel. 7525357, 7525032) or Leh (tel. 01982-42013).

TREKKING

The Kashmir Valley and Ladakh are popular trekking territories and you can choose between a backpack or a full team of porters and bearers. There are several local agencies organising all inclusive trekking. Equipment is available in Srinagar, Pahalgam, Sonamarg and Leh. Trekking in Ladakh is particularly demanding as it is a high-altitude desert with extreme temperatures, and you have to be self-sufficient in food.

There are short and easy, as well as long and tough, treks in Kashmir. A short trek from Acchabal near Srinagar will take you to Kounsarnag, a mountain lake at 3,700 metres (12,140 feet). From Pahalgam you can take a four-day trek to the Kolahoi Glacier and back, or extend it into the Sindh Valley. Pahalgam can also be the base for a trek to Amarnath, returning either to Pahalgam or going on to Sonamarg. A nine-day trek from Pahalgam will take you to the Suru Valley south of Kargil. From Sonamarg you can take the week-long Lake Trek to the splendid Gangabal Lake at 3,570 metres (11,710 feet) via Vishansar and Krishansar lakes. From Gulmarg there are treks to Alpather Lake and Tosa Maidan, an alpine meadow. Treks to Padam in Zanskar start either from Kargil (seven days), Ringdom (five days) or Manali (ten days). From Padam there are various routes to be taken to Leh, as well as the week-long trek to Kishtwar in southern Kashmir over the Umasi La at 5,234 metres (17,172 feet).

Warning: In view of the uncertain political situation, trekking in the Kashmir Valley is **not** recommended.

Himachal Pradesh

Himachal Pradesh is a small mountain state constituted originally after Indian Independence when 31 hill princes resigned their right to rule. Himachal was then known as the Simla and Punjab Hill States. In 1966 it was enlarged to include the hill districts of Punjab, and gained a new name in the process. The state has become increasingly popular as a holiday destination, especially since the recent troubles in Kashmir. Its most celebrated hill station is Shimla, formerly spelt as Simla, the summer capital of the Raj.

Dalhousie

Dalhousie still retains much of the style of the British Raj. Its tin-roofed, half-timbered houses are spread over 13 square kilometres (five square miles) of well-forested hills, at heights between 1,525 and 2,378 metres (5,003 and 7,802 feet). Dalhousie stands at the foot of one of the main spurs of the Dhauladhar range of the Himalayas. The views are spectacular to the north; range upon range of hills culminating in the snow of the Pir Panjal mountains of Kashmir and to the south the plains of Punjab. Far below, runs the valley of one of the five rivers of Punjab, the Ravi, which flows through the city of Lahore in Pakistan. Two others, the Beas and the Chenab, can be seen snaking across the plains.

Church and Mall Road, Dalhousie c 1910

BACKGROUND

Dalhousie was named after the Marquess of Dalhousie who, between 1848 and 1856, was one of the ablest and most controversial governor-generals of India. He believed in a westernised and united India — united under British rule. He masterminded the construction of the railway and postal systems and set out to 'rationalise the map of India' by annexing previously independent states. His expansionist policies are held partly responsible for the Mutiny or First War of Independence in 1857. One of the prize feathers in Dalhousie's cap was the wresting of Punjab from its Sikh rulers in 1548. The new British rulers needed a convenient hill retreat and in 1851 the ruler of Chamba, on the fringes of the former Sikh empire, was asked for land to build a sanatorium.

In 1853, four hills — Kathlog, Portreyn, Tehra and Bakrota were transferred to the Government of India against an annual payment of Rs2,000 to Chamba state. In 1866, a fifth hill, Balun, was acquired for a cantonment (a permanent military camp), as were Banikhet and Bakloh lower down the mountainside. These are still cantonments today

By the 1860s, Dalhousie was a nourishing hill station. It was not a summer capital, and so was never as prestigious as Simla but the elite from the Punjab capital of Lahore flocked here to their neat bungalows and well-laid-out gardens. The district army headquarters moved up to Dalhousie each summer. With the army came some of the leading families of the modern hill station. The Khannas were first-class canteen contractors who built their own empire in Dalhousie. Today they run the Aroma-n-Claire hotel.

Dalhousie also became a major educational centre. An order of Belgian nuns established the Sacred Heart Convent on Portreyn and, with it, the Sacred Heart College.

At Independence, Lahore was lost to Pakistan and Dalhousie was deserted. It has now regained popularity, although it remains a 'second string' hill station which fortunately has not yet developed the five-star video culture of the plains.

GETTING THERE AND AROUND

There are regular trains from Delhi, Mumbai, Calcutta and Jammu to Pathankot, 80 kilometres (50 miles) from Dalhousie. This is definitely the most convenient way to travel, but rail bookings should be made in

Sunset, moonrise, Himachal Pradesh

advance, particularly during the tourist season. Buses or taxis are readily available from Pathankot up to Dalhousie. The drive takes you through the strangely eroded, scrub-covered hills and ravines before you climb steeply into the Dhauladhar range. Indian Airlines can take you to Amritsar, 100 kilometres (118 miles) away, which again is connected to Dalhousie by regular buses and taxis. Taxis over these routes can prove expensive unless you share them. There are also direct buses from the Interstate Bus Terminal in Delhi to Banikhet near Dalhousie.

Dalhousie is well connected by bus with other destinations in Himachal Pradesh like Dharamsala and Chamba. Local services run to the village of Lakkar Mandi and the meadow of Khajjiar. There are also conducted tours during the season.

SIGHTS

Most visitors arrive at the bus stand, the scruffiest part of Dalhousie, near the Tourist Office and the taxi stand. The main parts of Dalhousie lie above this terminus. Of the station's five hills, the most important are **Portreyn**, with the Sacred Heart Convent, **Moti Tibba** (formerly Tehra) and **Bakrota**. Around Moti Tibba and Portreyn there is a figure-of-eight shaped **Mall**, a level walk, nearly half of which is restricted to pedestrians. This is the most popular place to stroll in as it runs through oak, conifer and rhododendron forest. Signs warn motorists that 'walking is the fashion in the hills'. Black-faced langurs and rhesus macaques leap through the trees.

You can sit to watch the sunset at two crossroads on the way — **Subhash Chowk** (formerly Charing Cross), site of **St Francis's Catholic Church**, and **Gandhi Chowk**, site of the Protestant **St John's Church** and the post office. There is no Protestant congregation now, so the priest doubles as postmaster. Hill ponies are available for hire and there are lines of small shops selling walking sticks and other necessities.

A road leads down from Gandhi Chowk past **Sat-Dhara** (Place of Seven Streams), where mica-rich springs trickle from the hillside to **Panjpula** (Five Bridges), two kilometres (just over a mile) away. Here is a memorial to the uncle of the freedom-fighter and martyr, Bhagat Singh, who was executed by the British for murdering a police officer. Official beautification of this spot has not improved its appearance. On the Panchpula road, at **Luhali**, is a house called **Tynance** where one of

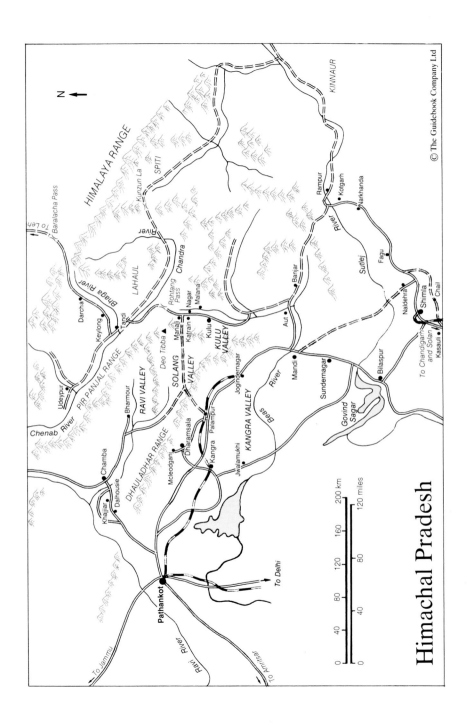

Himachal Pradesh

the foremost leaders of the freedom movement, Subhash Chandra Bose, came to work out his strategies, and after whom Subhash Chowk is named. Another pleasant walk is to **Jandri Ghat**, the summer palace of the Chamba rajas, two kilometres (one mile or so) from the post office. It has some remarkable hunting trophies, but these can only be seen with permission from the raja himself. Unless he is in Dalhousie, this is difficult to get. Above Gandhi Chowk is a path leading up **Bakrota Hill**. This is a steep climb but well worth the effort and the 'Bakrota Round' is famous. The Tibetans have their handicraft centre at Bakrota producing carpets and beaded jewellery. The Nobel prize-winning poet Rabindranath Tagore is said to have written part of his poem *Gitanjali* here at a house called **Snowden**. The watchman will open the house for Tagore fans.

Eight kilometres (five miles) from the post office, above Bakrota, is a village called **Lakkar Mandi**. A right turn here will take you to **Dainkund Peak**, known as the **Singing Hill** because of the sound of the wind blowing through the trees. The top of the hill is occupied by the Indian Air Force, but if you turn left before the main gate, you can take a path which leads to the **temple of the goddess Pholani Devi**. The temple has no image, just a forest of tridents (the type associated with Lord Shiva) stuck into the ground, but there are panoramic views.

A left turn at Lakkar Mandi brings you to the **wildlife sanctuary of Kalatop**, eight and a half kilometres (just over five miles) from the post office (altitude 2,440 metres or 8,005 feet). The forest is very thick and you need luck to sight any of the barking deer or Himalayan black bear in the sanctuary. However, it's a fine place for birdwatchers and, again, the views are remarkable. There is a Forest Resthouse for those wishing to stay overnight (reservations to be made in Dalhousie).

Some 17 kilometres (ten and a half miles) from the post office, straight on beyond Lakkar Mandi, you come to **Khajjiar** at 2,000 metres (6,562 feet). Here there is a saucer-shaped meadow a kilometre and a half (one mile) long and a kilometre (half a mile) across, with a small lake in the centre. The lake has a curious floating island and nearby is a 14th century, golden-domed temple devoted to Khajinag. On all sides are dense deodar forest. Lord Curzon called this 'the prettiest place I have seen in India'. It now has a tourist bungalow and a rarely used golf course.

Chamba

The road to Chamba runs along the valley of the fast-flowing Ravi, at first high above and then beside the river. The town, 53 kilometres (33 miles) from Dalhousie and connected by regular bus services, was the capital of the former rajas of Chamba. It is perched on a mountain shelf 996 metres (3,268 feet) above sea level, which drops cliff-like to the river below. At the centre of Chamba is the Chaugan, a large grassy park which runs for a kilometre (half a mile) along the cliff over the Ravi. From the **Chaugan** you can see the snows, while above it stands the elegant **Akhand Chandi Palace** of the royal family, part of which has now been converted into government offices and a college. For details of where to stay, see page 271.

Background

The kingdom of Chamba was ruled, without a break, by the same Rajput family from AD 550 to Independence in 1947. The first ruler, Maru Varma, established his capital at Brahmpura, today's Bharmour. Around AD 930, his descendant, Sahi Varma, moved the capital to Chamba at the request of his daughter Champavati after whom the town was named. Chamba was sufficiently remote to escape Muslim invasions; all the ruler was obliged to do was to accept the authority of the paramount power in the region. So the kingdom kept its ancient temples intact, and became a refuge for artists whenever there was turmoil in the plains.

The state had excellent relations with Ranjit Singh, the great 19th-century Sikh ruler of the Punjab, as one of the raja's chief ministers had prevented the Sikh ruler's palanquin from falling into a deep precipice. After Ranjit Singh's death, relations deteriorated and the state was about to face attack from Sikh forces when the Anglo-Sikh war broke out. After the British annexed the Punjab in 1849, the raja continued to run his own affairs, but under the supervision of a British Resident who lived in what is now the Circuit House at the end of the Chaugan.

Sights

Chamba is celebrated for its finely carved temples built in the *shikhara* or spired style of the Indian plains. They are devoted to forms of

Vishnu and Shiva, the Preserver and Destroyer respectively of the Hindu Trinity. The worship of Shiva was established earlier. Vishnu becoming a popular deity by the ninth century AD.

The 11th-century **Hari Rai Temple** at one end of the Chaugan, next to a ruined gateway, is devoted to the four-faced form of Vishnu. The idol was stolen some years ago and taken to a godown in Mumbai. Vishnu is said to have appeared to the owner of the godown and to have threatened his life if he didn't inform the police. The terrified owner immediately went to the police and the idol was restored to its rightful place.

The **main temple complex** is further up towards the palace. There are six temples. The largest temple of Lakshmi Narayan, and the temples of Radha Krishna and Lakshmi Damodar are devoted to Vishnu. The temples of Chandragupta, Gauri Shankar and Trimukhteshwara are devoted to Shiva. All of them are provided with pitched roofs to drain off the snows. The earliest date from the 10th-11th centuries, although they were restored in the 16th century, and one, the Lakshmi Narayan temple, was restored recently by the Archaeological Survey. The new slabs of stone have already begun to weather badly. However, nothing can mar the beauty of the carvings — floral and animal designs with scenes from Hindu mythology and daily temple worship. The splendid idol of Lakshmi Narayan stands on an altar of beaten silver, the Gauri Shankar temple has an equally ancient metal image of Shiva and his consort.

Outside the temples stand a number of fine images of Nandi, the bull which is Shiva's vehicle. Other smaller shrines dot the complex. The priests are very active and six times a day the temple musicians play drums and *shehnais* to accompany the ceremonies.

To one side of the palace is the **Bansi Gopal Temple**, which is dedicated to Krishna and has a collection of stone images. Higher still, a kilometre (half a mile or so) from the Chaugan, is the **temple of Chamunda Mata**, overlooking the town and the river. It is a popular picnic spot.

Chamba also has the fascinating **Bhuri Singh Museum**, named after the raja who ruled Chamba from 1904 to 1915. Most of the exhibits in the museum were donated by him. They were catalogued by the celebrated Indologist, Dr J P Vogel, who set up the museum. It has a unique collection of fountain slabs, carved stones set up in memory of the heroes of Chamba and their wives, many of whom committed *sati* (ritual immolation) on the funeral pyres of their husbands. The heroes were not necessarily warriors; also among them were men who had shown great compassion. The slabs were set up at wells and fountains because, besides being sources of water, they were also meeting places where villagers would sit together and talk. The museum collection of 18th- and 19th-century miniature paintings is also well worth seeing. The various hill or Pahari schools of painting originally developed when artists from the plains fled to the peaceful hills in times of unrest. The oldest school developed in Basholi, and the later Guler and Kangra schools are well represented, showing scenes of courtly life and Hindu mythology. There are also murals from the Rang Mahal palace at Chamba, which is now reduced to a **Handicrafts Centre**. An artist is attached to the museum to help continue the tradition of Pahari miniature painting.

FESTIVALS

The chief festival in Chamba takes place some time at the end of July or the beginning of August. Called the Minjar festival, it is named after the flower of the maize plant — the staple crop of the region. Men wear gold threads symbolising the maize flower for the week-long celebrations which include sports and folk dancing on the Chaugan. On the last day, the emblems of the royal house and local deities are carried in palanquins in procession to the banks of the Ravi and the golden threads are consigned to the waters.

Krishna, the pastoral god, a miniature from the Bhuri Singh Museum

Narasimha, an avatar of Vishnu, a painting from the Bhuri Singh Museum, Chamba

Shiva allowing the sacred Ganga to flow out of his top-knot, from the Bhuri Singh Museum

Dharamsala

Dharamsala lies on a spur of the Dhauladhar range of the outer Himalayas. Dhauladhar means 'white crest' or 'ridge' and this snow-capped range rises sheer out of the Kangra Valley to heights of between 4,300 and 5,200 metres (14,000 and 17,000 feet). It is a treacherous range, the weather being very unpredictable, but it has many passes between 2,400 and 4,570 metres (8,900 and 15,000 feet) which provide paths for the nomadic herdsmen of the Ravi Valley beyond to make their way to lower pastures.

The Kangra Valley is a wide fertile plain crossed by low hills which look, from a distance, like ripples on the surface of a lake. Rice and wheat are grown here, and tea too. Near the mountains are pine woods whilst the plains are dotted with clumps of bamboo. The scenery touched the heart of the British official who wrote:

> No scenery, in my opinion, presents such sublime and delightful contrasts. Below lies the plain, a picture of rural loveliness and repose; the surface is covered with the richest cultivation, irrigated by streams which descend from perennial snows, and interspersed with homesteads buried in the midst of groves and fruit trees. Turning from this scene of peaceful beauty, the stern and majestic hills confront us, their sides are furrowed with precipitous water-courses; forests of oak clothe their flanks and higher up give place to gloomy and funereal pines; above all are wastes of snow or pyramidal masses of granite too perpendicular for the snow to rest on.

There is less forest now than then, but the general effect is still the same.

Dharamsala is a hill station split into two. It lies between 1,250 and 1,982 metres (4,100 and 6,503 feet) on the steep mountainside. The lower part, known only as Dharamsala, is nine kilometres (five and a half miles) away by road from the upper part, known as Mcleodganj. It has a population of some 16,000 and is surrounded by pine, oak and deodar forest. Parts, however, are now sadly deforested. Mcleodganj is the present home of the Dalai Lama of Tibet.

For hotels in Dharamsala, see page 271.

BACKGROUND

Dharamsala means 'resthouse' for this is where Hindu pilgrims have traditionally stopped. But the original Dharamsala has long since been forgotten. In 1849, the British planned to accommodate only a regiment here, but it did not remain a military centre for long. By 1855, it was a flourishing small hill station and administrative headquarters of Kangra district which had been taken over by the British in 1848. The two main areas were Mcleodganj, named after a lieutenant governor of Punjab, and Forsythganj, named after a divisional commissioner. The Viceroy, Lord Elgin, loved the forests of Dharamsala, and before he died here in 1863, he asked to be buried in the graveyard of St John-in-the-Wilderness. If he had lived, Dharamsala, not Shimla might have become the summer capital of the Raj.

A severe earthquake in 1905 changed the face of Dharamsala. Many buildings collapsed; the whole villages, once destroyed, were never re-occupied. The local officials advised residents to move to the safety of lower Dharamsala which, until then, had boasted not much more than a jail, a police station and, possibly, a cobbler's shop.

At Partition when the British left and the Muslims were forced out or chose to go, Mcleodganj became a ghost town until the Dalai Lama of Tibet made it his headquarters in 1960. Mcleodganj is now very much 'Little Tibet', with modern buildings constructed in Tibetan style and many more under construction.

GETTING THERE

Dharamsala is 90 kilometres (56 miles) east of Pathankot railway station. There are regular buses to Dharamsala and a narrow-gauge train as far as Kangra, 17 kilometres (ten and a half miles) from Dharamsala. There are direct buses connecting the hill station with Delhi (470 kilometres or 292 miles away), Chandigarh (239 kilometres or 149 miles away), Mandi (147 kilometres or 91 miles away) and Shimla (278 kilometres or 173 miles away).

'Mrs Packletide's Tiger'

*I*t was Mrs Packletide's pleasure and intention that she should shoot a tiger. Not that the lust to kill had suddenly descended on her, or that she felt that she would leave India safer and more wholesome than she had found it, with one fraction less of wild beast per million of inhabitants. The compelling motive for her sudden deviation towards the footsteps of Nimrod was the fact that Loona Bimberton had recently been carried eleven miles in an aeroplane by an Algerian aviator, and talked of nothing else; only a personally procured tiger-skin and a heavy harvest of Press photographs could successfully counter that sort of thing. Mrs Packletide had already arranged in her mind the lunch she would give at her house in Curzon Street, ostensibly in Loona Bimberton's honour, with a tiger-skin rug occupying most of the foreground and all the conversation. She had also already designed in her mind the tiger-claw brooch that she was going to give Loona Bimberton on her next birthday. In a world that is supposed to be chiefly swayed by hunger and by love Mrs Packletide was an exception; her movements and motives were largely governed by dislike of Loona Bimberton.*

Circumstances proved propitious. Mrs Packletide had offered a thousand rupees for the opportunity of shooting a tiger without overmuch risk or exertion, and it so happened that a neighbouring village could boast of being the favoured rendezvous of an animal of respectable antecedents, which had been driven by the increasing infirmities of age to abandon gamekilling and confine its appetite to the smaller domestic animals. The prospect of earning the thousand rupees had stimulated the sporting and commercial instinct of the villagers; children were posted night and day on the outskirts of the local jungle to head the tiger back in the unlikely event of his attempting to roam away to fresh hunting-grounds, and the cheaper kinds of goats were left about with elaborate carelessness to keep him satisfied with his present quarters. The one great anxiety was lest he should die of old age before the date appointed for the memsahib's shoot. Mothers carrying their babies home through the jungle after the day's work in the fields hushed their singing lest they might curtail the restful sleep of the venerable herd-robber.

The great night duly arrived, moonlit and cloudless. A platform had been constructed in a comfortable and conveniently placed tree, and thereon crouched Mrs Packletide and her paid companion, Miss Mebbin. A goat, gifted with a particularly persistent bleat, such as even a partially deaf tiger might be reasonably expected to hear on a still night, was tethered at the correct distance. With an accurately sighted rifle and a thumb-nail pack of patience cards the sportswoman awaited the coming of the quarry.

'I suppose we are in some danger?' said Miss Mebbin.

She was not actually nervous about the wild beast, but she had a morbid dread of performing an atom more service than she had been paid for.

'Nonsense,' said Mrs Packletide; 'it's a very old tiger. It couldn't spring up here even if it wanted to.'

'If it's an old tiger I think you ought to get it cheaper. A thousand rupees is a lot of money'.

Louisa Mebbin adopted a protective elder-sister attitude towards money in general, irrespective of nationality or denomination. Her energetic intervention had saved many a rouble from dissipating itself in tips in some Moscow hotel, and francs and centimes clung to her instinctively under circumstances which would have driven them headlong from less sympathetic hands. Her speculations as to the market depreciation of tiger remnants were cut short by the appearance on the scene of the animal itself. As soon as it caught sight of the tethered goat it lay flat on the earth, seemingly less from a desire to take advantage of all available cover than for the purpose of snatching a short rest before commencing the grand attack.

'I believe it's ill,' said Louisa Mebbin, loudly in Hindustani, for the benefit of the village headman, who was in ambush in a neighbouring tree. 'Hush!' said Mrs. Packletide, and at that moment the tiger commenced ambling towards his victim.

'Now, now!' urged Miss Mebbin with some excitement, 'if he doesn't touch the goat we needn't pay for it.' (The bait was an extra).

The rifle flashed out with a loud report, and the great tawny beast sprang to one side and then rolled over in the stillness of death. In a moment a crowd of excited natives had swarmed on the scene, and their shouting speedily carried the glad news to the village, where a thumping of tomtoms took up the chorus of triumph. And their triumph and rejoicing found a ready echo in the heart of Mrs Packletide; already that luncheon-party in Curzon Street seemed immeasurably nearer.

It was Louisa Mebbin who drew attention to the fact that the goat was in death-throes from a mortal bullet-wound, while no trace of the rifle's deadly work could be found on the tiger. Evidently the wrong animal had been hit, and the beast of prey had succumbed to heart-failure, caused by the sudden report of the rifle, accelerated by senile decay. Mrs Packletide was pardonably annoyed at the discovery; but, at any rate, she was the possessor of a dead tiger, and the villagers, anxious for their thousand rupees, gladly connived at the fiction that she had shot the beast. And Miss Mebbin was a paid companion. Therefore did Mrs Packletide face the cameras with a light heart, and her pictured fame reached from the pages of the Texas Weekly Snapshot *to the illustrated Monday supplement of the* Novoe Vremya. *As for Loona Bimberton, she refused to look at an illustrated paper for weeks, and her letter of thanks for the gift of a tiger-claw brooch was a model of repressed emotions. The luncheon-party she declined; there are limits beyond which repressed emotions become dangerous.*

H H Munro (Saki)

SIGHTS

Little Lhasa in India

Mcleodganj's small bazaar consists of lines of Tibetan restaurants and hotels. In the centre of the bazaar is the **Namgyalma Stupa** surrounded by golden prayer wheels turned by devotees circumambulating the shrine. There are numerous shops and stalls selling Tibetan handicrafts, and a **Tibetan Handicraft Centre** where they are made. A video parlour screens films on Tibet. One of the original residents of the bazaar is the proprietor of **Nowrojee's Wine and General Merchants** which has been selling 'High Class Mineral Water' since 1860. The old-fashioned shop still advertises Peak Freen's biscuits made in Britain, and State Express 555 cigarettes as smoked by Madeleine Carroll, a star of British Gaumont Pictures.

At the opposite end of the bazaar from Nowrojee's is a road leading down to a complex of buildings housing the **Central Cathedral (Tsuglag Khang)**, the **Namgyal Monastery** and the **residence of the Dalai Lama**. The path to the cathedral takes you past the monastery where you can often see young monks playing badminton. The residence of the Dalai Lama is not open to visitors but the cathedral is. It is a simple, yellow-painted hall hung with Tibetan paintings. At one end is a raised dais. The principal image there is a three-metre- (nine-foot-) tall Buddha. To one side are two other large images of the bodhisattvas Avalokiteshvara, the patron deity of Tibet, and Padmasambhava, the Buddhist saint who, in the eighth century AD, was invited to Tibet from India to teach the Middle Way. The tall cupboards are full of Tibetan scriptures and in the centre of the dais is the seat of the Dalai Lama who gives discourses here. Religious festivities, including monastic dances, are also held and there is a constant stream of devotees.

A road from the cathedral complex leads steeply down to **Kotwali Bazaar**. Halfway down is the **Central Tibetan Secretariat**. In this complex of buildings is a fascinating library of Tibetan works. The library also arranges lectures on Buddhist philosophy. Nearby is the small **Nechung Monastery**, the seat of the Nechung Oracle who plays an important part in the search for new Dalai Lamas.

A kilometre (half a mile or so) uphill from Mcleodganj is the **Tibetan Institute of Performing Arts** which in April every year holds a ten-day folk opera festival. Other Tibetan institutions include a **Tibetan Medical Institute** and **children's villages** which give education to thousands of Tibetan children. A two-hour climb above Mcleodganj and beyond the **Bhagsunath Waterfall** are the Retreat Caves where monks stay for meditation.

Down the Hill
The **Church of St-John-in-the-Wilderness** lies 15 minutes' walk from Mcleodganj on the longer and thickly forested road to the Kotwali Bazaar. This road takes you to the bazaar of Forsythganj and through the cantonment. The grey-stone church lies in a glade of deodar cedars at 1,768 metres (5,800 feet). It was built in 1852 and has some fine Belgian stained glass windows donated by Lady Elgin. The memorial to her husband, Lord Elgin, stands in the churchyard. Below the windows devoted to Justice and Sacrifice is a shield showing the Stars and Stripes. Brass plaques and a large brass eagle lectern show the long connection between this church and the Gurkha Rifles. The church miraculously survived the earthquake of 1905 — only the spire collapsed. A new bell was sent out from London and stands suspended a metre or so from the ground outside the ruined tower. After Independence the church was neglected and the activities of local monkeys caused the roof to collapse. The church reopened in 1986 and you can visit between 10 am and 5 pm each day.

There are many pleasant houses in lower Dharamsala, but the main Kotwali Bazaar holds little attraction. The bus stand makes it a convenient place to stay if travelling early in the morning, and, if you have questions about the region, the **Himachal Pradesh Tourist Development Corporation** (HPTDC) has an office on the first floor above its own restaurant.

The Tibetan Library (above) and monks (below), Dharamsala

The Kangra Valley

Y ou can best see the scenery of the Kangra Valley by taking a journey on the narrow-gauge railway which runs for 164 kilometres (102 miles) from Pathankot in the west to Jogindernagar in the east, via Kangra and Palampur, the two major towns in the valley. The line was constructed in less than three years and opened for traffic in April 1929. Until 1973 steam engines imported from Britain hauled the trains over the 932 bridges (35 of them major), through the two tunnels, and round the 456 curves on the railway. Now all engines on the line are diesel. The track is cleverly aligned and runs along the foot of the hills. At the same time it has panoramic views of the valley. From the outskirts of Palampur the line comes within 16 kilometres (ten miles) of the snows, and stays close to them until it turns southwards to the terminal of Jogindernagar.

About 17 kilometres (ten and a half miles) south from Dharamsala is Kangra, situated at the confluence of the Bener and Majhi streams and overlooking the Banganga torrent. On a ridge stands **Nagarkot**, the fort of the rajas of Kangra, which now lies in ruins. Kangra was subjected to numerous invasions from the 11th century onwards. Part of its attraction were the riches belonging to the golden-domed **Vajeshwari temple** next to the fort.

After an invasion by the Mughal emperor Jahangir in the 16th century, the state enjoyed a more peaceful period and its raja, Sansar Chand (1775-1823), was a great patron of the arts. It was then that the celebrated Kangra school of miniature paintings evolved. This creative period, however, was interrupted when the Sikh ruler, Ranjit Singh, invaded Kangra and the raja was forced to move his capital elsewhere.

Walks

Triund is one of the most scenic places within easy reach from the town. The direct route leads nine kilometres (five and a half miles) steeply up from the Mcleodganj bus stand, past the **Mountaineering Institute**, and through deodar and rhododendron forest. It offers views of the Dhauladhars which rise directly behind Dharamsala.

The other route to Triund is via **Bhagsunath**, a couple of kilometres (just over a mile) from the bus stand down the road to Green's Hotel.

Nagarkot and the Vajeshwari temple are the main places of interest for visitors.

Palampur, 1,219 metres (3,999 feet) above sea level, is in the centre of the tea-growing area and the home of an Agricultural University. The town offers fine views of the mountains and there are some pleasant walks, for example, to **Buddha Chasm**. Near Palampur is the village of **Andretta** where there is a gallery displaying pictures by the late Sardar Sobha Singh, the artist who was the village's most famous resident. Some of his most famous paintings depict scenes from the great folk love stories of Punjab. A few kilometres out of town is **Al-Hilal**, the summer retreat of Ranjit Singh. The palace was subsequently sold to the rulers of Jammu and is now run by the last ruler of Jammu and Kashmir as a hotel.

Another stop on the railway line is **Baijnath**, a pilgrim centre with a ninth-century temple dedicated to Vaidyanath.

Jogindernagar, with its hydro-electric plant, is the last stop on the line.

Some 30 kilometres (19 miles) from Kangra and 56 kilometres (35 miles) from Dharamsala is the famous **temple of Jwalamukhi**, the flame-faced one, which has festivals in early April and mid-October. There is no idol but an undying flame which burns in a rock sanctum. The temple has a golden dome donated by the Mughal emperor Akbar. Some 15 kilometres (ten miles) south of Kangra is **Masroor**, known for its 15 richly carved rock-cut temples. Although they are now partly ruined, their resemblance to the great Kailash Temple at Ellora in Maharashtra can clearly be seen.

At Bhagsunath there is an old temple. There is also a waterfall, but the scenery has been ruined by the depredations of a stone quarry.

Beyond Forsythganj, 11 kilometres (seven miles) from Kotwali Bazaar, is the small **Dal Lake** surrounded by cedars, and near one of the Tibetan children's villages.

A more impressive lake to visit is **Kerei**, 33 kilometres (14 miles) from Kotwali Bazaar. There is also a resthouse 13 kilometres (eight miles) from the lake for overnight halts.

The Kullu Valley

The Kullu Valley, with its two main tourist centres of Kullu and Manali 41 kilometres (25 miles) apart, is one of the most enchanting parts of Himachal Pradesh. The valley is 80 kilometres (50 miles) long and no more than two kilometres (just over a mile) wide. The land slopes northwards from the town of Mandi, at 760 metres (2,493 feet), to the Rohtang Pass at 3,978 metres (13,050 feet). Through the Valley runs the Beas River, bordered by paddy fields in the monsoon and wheat fields in the winter. In March you can see the fruit trees in bloom and by June begin to taste the fruit. Conifers and rhododendrons fringe the upper slopes which are covered by snow in winter. To the northwest of the valley is the white mass of the Solang Valley and to the north is the Rohtang Pass, the gateway to the Great Himalayas. The road to Lahaul and on to Leh in Ladakh crosses the Rohtang Pass at 4,075 metres (13,370 feet). The Solang Valley is a winter ski slope. The views in the Kullu Valley are clear even in May and June when a pall of dust generally hangs in the air around most hill stations.

PEOPLE OF THE VALLEY

The Kullu Valley is in the happy position of being a well-developed tourist destination without having been ruined by tourists. The local people still largely preserve their way of life and are not economically dependent on visitors. They have their orchards and also their looms from which to earn their living. The production of woollen Kullu shawls with their geometrically patterned borders is becoming increasingly commercialised, but many local woollen items are still made at home. The women of the area wear homespun tunics, called *pattus*, fastened with pins. They do much of the work in the fields and collect fodder which they carry back home on their backs in conical baskets called *kiltas*. The characteristic dress of the men is the round Kullu cap, which has a decorated band across the front.

The traditional stone and wood village houses are particularly attractive. The lower floors are occupied by cattle and often stacked high with hay and straw. Delicately carved wooden balconies run round the upper storeys.

Manali Valley in spring

Near Mandi, Himachal Pradesh

The Gaddis are a separate community of nomadic shepherds who visit the valley between March and September and who originally come from Bharmour. They take their herds of long-haired goats up as far as Lahaul and Spiti to graze. The fair-skinned Gaddis are believed to be descendants of the armies of Alexander the Great. They wear pleated skirts bound at the waist with great lengths of woollen cord to keep out the cold. Another nomadic community are the Muslim Gujars who bring their buffaloes to the valley in the summer and sell their milk to local hotels and sweet shops.

Despite its remoteness, Kullu has always attracted outsiders. Like other hill states, it was annexed by the Sikh ruler of Punjab, Ranjit Singh and fell under British control when the Sikh armies were defeated in the Anglo-Sikh War. British army officers who originally visited the valley to hunt came back to settle. They formed a colony of planters and tried growing tea, but failed to make commercial success of it. According to some, the first man to think of planting apple trees here was an Irishman, Captain A T Bannon, who imported 200 trees in the 1860s. He seems to have stolen a march on the other orchard pioneer, Captain R C Lee of the Royal Sussex Regiment, who bought land in Kullu in 1870 and began to plant fruit trees. Their experiments proved successful. However, there was no road into the valley until after Independence and the entire orchard produce had to be carried 130 kilometres (81 miles) over the passes by porters. Like several of the planters, Captain Bannon came to stay and married a local girl. His grandson now runs the John Bannon Guest House in Manali and still owns some orchards. Independence and the construction of the road broke up the British colony and brought in the new age of tourism.

GETTING THERE AND AROUND
There are regular flights between Bhuntar airport, ten kilometres (six miles) south of Kullu and Delhi. Some also connect with Shimla and Chandigarh. There are also direct taxis and buses (including air-conditioned video coaches) to Kullu from Delhi, a distance of 512 kilometres (318 miles), Shimla, 235 kilometres (146 miles) and Chandigarh, 270 kilometres (168 miles) away. The journey from Delhi

can take 15 hours and only those with strong dispositions should take the video coach. Rail enthusiasts may prefer to take an overnight train to Chandigarh and take the bus from there in the early morning. If you have time to spare take a broad-gauge train to Pathankot, then catch the narrow-gauge train to Jogindernagar, and a bus from there to Kullu. There are also direct bus connections between Dharamsala, Pathankot and Mandi. Many buses to Kullu go on to Manali, 42 kilometres (26 miles) further up the valley.

There are frequent bus services between Mandi, Kullu and Manali. Taxis are also available, but the local taxi drivers' unions have fixed prices which are not low, but bargains can still be struck when business is slack. The Himachal Tourism office in Manali arranges conducted tours from there to the Rohtang Pass, Nagar and Manikaran during the main tourist season. At the height of the season, it's best to buy tickets in advance.

For details of where to stay, see page 272.

SIGHTS
On the Way There
The Chandigarh, Delhi and Shimla roads to Kullu all meet near Bilaspur, which is on the shores of the **Govind Sagar reservoir**. Further on, where you can see half submerged temples, is the pleasant valley of **Sundernagar** which has been transformed by the Beas/Sutlej scheme, the biggest irrigation project in Asia. There is a large canal and dam and the roadsides are planted with poplars and eucalyptus.

The valley narrows again before reaching the old princely capital of **Mandi**, a small town which is fast losing its character through new construction and the decay of its old buildings. A section of one palace has been turned into a very ramshackle hotel. It is, however, celebrated for its temples: **Bhutnath, Triloknath, Panchvaktra** and **Shayamalkoli** at **Tarna Hill**.

Beyond Mandi the road passes through a 40-kilometre- (25-mile-) long gorge. This is particularly spectacular beyond the **Pandoh Dam**. The gorge has tantalising glimpses of the snows, before it widens and the road runs through orchards up to Kullu.

Goddesses from all over the Kullu Valley
are brought in procession to Mandi for the festival of Shivratri

Kullu

Kullu, at 1,220 metres (4,003 feet), on the banks of the Beas River, is the local district headquarters and the largest settlement in the valley. The town is divided into three parts. In the south is the **Dhalpur Maidan**, a large, grassy area where the Dussehra festival takes place. On the edge of the maidan are the tourist office and one of the two bus stations in Kullu. From the **Dhalpur Bazaar** the main road crosses the Sarvari River, a tributary of the Beas. Across the Sarvari is the **Adhara Bazaar**, a maze of narrow lanes lined with haphazardly built shops. On the hill above is the tranquil **Sultanpur**, where Raja Jagat Singh built his capital in the 17th century. The descendants of the raja still own the Rupi Palace in Sultanpur, parts of which have been converted into Home Guard offices. Near the palace, around a courtyard of jasmine bushes, are the buildings of the **Raghunathji Temple** dedicated to Ram and Sita, the temple images of whom lead the Dussehra procession and festival. These richly adorned images are only 15-20 centimetres tall — the height, according to some Hindu pandits, of the human soul.

Around Kullu

Some three kilometres (two miles) out of Kullu, up a steep path off the main road to the Akhara Bazaar, is the **Jagannath Devi Temple** in the village of Bhekhli. From here you can look down over the town and valley. Also worth seeing is the small **cave temple of the goddess Vaishno Devi**, which lies four kilometres (two and a half miles) further along the Kullu-Manali road.

One of the most striking views is from the **temple of Bijli Mahadev** high up on the mountainside, across the Beas and 14 kilometres (nine miles) from Kullu. There is a motorable road up to the temple which has a 20-metre- (65-foot-) high staff said to attract divine blessings in the form of lightning. Another famous temple is at **Bajaura**, 15 kilometres (just over nine miles) short of Kullu. The *shikara*-style temple of **Basheshwar Mahadev** is just outside the village and dates from the mid-eighth century. Some of the elaborate carvings have been mutilated, probably by the invading armies of the Kangra kingdom in the 18th century.

Manikaran, at 1,737 metres (5,699 feet) and 45 kilometres (28 miles) east of Kullu, lies in the valley of the Parvati River which joins the Beas south of Kullu at Bhuntar. The Parvati is named after the consort of Lord Shiva who lost her earrings — *manikarna* — and recovered them at the spot from which the hamlet's famous hot springs bubble up. Sulphur baths are available here for the devout or simply weary traveller. The water from the springs is boiling hot and rice and lentils are cooked at the temple by lowering pots into it. There is also a Sikh temple, or *gurudwara*, at Manikaran and a Himachal Tourism bungalow.

Largi, a small hamlet 34 kilometres (21 miles) south of Kullu via Aut, offers the best trout fishing in the valley. The resthouse there is in a stunning location where two Himalayan torrents, the Sainj and Tirthan, meet. Fishing permits can be obtained from Kullu and Largi itself (the tourist office will give details). Bring your own tackle and remember that trout in the Kullu Valley respond more often to spinners than flies.

There are two roads, one on each side of the Beas, from Kullu to Manali. The eastern side of the river is known as the 'left bank' and locals will tell you this is the more picturesque. But the main road runs along the western side. Some 12 kilometres (seven and a half miles) from Kullu on this road is **Raison** (altitude 1,433 metres or 4,700 feet), which has many orchards and is a good trekking base. There is a camp site, as well as Himachal Tourism huts, here. **Katrain**, 20 kilometres (12 and a half miles) from Kullu, lies at 1,463 metres (4,800 feet). It has a small hotel. This village too is famous for its orchards, bee-keeping and nearby trout farms. The valley is at its widest here and above it towers the 3,325-metre- (10,908-foot-) high **Baragarh Peak**.

Opposite Katrain, on the eastern side of the Beas, is **Nagar** which was the capital of the state for 1,400 years prior to the move to Kullu in the 18th century. The village clings to the hillside at an altitude of 1,770 metres (5,807 feet). The survival of the 500-year-old castle of Nagar, built of wood and stone, proves the earthquake-resistant properties of local architecture. The castle is now a small hotel, worth staying in for the views alone. In one of its courtyards is the small shrine of **Jagati Pat** containing a stone slab which, according to tradition, was carried down from the peak of Deo Tibba by the gods in the form of a swarm of bees. It is said that Nagar is the seat of the gods and that, at times of crisis, the gods all gather by the shrine. The castle also has a verandah said to be haunted by the ghost of a young *rani* who leapt from there to her death.

Among the traditional houses of the village was until recently the pagoda-style **temple of the goddess Tripura Sundari**. This ancient and beautiful temple was recently demolished to make way for a modern one. The two other main temples are the little stone **shrine of Gaurishankar** (Shiva and Parvati) and the **temple of Murlidhar** (Krishna, the flute player), 15 metres (49 feet) above the present village. These are both in the *shikhara* style, while a miniature chalet-style **temple to Narasingh** (the lion incarnation of Vishnu) stands opposite the main entrance to the castle.

A Russian painter, Nicholas Roerich, made his home in Nagar, a kilometre (less than a mile) above the village. In his house, surrounded by rose beds and covered with wisteria, is a collection of his paintings of the Himalayas, together with local folk carvings. Roerich aimed to unify humanity through art. For many years he was an exile from his own country although the Soviet Union finally accepted him as a Russian artist. Roerich died in 1947 and was buried according to Hindu rites. A memorial stone to him inscribed in Hindi lies on a terrace below his house.

Jagatsukh, the most ancient Kullu capital, is on the left bank, between Nagar and Manali. Little remains of the glory of this former state capital where rice was first cultivated in the valley. Around the Jagatsukh secondary school playground there are two ancient temples — the small **shrine of Gaurishankar** and the larger chalet-roofed **temple to the goddess Sandhya Devi**, the stone base of which is much more ancient than the 19th-century wooden verandah and roof.

Manali

Manali is the main tourist resort in the valley. It is ideally situated along the western bank of the Beas, close to the snows of the Rohtang Pass and Solang Valley. Since it is at an altitude of 1,830 metres (6,004 feet), it is never hot. The mean maximum temperature in summer is 25°C (77°F) so light woollen clothing and blankets are needed even in May and June. It is well organised for tourists, with an efficient, though sometimes oversubscribed, tourist office in the main bazaar. This is also the site of the taxi stand, bus stand and ponies-for-hire stand. A host of

Temples in the shikhara style: the Radha Krishna temple, Nagar (left): the 12th-century stone temple in Jagatsukh (right):

The steep terrain of the Sutlej Valley, Himachal Pradesh

small shops, restaurants and small hotels (see page 272) provide the neccessities of daily life. The bazaar is not large, but is becoming progressively built up. The crowds of tourists have increased since the recent troubles in Kashmir began. Those who like peace and quiet will be relieved to hear that most established guest houses are on the quieter roads to the north of and above the bazaar. Walking just a couple of kilometres (just over a mile) outside the town you can still reach undisturbed countryside.

SIGHTS

To the north of the bazaar the main road leads past a forest reserve, fringed by introduced species — English limes and oaks. Marijuana, which once made Manali a hippie haven, still grows wild under the trees. A left turn leads to the pagoda-style **Hadimba Temple** surrounded by deodar cedars of the Doongri forest. There is a steep footpath to the temple or a longer motorable road. The four-tiered pagoda built in 1553 is constructed around a small natural cave which enshrines the footprints of the goddess Hadimba. Outside hang deer antlers and markhor horns donated by local hunters. Hadimba, the demoness, married Bhima, one of the great heroes of the Hindu epic, the *Mahabharata*, and eventually was adopted as the patron goddess of the Kullu royal family. Other gods in the valley recognise her seniority and, mounted on palanquins, their images attend a festival in her honour every May.

North of the road to the Hadimba Temple is the Manalsu River which flows into the Beas. Across the river lies old Manali, the original village which seems centuries behind the not-very-modern Manali of hotels. Slippery stone paths lead through the old village houses up to the **temple of Manu**. Manali is named after the sage Manu who is believed to have resided here.

Tibetans have a base in Manali too. There is a large modern Tibetan temple to the south of the bus stand and also a small handicrafts centre.

On the left bank of the Beas, five kilometres (three miles) from Manali near the village of Prini, is the **Arjun Gufa** or cave of Arjuna. One of the heroes of the *Mahabharata*, Arjuna is said to have performed penance here.

On the same side of the Beas is the **Mountaineering Institute**, which offers training courses to organised groups. The institute staff will offer expert advice to trekkers.

North of the institute and a little more than three kilometres (two miles) from the centre of Manali is the village of **Vashisht**, famous for its hot **sulphur springs**. There are two sets of sulphur baths. The first is by the temple in the centre of the village dedicated to the sage Vashisht. The black stone image of ʼthe sage, with silver eyes and wearing a sacred thread, stands in a shrine within a shrine. Next to the shrine are two open-air baths, one for men and one for women. If you are particularly weary, however, try the other, more comfortable sulphur baths in the nearby Himachal Tourism complex.

Beyond Vashisht the motor road leads to the **Rohtang Pass**, the gateway to the districts of Lahaul and Spiti.

Six kilometres (four miles) from Manali is **Nehru Kund**, a spring named after the late prime minister, Jawaharlal Nehru, who was very fond of the area. Northwest of the resort is the splendid **Solang Valley**. The nearest glacier to Manali (only 13 kilometres or eight miles away) is here, as are ski slopes which are generally operational in January and February. Also in the Solang Valley is a hostel of the Department of Mountaineering and Allied Sports, Manali. Beyond the turning to the Solang Valley, 12 kilometres (seven and a half miles) from Manali, is the beautiful village of **Kothi**. The views are particularly fine at this point, and the Beas River here runs through a narrow gorge. The well-situated Public Works Department (PWD) Resthouse is a popular place for overnight stays. Four kilometres (two and a half miles) further on from Kothi are the beautiful **Rahalla Falls**.

From the Rahalla Falls the road climbs to the Rohtang Pass, 51 kilometres (32 miles) from Manali and 3,978 metres (13,050 feet) above sea level. The Pass, which provides the only access to the Lahaul Valley, is open from June to November each year. Snowfall is, however, unpredictable and blizzards can close the pass even during this period. When the pass is open, it offers panoramic views of the mountain scenery. A few kilometres away is the **Sonapani Glacier**; slightly to the left is the jagged twin peak of **Gaypan**. The **Beas Kund**, the lake which is the source of the Beas River, is accessible from the pass. It is a holy place for Hindus who believe that the sage Vyas meditated here.

Lahaul and Spiti

The remote valleys of Lahaul and Spiti, at an altitude of some 2,750 metres (9,022 feet), border Zanskar and Tibet and are much drier and more barren than the fertile Kullu Valley. There is no monsoon here, although in the cool summers the valleys are green with grass, alpine flowers and the famous seed potato crop. Two rivers, the Chandra and the Bhaga, run through the Lahaul Valley which is surrounded by the great Himalaya to the north, the Pir Panjal to the south and the Spiti-Chandra watershed to the east. There are many high glaciers in Lahaul, the largest being the Bara Shigri.

Lahaul is also culturally very different from Kullu. The, area has a strong Tibetan Buddhist tradition and the monasteries, known as *gompas*, have rich collections of Buddhist art.

Much of the area is now open to tourists during the short period from July to October. During the summer buses ply regularly to **Keylong**, the administrative headquarters of Lahaul, 117 kilometres (73 miles) north of Manali and to Kaza in Spiti. Between July and mid-September the bus route extends as far north as Leh. There is a PWD

Resthouse and a Tourist Bungalow in Keylong, which makes it a good base for exploring the surrounding countryside.

There are several fascinating monasteries within easy reach of Keylong. The **Kharding Monastery**, three kilometres (two miles) from Keylong, overlooks the town and is located at the former capital of the area. Other monasteries to see are the **Shashur**, three kilometres (two miles) away, **Tyal**, six kilometres (four miles) away and **Guru Ghantal**, 11 kilometres (seven miles) away. One of the most striking buildings in the region is the eight-storey **castle of the Thakur**, or ruler, of **Gondla**. Gondla also has a historic *gompa* lying a short distance from Keylong on the Manali Road.

Between Keylong and Gondla is the village of **Tandi** at the confluence of the Chandra and Bhaga rivers which become the Chenab River of the Punjab. Further up the Chenab Valley to the northwest is the pilgrimage site of **Triloknath**, sacred to both Hindus and Buddhists, where there is a six-armed marble image of the Avalokiteshvara Bodhisattva. In the nearby village of **Udeypur** is the 11th-century **temple of Mrikula Devi**, remarkable for its fine woodcarvings.

Chandra River, Lahaul, Himachal Pradesh

Valley of the Gods

In the Kullu Valley over 365 gods are worshipped and the stories of many of them are bound up with the history of the royal house of the former Kullu state. According to tradition, drought brought the first raja, Bihang Mani Pal, to Kullu many centuries ago. He had left his home near Haridwar in search of water, carrying with him a stone symbolising the goddess Tripura Sundari, 'Beauty of the Triple World', a form of Shiva's consort Durga. The original deity is still in the possession of the royal family. Bihang Mani Pal became an apprentice to a potter and was taking pots to the market when he came across a local demoness called Hadimba in the guise of an old woman. She lifted him on her shoulders and promised to make him raja of all he surveyed if he would worship her as a goddess. Bihang Mani Pal became king and Hadimba his patron deity. The people of Kullu originally worshipped mountain gods like Hadimba as well as the great god of destruction, Shiva. A famous legend explains how the worship of Vishnu, the Preserver, was introduced in the 16th century.

The then raja, Jagat Singh, was told that a pious Brahmin had a store of pearls. But the Brahmin had no pearls and, rather than await the king's displeasure, took his own life and that of his family. The king stood cursed from that day onwards. He could neither eat nor drink; rice seemed like worms, and water like blood. Finally a holy man advised that the curse could be lifted only if the king brought the image of Ram (an incarnation of Vishnu) from its home in Ayodhya, installed it as king, and then ruled as Ram's regent. One of the disciples of the saint was employed to steal the idol. For a whole year he studied the ceremonial routine of the Ayodhya temple before spiriting away the idols of Ram and his consort Sita. Since then Ram has been the presiding deity in the valley.

The gods of the valley are brought over to pay homage to Ram, here known as Lord Raghunath, at the famous Kullu Dussehra Festival, which celebrates the victory of Ram over King Ravan of Lanka and the release of Ram's wife, Sita, whom Ravan had abducted. The seven-day festival takes place in October, beginning as the Dussehra festivities in the plains come to an end. The gods from all over the valley, led by Hadimba, are carried in garlanded palanquins to the temple of Lord Raghunath in Kullu. The chief deities, Ram and Sita, and the other gods are taken in procession to the Dhalpur Maidan (or field). Ram and Sita are placed on a golden chariot and pulled across the maidan by devotees. On the seventh day, the gods move to the banks of the Beas and the head of the former royal family and his male relatives go to the riverside to make sacrifices to Durga for the destruction of Ravan. There are, traditionally, five sacrifices — a buffalo, symbolising Ravan, a ram, a cock, a crab and a fish.

The festival attracts thousands of people every year although now only some hundred gods arrive instead of the former 365. This is because the temples have lost their lands to their tenants under land reform measures and they are no longer as rich as before. The government now sponsors the annual journey of the palanquins to Kullu. Also the tradition that one male member of every family should accompany the local god is not as strong as it once was. The week-long festivities include a local dance called *natti*. On the last day, the gods are taken back to their respective temples.

The Kullu Valley has four distinct styles of temple. The first is the *shikhara* form of the plains. This style is distinguished by a curvilinear tower as in the Gauri Shankar temple at Nagar. The second style is built after the fashion of the local houses. It features alternative bands of wood and dry stone in the form of a rectangular tower, topped by a carved wooden verandah and a gabled roof. This is a thoroughly earthquake-proof design. The third style is the chalet style, a good example of which is the temple of the sage Manu in old Manali. The fourth, the pagoda style, is described as 'a folk version of the much more sophisticated and highly finished Nepalese court architecture'. This is the rarest type and can be seen at Hadimba Temple in Manali.

Shimla

Much has changed in Simla since the days when the British ruled one-fifth of mankind from this small Himalayan settlement. Simla has become Shimla in a gesture of Indianisation. The official summer capital of the Raj from 1864 to 1947 has become the permanent capital of one of India's smallest and better run states, Himachal Pradesh. The tourists are overwhelmingly Indian and the resident and seasonal populations have burgeoned. As a result, the summer brings water shortages and the winter, electricity cuts. An army of trucks delivers supplies to the hill station from the plains and another army of trucks travels to the plains loaded with apples and out-of-season vegetables — the cash crops which have brought prosperity to the state. Unruly buses choke the old cart road and new concrete hotels and offices stalk the hillsides.

Much has changed, but much remains the same. Fire has destroyed a few of the oldest Raj buildings but neither fire nor the developers could efface the omnipresent signs of the past — the 'wild west Swiss' of the Mall and the Ridge, and the two buildings which still dominate the skyline — Christchurch and Viceregal Lodge. The Mall is still the social centre of the station; the lower bazaar is still the same rabbit warren it was in Rudyard Kipling's time; and the Ridge still looks out over snows. In short, Shimla remains one of the largest and most successful hill stations.

Because Shimla lies at a height of 2,215 metres (7,267 feet) above sea level, it is comfortable to visit throughout the year, although the summer months of May and June are the most crowded. The climate is, as it always was, a great attraction in the summer, despite the heat haze which can block out views. At night, forest fires burn on distant hillsides. The monsoon, generally a quiet time of the year, reveals beautiful sunsets with clouds settling below in the valleys. The winter months show the surrounding mountains at their best and Shimla too has snow which sparkles in the 'long moon-nights'.

GETTING THERE AND AROUND
Shimla has a new airport, 22 kilometres (14 miles) away, with regular Jagson Airlines flights to Delhi. Chandigarh airport, 120 kilometres (74

Lithographs of Fancy Fair at Annandale in 1839 *(above) and of* The View of Simla from Colonel Chadwick's House at Mahasu *(below) from G P Thomas's book,* Views of Simla, *London, 1846*

miles) away on the plains below, has more flights. However, it is more comfortable to travel by rail. The broad-gauge train runs to Kalka, a small town at the foot of the hills. Trains connect Kalka with several major cities, although the most convenient base for the journey is Delhi, 268 kilometres (167 miles) from Kalka. The overnight Kalka Mail deposits you at Kalka in the early morning in time to catch connecting trains on the splendid narrow-gauge train to Shimla (see page 104). The rail car is the most luxurious way to reach the Shimla summit, and the journey takes five to six hours. It's a lot quicker by bus, but you miss the views. There are regular buses from Kalka to Shimla, as well as long-distance buses (including video coaches) from Chandigarh and Delhi.

Taxis are available for hire in Shimla from the car park at the bottom of the lift which operates between the Cart Road and the Mall above. Also on the Cart Road is the bus stand from where buses leave for other destinations in Himachal Pradesh, as well as for the cities of the plains. On the Ridge and the Mall there are ponies for hire and you can spot a few mouldering handpulled rickshaws, no longer in use. There's no shortage of porters if you prefer to walk from the bus or railway stations but can't manage your luggage. Sightseeing tours, arranged by Himachal Tourism, take you around the neighbouring hills.

SIGHTS
On the Way to Shimla
Both road and railway climb steeply from Kalka via Dharampur, where a turning takes you to Kasauli, the nearest hill station to the plains. Beyond Dharampur lies Barog, the half-way point of the journey where there is a well-run Himachal Tourism Hotel. After **Barog** comes **Solan**, a developing hill town. The land was first acquired by the British for a rifle range but its chief claim to fame today is the **Mohan Meakin Brewery** founded in 1935, which has its own stop on the railway line. The roofs of its **oast houses** dominate the town. Beyond Solan is the small settlement of **Khandaghat** where a right turn takes you down into a valley and then up to the heights of the small hill station of **Chail**. As you climb the hills, the flora changes. At Dharampur you have entered the realm of the chir pine, and beyond Khandaghat you travel past terraced hillsides until you see Shimla and its covering of deodar cedars.

The Town

The best view of Shimla is from Jakhu (formerly Jakho) Hill at an altitude of 2,445 metres (8,022 feet). In ancient times the monkey god Hanuman is said to have rested here on his way from the Himalayas with the magical *sanjeevani buti* — the herb that saved the life of Ram's brother Laxman. Hanuman is one of the great figures of the *Ramayana* epic, and a temple to him stood on the summit of Jakhu before Shimla was 'discovered' by the British. There are still large numbers of his latter-day relatives to guard the temple.

Looking down from the peak you can see Shimla stretching along a 12-kilometre (seven-and-a-half-mile) mountain ridge. Immediately below is the spot known as the **Ridge**, a popular promenade dominated by the yellow-painted **Christchurch**. Work began on this Gothic church, designed by Colonel J T Boileau, in 1844, but it was only consecrated after 1857. It was never a large church and one vicar preached a sermon against the space taken up by the women's crinolines and the extravagance of their attitude. Next Sunday, the chastened ladies all turned up in riding habits. Now the congregations have dwindled and there is no lack of space. Around the chancel window is a fresco designed by Rudyard Kipling's father, Lockwood Kipling, who was the principal of the Mayo School of Art in Lahore. There is also a fine stained-glass window representing Faith, Hope, Charity, Fortitude, Patience and Humility.

Outside the church, visitors can stroll or sit on benches and enjoy a scenic view of the Himalayas. There are lines of ponies for hire and the stalls of Tibetan shawl-sellers.

The Ridge slopes down past the tourist office towards Shimla's main thoroughfare (restricted for motor vehicles), the **Mall**. There is a statue of the Punjabi Nationalist leader, Lala Lajpat Rai, at the point where the Mall meets the Ridge. It was here that the dashing Maharaja of Patiala was reputed to have abducted the beautiful daughter of an English gentleman, and whisked her off to his palace at Chail. The incident was hushed up, the lady never complained and only the name, **Scandal Point**, remains to remind visitors of the story. Near Scandal Point are the post office, the town hall, the library and the **Gaiety Theatre**, opened in 1887 and now more frequented as a club. This area is one of the most crowded during the evening promenades. Tourists

Shimla after snowfall

The entrance to Chapslee Hotel

The drawing room at Chapslee

Gorton Castle, formerly the main secretariat of the Government of India

Institute of Advanced Studies, formerly Viceregal Lodge, Shimla

wander along, honeymooners hold hands and local journalists meet friends to exchange the latest gossip.

The Mall is the main shopping centre, and also has a number of not very distinguished restaurants. Numerous pathways lead steeply down through the ramshackle bazaars and alleyways of the middle and lower bazaars, where you get a different view of hill life. Walking westwards along the Mall you pass the **Roman Catholic Cathedral**, established in 1885. Further on is **Gorton Castle**, now the office of the accountant-general, but once the main secretariat of the Government of India. This peculiar building has been described as 'a gaunt, sinister edifice built in a style resembling Scottish baronial'. A turning to the left leads to the railway station, while straight on you come to the **State Legislative Assembly**. To the north is the famous glen of **Annandale**, site of many a Raj picnic and fête, but now in army hands.

Also in this direction are the Cecil Hotel and the **Himachal State Museum** (closed on Monday) which has a collection of Pahari miniature paintings as well as statues and carvings from various parts of the state. Eventually you reach the **Indian Institute of Advanced Studies** (IIAS), formerly Viceregal Lodge, which was built in 1888 by Viceroy Lord Dufferin. Dufferin had long dreamed of building a great house under his own direction and in Shimla his dream came true. The result has been uncharitably compared to Pentonville Prison in Britain but, in fact, it is an imposing country house designed more or less in Elizabethan style. It has a huge teak staircase, entrance hall and gallery and a panelled state dining room. Even in 1888 it had, unusually for the times, electric light and an indoor tennis court. The students of the new IIAS are few and cannot fill the emptiness of this eerie building. The IIAS stands on **Observatory Hill** and nearby is **Observatory House**, once the home of the eccentric Colonel Boileau who, besides being the architect of Christchurch, was a keen astronomer. He built his observatory here in 1844 and gave his name to the neighbouring locality of Boileauganj.

Taking the Mall eastwards from Scandal Point you pass the lift to and from the car park on the Cart Road below and across what was once Combermere Bridge over a deep ravine, to Hotel Clarke's and the long spur of Chota Shimla or Shimla Minor. In this quieter part of Shimla are the **State Government Secretariat** and the governor's

residence, **Raj Bhawan**. This building was formerly known as Barnes
Court after Sir Edward Barnes, commander-in-chief in 1832-3, who had
been the Duke of Wellington's adjutant-general at the battle of
Waterloo. Below the Mall is **Bishop Cotton School**, founded at the
request of the Bishop of Calcutta as a thanksgiving to God for
delivering the British people from the Indian Mutiny in 1857. The
school, completed in 1869, was designed for the sons of government
officers on small salaries and aimed to be 'not less useful than
Winchester, Rugby, and Marlborough'. Today it is one of India's
foremost public schools and still has its large chapel and fine stained-
glass intact.

Another road leads from the Ridge below Jakhu through **Lakkar**
(wood) **Bazaar** where carved walking sticks are on sale amongst other
items. The road winds around **Elysium Hill**, site of **Chapslee** and
Auckland House girls' school where Emily Eden and her brother, the
Viceroy Lord Auckland, had their summer home in the 1830s. Another
building on Elysium Hill is **Stirling Castle**, built in 1833, where Sir W
W Hunter wrote his *History of the Indian People*. The road doubles from
Elysium Hill, past **Snowdown**, residence of several commanders-in-chief
of the British Indian Army, including Lord Kitchener. The building is
now a hospital. The road then leads to Sanjauli and to Wildflower Hall,
a later residence of Lord Kitchener.

To cross **Sanjauli** you have to pass through a 170-metre- (186-
yard-) long tunnel built by 10,000 convicts and 8,000 labourers. It was
completed in 1851-2. The lighting, now quite adequate, was not so in
the 19th century and it was here that Lord Kitchener fell from his horse
and broke his leg. His Indian attendants ran away and the commander-
in-chief lay in the tunnel for over half an hour before he was rescued.

Walks around the town can take you to **Jakhu Hill** and **the Glen**, a
popular picnic spot reached by a path near the Cecil Hotel. A large
spur separates the Glen from **Chadwick Falls**, a 65-metre- (213-foot-)
high waterfall, at its best during the monsoon. About five kilometres
(three miles) from the centre of town is **Prospect Hill** (15 minutes'
walk from Boileauganj), which is one of the most popular viewpoints. It
is surmounted by a shrine to the goddess Kamana Devi. There are also
some shady paths around the suburb of **Summer Hill**, the site of
Himachal University.

An Evening at the Club

Let us go over to the Simla Club. It is nightfall, for the last moments of the day are absorbed in the canter round Jacko, the closing gallop down the Mall, billiards, the racket-court, the library, or lounging from one shop into another. Lights are gleaming from the long row of windows in the bungalow. Syces holding horses, and jampanees sitting in groups by their masters' chairs, are clustering round the verandah. Servants are hurrying in to wait on the sahibs, who have come to dinner from distant bungalows. The clatter of plates and dishes proclaim that dinner is nearly ready. The British officers and civilians, in every style of Anglo-Indian costume, are propping up the walls of the sitting-room, waiting for the signal to fall on. The little party in the corner have come down from the card-room, and it is whispered that old Major Stager has won 700 rupees from young Cornet Griffin, since tiff; but Griffin can never pay unless he gets his Delhi prize-money soon; and that little Shuffle, the Major's partner, who does not look twenty yet, but who is well known as a cool hand, has extracted nearly twice as much from that elderly civilian, who has come up with a liver and full purse from the plains. The others are the soldierless officers of ex-sepoy regiments, Queen's officers, civilians, doctors, invalids, unemployed brigadiers, convalescents from wounds or illness in the plains; and their talk is of sporting, balls, promotions, exchanges, Europe, and a little politics, rechauffed from the last Overland Mail; but, as a general rule, all serious questions are tabooed, and it is almost amusing to observe the excessive esprit de crops which is one of the excellences as one of the defects of the English character, and which now breaks up the officers of the Queen's, of the Company's service, and of the civil departments into separate knots. Dinner is announced, and the members and guests file into a large room with a table well laid out with flowers and plated epergnes, round which there is a double file of the club servants and of the domestics which each man has taken with him. The dinner is at all events plentiful enough, the pastry and sweets being, perhaps, the best department. Conversation is loud and animated. Among Indians the practice of drinking wine with each other has not yet died out, and the servants are constantly running to and fro with their masters' compliments, bottles, and requests to take wine with you, which are generally given to the wrong persons, and produce much confusion and amusement.

Cheroots follow closely on the removal of the last jelly-brandy-panee, and more wines not very infrequently succeed, while parties are formed and set to work in the inner room, and the more jovial of the gentlemen proceed to the execution of vocal pieces such as were wont to be sung in Europe twenty years ago, generally enriched by fine choral effects from the combined strength of all the company. The usual abandon of such reunions in Europe is far exceeded by our Indians, who when up at the hills, do not pretend to pay the least attention to the presence of old officers, no matter what their rank or age. The 'fun' grows louder and faster as the night advances. The brigadiers look uneasily or angrily over their cards at the disturbers, but do not interfere. There is a crash of glass, and a grand row at the end of the room, and the Bacchanalians, rising with much exultation, seize 'Ginger Tubbs' in his chair, and carry him round the room as a fitting ovation for his eminent performance of the last comic ballad, and settle down to 'hip-hip-hurrah, and one cheer more', till they are eligible for their beds or for 'a broiled bone' at old Brown's. Hinc illae lachrymae. Hence the reports of the bazaar people of the rows and scrapes that reach us in the mornings. But by midnight nearly all the guests and members have retired to their rooms or bungalows.

'Dr Russell' quoted in
Edward J Buck, Simla Past & Present

The Mountain Railway to Shimla

Before 1903 the journey to Shimla, then Simla, was not an easy one. Britons made their way by train from the imperial capital Calcutta to Kalka, where the steep climb into the Himalayas began. One who made the journey in 1892 recorded a particularly alarming reception.

At last we arrived at Kalka and here detrained. There was no platform in those days. We just got out where the train stopped; the ladies being assisted down by small ladders which were placed against the sides of the carriages. There now fell upon us a marauding horde of savages, coolies, tonga wallahs, camel drivers and mahouts yellings, shouting and gesticulating wildly. They seized upon our luggages. Bedding and boxes were torn apart in the melee. In vain, my father, brandishing his stick, shouted commands; nothing availed until a bearded dacoit [bandit] informed us with an engaging smile that our luggage was all packed and stored away in his tonga [horse drawn cart] and that he would now have the honour to convey us to Simla.

A mountain railway was obviously needed. A correspondent of the *Delhi Gazette* first sketched out a route in 1847 and expressed the hope that, when the railway was complete, ' we might then see these cooler region become the permanent seat of a government daily invigorated by a temperature adapted to refresh an European constitution and keep the mental powers in a state of health beneficial both to the rulers and ruled alike.' Numerous surveys were made of the route before work began on the Kalka-Shimla section which was to be 59.44 miles (96 kilometres) long with a two foot six-inch (0.75-metre) gauge. Among the problems faced by the engineers was the construction of a tunnel over a quarter of a mile long under Taradevi Hill, which had long been a place of pilgrimage for Hindus. From the day work commenced the local people declared that the goddess Taradevi would never permit the tunnel to be completed. The workers fled in panic when there was a report that a huge snake, several hundred feet long, had been uncovered in the tunnel. This remarkable reptile, however, turned out to be an iron pipe which was pushed into the tunnel to ensure a supply of fresh air!

The line was opened on 9 November 1903, and represents the most remarkable feat of engineering of any of the hill railways. The trains travel up from Kalka, at 640 metres (2,100 feet), to Shimla station, at 2,073 metres (6,801 feet), through 102 tunnels (they are numbered up to 103 but tunnel 46 does not exist) and over 869 bridges, including multi-arched galleries like ancient Roman aqueducts, which carry the line over the ravines between the spurs of the hills. The line passes through 20 picturesque, cottage-style stations where the driver is handed the token which guarantees him sole possession of the next section of line. The first large station outside Kalka is Dharampur where the gradient is very steep and the line climbs the mountainside in three graceful loops, one above the other. The longest tunnel (1,144 metres or 3,753 feet) passes 275 metres (90 feet) below the road at Barog. Barog, with its carefully tended hanging baskets of pink geraniums, is one of the prettiest stations on the Shimla line, and is where the morning trains halt for breakfast. Omelette, toast and tea is the standard fare. From Barog the line descends gently to Solan (1,494 metres or 4,902 feet), where there is a separate station for the brewery, and Kandaghat (1,422 metres or 4,665 feet), from where the final ascent to Shimla begins. Finally the train winds around Summer Hill and burrows under Inverarm Hill to emerge below the road on the south side of the hill and reach its terminus.

The trains carry nearly 350,000 passengers each year, mainly during the summer months, proving that many would still prefer to spend over five hours on a train than half the time on a bus. All the engines are now diesel but a journey on the comparatively highspeed first-class railcar, with its white cotton seat covers, is still a unique and luxurious experience for rail enthusiasts. In the summer there are generally eight passenger trains a day (four up and four down), as well as the railcar services, between Kalka and Shimla. The *Shimla Queen* does not run in the winter months.

The steam locomotive taking on water and coal at Coonoor (top and bottom); pulling into Ooty Station (middle); riding the toy train, Darjeeling (right)

Out of Town

Beyond Wildflower Hall is **Mashobra**, at 3,150 metres (7,054 feet). Every June, the **Sipi Fair** is held here and local people gather in their traditional dress. Mashobra was used as a suburban retreat by the viceroys and the most famous house is the **Retreat**. Here Indira Gandhi and the former Pakistan prime minister, Zulfiqar Ali Bhutto, signed the Shimla Agreement between the two countries in 1972. Three kilometres (two miles) away is the **Craignano Rest House** perched on a hill at a height of 2,280 metres (7,480 feet). Further on, at **Naldehra**, 23 kilomeres (14 miles) from Shimla, is a **nine-hole golf course**. At Naldehra you can see the deep gorge of the Sutlej River. Next to the Sutlej at **Tatta Pani**, 50 kilometres (31 miles) from Shimla, and only 665 metres (2,182 feet) above sea level, are hot sulphur springs which are believed to work miracles.

An alternative route from Wildflower Hall leads to the resorts of **Kufri**, 16 kilometres (ten miles) from Shimla, and at 2,633 metres (8,683 feet), and **Narkhanda**, 65 kilometres (41 miles) away to the northwest and at 2,700 metres (8,858 feet). The skiing season is from the end of December to early March, depending on the snowfall. Himachal Tourism runs ski courses at Narkhanda, details of which are available from the tourist office in Shimla. (For hotel addresses, see page 273). In between the two hotel resorts is **Fagu**, 22 kilometres (14 miles) from Shimla, at a height of 2,510 metres (8,235 feet), which has extensive views. From Narkhanda you can explore the apple-growing area of **Kotgarh** where orchards were pioneered by an American called Stokes who married a local girl and whose family still lives in Himachal Pradesh. Alternatively, you can head north to Kullu and Manali.

There are many places in the Shimla region which have resthouses or tourist bungalows, but only two other hill stations in the area are worthy of the name; Kasauli, 77 kilometres (48 miles) from Shimla, and Chail, 45 kilometres (28 miles) away.

Kasauli

Kasauli, 1,927 metres (6,325 feet) above sea level, is the first hill station you see as you approach the Shimla hills. Easily recognisable by a huge television tower, it runs along the first high ridge of the Himalayan foothills. Kasauli was developed as a cantonment-sanatorium over 20 years after the British had established themselves at Shimla. This was despite the fact that Kasauli was in a much more accessible position than the summer capital. Its attraction today remains its accessibility; only 15 kilometres (nine and a half miles) from Dharampur; 35 kilometres (23 miles) from Kalka, and 65 kilometres (40 miles) from Chandigarh, and the fact that it is kept quite clean and small by the cantonment. Most of the houses, old-fashioned bungalows in secluded gardens, have had the same owners for many years. There are a couple of hotels here (see page 274).

Even at the peak of summer, Kasauli cannot be called crowded and the only time it should be avoided is during the first four days of October when it is overrun with parents attending Founder's Day at the nearby Lawrence School, Sanawar.

The Upper and Lower Mall are the two main roads which run along the length of Kasauli, bordered by chir pine, horse chestnuts, Himalayan oak and the odd juniper. Traffic is restricted on these roads which also helps to keep Kasauli one of the quietest hill stations. The small, sleepy bazaar has two first class general stores. **Gupta's** is next to the splendidly old fashioned **Jakki Mull's drapers. Daily Needs**, around the corner, stocks tasty chicken salami. A number of Tibetan stalls offer bargain woollens of the best quality.

The **Hotel Alasia's** pies provide excellent picnic fodder. A remnant of the Raj, the attractive **Christchurch** has some fine stained-glass, while a new arts centre has been set up at **Ivy Cottage** by a nephew of the celebrated Indian artist, Amrita Sher-Gill. The centre organises occasional seminars and exhibitions.

Walks

From the many paths leading over the hillsides you can look out over the plains towards Delhi and northwards towards Sanawar, Shimla and the snows (especially good in the cooler months).

Chail

Chail lies at a height of 2,250 metres (7,382 feet) and is one of the smallest Himalayan hill stations. It is 45 kilometres (28 miles) from Shimla, and 86 kilometres (54 miles) from Kalka via Khandaghat and the picturesque Sadhupul village. It was developed as the summer

Trekking in Himachal Pradesh

Himachal Pradesh is only beginning to make the most of its mountains. The main trekking areas are Kullu-Manali, Lahaul-Spiti, Chamba-Kangra and Shimla, but the only really well-organised centre is Manali. Here there are a number of government recognised companies organising treks, and the tourist office has up-to-date information on them. These companies can provide tents, guides, cooks and porters, and have different grades of treks depending on their clients' budgets. Some companies also offer jeep treks as far afield as Ladakh and short skiing treks between January and June. Local guides are invaluable as no detailed contour maps are available.

Many visitors come to Manali and then arrange their treks. If you want to book well in advance, there are a few well-established companies which also have London offices. Chandertal Tours, run by Robert Newbury, at 20 The Fridays, East Dean, East Bourne, Sussex, England. tel. 01323–422213. (Manali office: Himalayan Folkways, run by Roop Katoch, tel. 01902–53026, 52490, fax 01902–52378.) They offer a series of treks, jeep safaris, fishing and bike tours between July and September. Paddy's Treks and Tours Pvt. Ltd. 12/14 Sarvapriya Vihar, New Delhi 110 016; tel. 6510703; fax 011-6179951; Manali tel. 52490; fax 52378 is another well organised company. It is named after Captain Padam Singh who runs it and has an unbeatable knowledge of treks in Himachal. Other trekking companies in

residence of the maharajas of Patiala and was a favourite place of Maharaja Bhupinder Singh who distinguished himself in the First World War and became one of the ADCs to King George V. It was his son and successor who demolished the old palace and built a new one, known as **Rajgarh**, after Independence. Rajgarh means 'fort of the rule' but in fact it is a simple, stone country house surrounded by sprawling lawns laid out on the flattened hilltop amid beautiful orchards and gardens. The Patiala family sold Rajgarh and today it is known as the **Chail Palace Hotel**, and is run by Himachal Tourism.

The gardens, judging by the decrepit state of the maharaja's greenhouse, are not what they once were. However, the lawns ringed by deodar cedars are captivating, as are the annual beds when water is available for them. The grounds and slopes immediately around the station are forested with deodars. A short walk leads to a small bazaar.

Manali include Himalayan Adventurers (tel. 52185) run by R C Negi, Arohi Travels (tel. 52139), International Trekkers (tel. 52372), Trans Himalayan Expeditions (tel. 52489) and Tourist Adventure Holidays (tel. 53562, 53219) run by Dev Raj Thakur.

A week's round-trek can take you to the Malana Valley across the Chandrakhani Pass around 3,600 metres (11,810 feet) above sea level, open from March to December. Malana is also accessible from the Parvati Valley. The inhabitants of Malana are a law unto themselves — they are considered one of the oldest democracies in the world. They do not intermarry with people from neighbouring villages and have a distinct language. Their god, Jamlu, is a very powerful and aloof deity who attends but does nor participate in the Dussehra festival.

One of the finest treks in the region is from Manali to Keylong (11 days) via the Hemta Pass, the Chandratal (the Lake of the Moon) and the Baralacha Pass where routes from Zanskar, Ladakh, Lahaul and Spiti meet. There are two routes for trekking from Banjar (near Kullu) to Narkhanda or Rampur (near Shimla) and they can be made in either direction. A four-day trek takes you from Banjar via the 3,250-metre- (10,663-foot-) high Bashleo Pass to Rampur. The alternative route is in five stages and takes you across the spectacular Jalori Pass, at 3,135 metres (10,285 feet).

The office of the range officer in charge of the newly formed **Chail Wildlife Sanctuary** also is here.

A steep road up from the bazaar leads you past the small *gurudwara* (Sikh temple) to the military school, surrounded by Himalayan oaks. Towards the top of the hill is the highest cricket ground in the world, which now has a concrete wicket. Both Bhupinder Singh and Yadevendra Singh, the last ruler of Patiala before Independence, were avid cricketers and captained the Indian team. The season began in April and continued during the monsoon when mists sometimes made it impossible for fielders on the boundary to see the batsmen. When that was the case, team members nearer the wicket would shout to let the outfield know when the ball was heading their way. The pitch is now mainly used by local schoolboys.

Uttar Pradesh

Uttarakhand

The mountain districts of Uttar Pradesh, India's largest and most populous state, make up Uttarakhand, the holiest area of the Himalayas. These districts are more commonly known as Garhwal and Kumaon, the names of two former mountain kingdoms. Garhwal consists of the districts of Pauri, Chamoli, Tehri, Dehra Dun and Uttar Kashi; Kumaon of Nainital, Almora and Pithoragarh. Uttarakhand has some of the most celebrated of the Indian hill stations like Mussoorie and Nainital, but in India it is most famous for the Dev Bhumi, Land of the Gods, in Garhwal.

THE DEV BHUMI

Garhwal is believed to be the land where the most ancient Hindu scriptures, the *Vedas*, were composed. The *Vedas* refer to the land of the *Saptasindhu* — the seven rivers — as the home of the Vedic people, the Aryans. These seven rivers are the seven streams of the Ganga or Ganges which flow through Garhwal. They are the Vishnu Ganga (Alaknanda), the Dhauli Ganga, the Nandakini, the Pinder, the Mandakini, the Bhagirathi and the Nayar.

Jawaharlal Nehru, in his book *The Discovery of India*, attempted to describe the incredible influence that the Ganga has over the lives of Indians, and which draws so many of them to her in death:

> The Ganga, above all, is the river of India, which has held India's heart captive and drawn uncounted millions to her banks since the dawn of history. The story of the Ganga; from her source to the sea, from old times to the new, is the story of India's civilization and culture, of the rise and fall of empires, of the great and proud cities, of the adventure of man, of the quest of the mind which has so occupied India's thinkers, one of richness and fulfilment of life as well as its denial and renunciation, of ups and downs, of growth and decay, of life and death.

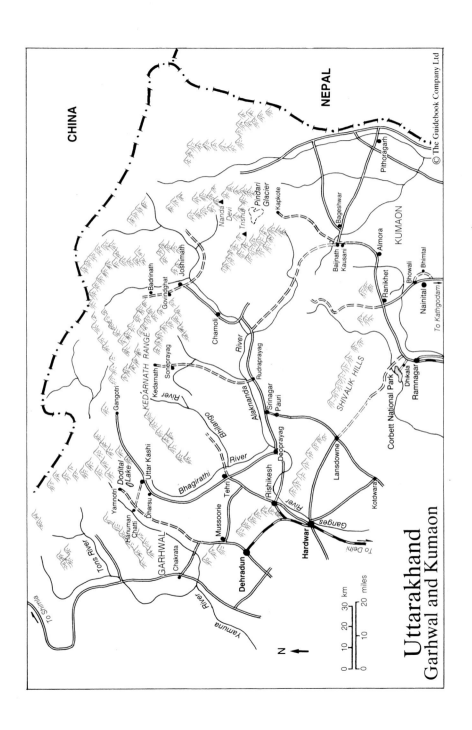

Uttarakhand
Garhwal and Kumaon

© The Guidebook Company Ltd

The Ganga begins its long journey at the Gangotri Glacier in Garhwal. According to popular belief, the goddess Ganga was brought to earth as a result of austerities performed by the sage Bhagirath. Lord Shiva received the full force of the great river in his matted locks so that Ganga would not fall directly upon the earth and destroy it. The stream which fell from Shiva's hair was the Bhagirathi, which is the name of the Ganga at its source. The sage purified the ashes of 60,000 of his kinsmen in Ganga's waters and they found eternal rest.

The sanctity of the Dev Bhumi is not only due to the Ganga. It also possesses the four principal mountain pilgrimage sites, the four *dhams*, visits to which are believed to ensure salvation. These are: Yamunotri, the source of the River Yamuna or Jamuna; then Gangotri, the source of the Ganga; then Kedarnath, the Abode of Lord Shiva; and finally Badrinath, the Valley of Lord Vishnu. Shiva is the great Destroyer and Vishnu the Preserver, but this shorthand definition conveys very little of the significance these deities have for their devotees.

GARHWAL AND KUMAON: THE TWO MOUNTAIN KINGDOMS

The history of both these kingdoms is based mainly on oral accounts recorded in the 19th century. From these it appears that the first great raja of Garhwal was Ajai Pal who overcame 52 petty chieftains and their fortresses (*garh*) in the 15th century. Until that time, every hill had its own princeling. Ajai Pal established his capital at Srinagar in Uttar Pradesh, and his descendants set about enlarging his kingdom.

Their relations with the neighbouring and equally ancient house of the Chand rajas of Kumaon, to the east of Garhwal, were often strained. From the 17th century, the capital of the Kumaon rajas was Almora. There was much intrigue in the two courts and, on occasion, the two armies faced one another on the battlefield.

Both royal houses were eclipsed at the end of the 18th century when Gorkha armies from Nepal overran them. The Gorkhas remained firmly entrenched at Almora until they began to encroach on British territory. The British responded by declaring war in 1814.

On 14 October that year a British contingent led by Colonel Mawby reached the Doon Valley to take the fort of Kalanga from the

The Ganga close to its source at Gaumukh

Gorkha commander, Balbhadra Singh Thapa, and his small force. The struggle for Kalanga lasted for over a month, but from the first day it was marked by an almost medieval etiquette as one contemporary account records:

> Colonel Mawby sent a messenger the same night to demand the surrender of the fort, and it found Balbhadra Singh at midnight enjoying a well-earned repose. The Gurkhali commander read the letter and tore it up, vouchsafing no other answer than that 'It was not customary to receive and answer letters at such unreasonable hours'; but he sent his salam [greeting] to the English sardar [general], assuring him that he would soon pay him a visit in his camp!

After a gallant defence, the fort was captured on 30 November and the Gorkha base at Almora fell in 1815.

The Gorkha defeat delivered the entire Garhwal and Kumaon kingdoms into the hands of the British. But during the war the British had realised the worth of hill troops. They subsequently recruited many Gorkhas, Garhwalis and Kumaonis to the Indian army.

As 'an act of clemency', the raja of Garhwal was handed back half his former territory, and he set up a new capital at Tehri. His old capital, Srinagar, came under British Garhwal and was destroyed by floods in 1893. The. British ruled their portion of the state from Pauri.

Most importantly, the British gains in Kumaon and Garhwal made hill stations possible. Many were built on land made available after the Gorkha Wars — Shimla, Nainital, Ranikhet and the 'Queen of the Hills', Mussoorie — while a major army cantonment was established at Dehra Dun.

Dehra Dun

Dehra Dun, at 700 metres (2,297 feet) is the gateway to Mussoorie. It lies in the fertile Doon Valley on the watershed of the rivers Ganga and Yamuna and is one of the most important towns in the Himalayan foothills.

Dehra means 'camp', and the town took its name from the camp of Ram Rai, the son of the seventh guru of the Sikhs, Har Rai. Ram Rai was not made guru after his father and disputed the succession. He lost his case and came to the Doon Valley in the latter half of the 17th century where he was welcomed by the Garhwal raja. The Sikh temple, or *gurudwara*, he founded still stands in the Jhanda Mohalla area and attracts many devotees on the fifth day after the Holi festival (February/ March), the day Ram Rai arrived in the valley.

After the British annexed the town it developed swiftly. It became an educational centre and a military cantonment and was the summer base of the Viceroy's Bodyguard. Today it is the site of the prestigious Indian Military Academy. The Doon School, *alma mater* of the former Indian prime minister, Rajiv Gandhi, is one of the best Indian public schools. The Forest Research Institute, founded during British rule, and the new Wildlife Institute of India are also among Dehra Dun's many outstanding institutions.

GETTING THERE

Dehra Dun is also a main railhead of the Northern Railway with direct trains to Delhi, Mumbai, Calcutta, Lucknow and Varanasi. The most convenient train from Delhi is the 2018 Shatabdi Express (everyday except Thursday) which leaves New Delhi Station at 7.25 am and reaches Dehra Dun at 12 noon; and the Mussoorie Express which leaves Delhi late at night and arrives the next morning. The day train, the Dehra Dun Express, takes almost a whole day to reach its destination.

For places to stay in Dehra Dun, see page 274.

SIGHTS

Institutions like the imposing **Forest Research Institute** and mulberry demonstration farms of the **Sericulture Institute** are worth a look. Eight kilometres (five miles) from the town centre is **Robber's Cave (Gucchu Pani)**, a picnic spot. Two places with religious connections are **Tapovan**, five kilometres (three miles) from Dehra Dun, where the legendary guru of the heroes of the *Mahabharata*, Dronacharya, is said to have performed penance; and **Lakshman Siddh**, 11 kilometres (seven miles) away, a forest memorial to a modern saint. Eight kilometres (five miles) from the town is a **monument to Balbhadra Singh Thapa**, the hero of the siege of Kalanga. Sulphur springs now at **Shahastra Dhara** ('1,000 springs') 15 kilometres (nine and a half miles) from the town. For students of history, however, the place to head for is **Kalsi**, 50 kilometres (31 miles) from town, site of a rock inscription of the great Mauryan emperor, Ashoka, who united India in the third century BC.

Mussoorie

Mussoorie, 2,000 metres (6,560 feet) above sea level, straddles a horseshoe-shaped Himalayan ridge. If you look out over the valley of Doon in summer, you will have the satisfaction of being able to see the plains and know you are safe from the sweltering heat. To the north, Mussoorie looks out to the snowy line of the Garhwal Himalayas. As one of the hill stations most accessible from Delhi, it is a very popular destination for Indian tourists during the season (April-June and September-October) and wanderers in search of peace and quiet are recommended to visit in the monsoon or the winter months — especially when there's snowfall.

BACKGROUND

Mussoorie was only visited by local cowherds until it was 'discovered' by Captain Young in the 1820s. His house, built in 1829, still stands below Landour, an area first developed as a military convalescent centre, but which became an integral part of the resort. The ascent to Mussoorie was originally described as 'difficult and perilous in the extreme', but that did nothing to deter the British fleeing there from the plains. By the mid-19th century Mussoorie was a flourishing resort, with its own brewery. The holiday spirit was uncloyed by the presence of officialdom. As one Delhi bureaucrat advised the government in later years: 'Our young people need a place where they can let their hair down, free of protocol and poodle faking, paying polite calls. Let them have Mussoorie.'

One of the most famous early residents of Mussoorie was the surveyor, Sir George Everest, who gave his name to the world's highest mountain. Everest lived in the town (1832-43) and his house, including the ruins of the *bibi-khana* or harem, can still be seen seven kilometres (four and a half miles) west of the Library.

In 1880 the ex-Amir of Afghanistan, Yakub Khan, was detained at the Bellevue Estate, while during 1884 the Duke and Duchess of Connaught chose to spend the summer in Mussoorie. By this time the station had also become popular with the Indian princes, many of whom built summer residences here.

The lights of Mussoorie

GETTING THERE

Mussoorie is most easily reached from Dehra Dun, 35 kilometres (22 miles) away, which also has the nearest railhead. Bus services from Delhi, 290 kilometres (180 miles) away, take seven to nine hours. There are regular services for closer destinations like Haridwar, 103 kilometres (64 miles) and Tehri, 72 kilometres (45 miles) away. Private taxis are available, as are conducted tours. One of the most convenient ways of reaching either Dehra Dun or Mussoorie from Delhi is to share a taxi from the stand at the Ajmeri Gate at the end of Asaf Ali Road.

SIGHTS

Despite new construction, Mussoorie is still a typically 'wild west Swiss' hill station. The heart of the town is of course the **Mall**. Here are the tourist office, rows of Tibetan trinket and sweater vendors, and shops selling walking-sticks. Hand-pulled rickshaws still ply down the Mall past lamp-posts, manufactured in Glasgow, and the **State Bank** (formerly imperial Bank) building which still has wrought-iron grills marked with the insignia of Queen Victoria.

Above all, the Mall is a social centre. In the season it's crowded with people wearing their best clothes. In the informal atmosphere new friends are easily made.

The Mall is the starting point for the cablecar which takes you to the summit of **Gun Hill**, 2,142 metres (7,028 feet) above sea level. A two-kilometre (just over a mile) bridle path also leads to the summit. In British days, a gun was fired there at precisely 12 noon every day to inform residents of the correct time. The gun has since been removed and now the hill houses the water reservoir for Mussoorie. On clear days you can see Kedarnath, Badrinath and Nanda Devi from the peak.

You can take a pony trip along the north-facing **Camel's Back Road**, so named because on the map it resembles a camel's hump, as does the rock formation on the summit above. The road runs in a loop from Kulri Bazaar at one end of the Mall to the Library at the other, western, end.

A footpath leads from near the Library to the **Municipal Gardens**, which could be better maintained. The garden is a good viewpoint and there is a children's park and a café.

The Lal Bahadur Shastri National Academy of Administration is the premier institution of Mussoorie. It trains new entrants to the elite Indian Administration Service (IAS), the successor to the British Indian Civil Service (ICS). Near the gateway to the academy is a **coffee house** which serves Tibetan *momos*, while a road descending from the gateway leads to the pine-covered **Happy Valley**, the centre of the Tibetan community in Mussoorie·.

At the opposite end of the Mall is **Landour Bazaar**, which runs for a kilometre and a half (a mile) from the **Mullingar Hotel** to the Landour clock tower. This is very much an Indian-style bazaar and local hill jewellery is on sale. Roads leading from it wind around the hillside and offer excellent views. **Lal Tibba**, at 2,438 metres (7,999 feet) and the highest point in Mussoorie, is the peak above Landour, five kilometres (three miles) from the centre of town.

EXCURSIONS

From Mussoorie, 15 kilometres (nine and a half miles) along on the Chakrata road is the most popular and picturesque, though in summer rather litter-strewn, picnic spot at Kempty Falls. It's a pleasant day-long outing by foot, but buses and taxis are also available. The area from **Kempty Falls** west to the **Yamuna gorge** is being declared a sanctuary. Rich in birdlife, it also has goral (a kind of mountain goat) and a few leopards.

The **Mossey Falls** is a picnic spot six kilometres (four miles) from the centre and four kilometres (two and a half miles) by bridle path. Another waterfall is the smaller **Bhatta Falls**. Twelve kilometres (seven and a half miles) from Mussoorie on the Dehra Dun road, and six and a half kilometres (four miles) by bridle path. From Mussoorie, 24 kilometres (15 miles) along the Tehri road, is **Dhanoulti**, which is surrounded by dramatic scenery. Beyond Dhanoulti is the **Sukhanda Devi temple**, the highest point in the area — 3,021 metres (9,913 feet) and 45 kilometres (28 miles) from Mussoorie. There is a steep three-kilometre (two-mile) climb to the summit from where you look out over 200 kilometres (124 miles) of snows. The temple marks the place where, according to legend, the head of Shiva's consort fell after it was cut off to stop his cosmic dance which was rocking the universe dangerously.

Mustard growing on the terraces of the Kumaon Hills

The peach blossoms of the Himalayan spring

Rishikesh

Rishikesh, 24 kilometres (15 miles) from Haridwar, is a town of ashrams and temples, overlooked by tree-covered hills. At Rishikesh you get a strong impression of the Ganga tumbling from the mountains. Here the Chandrabhaga River joins the Ganga.

GETTING THERE

Rishikesh is among the last railheads for Garhwal. Most trains terminate at Haridwar, from where Rishikesh is 24 kilometres (15 miles) away, and Mussoorie, 77 kilometres (48 miles) away. Tours are available from here to Yamunotri, 288 kilometres (179 miles) away, Gangotri 258 kilometres (160 miles) away, Kedarnath, 228 kilometres (142 miles) away, and Badrinath, 301 kilometres (187 miles) away.

For a list of hotels in Rishikesh, see page 275.

SIGHTS

In the southern part of the town are the bus and railway stations, and the tourist office, on Railway Station Road. The northern part, known as **Muni-ki-Reti** is more attractive.

As at Haridwar, neither the ashrams nor the temples can lay claim to antiquity, and some areas are downright scruffy. The best views of the town and the river can be had walking across either of the two suspension bridges which sway across the river — the **Ram Jhula** and the older **Lakshman Jhula**.

Many ashrams cater to foreigners who want to learn yoga and more about Hinduism. One with excellent credentials is the **Divine Life Society** founded by Swami Sivananda. Then there is always Maharishi Mahesh Yogi's **Transcendental Meditation Centre**, which drew the Beatles to Rishikesh in the 1960s. On the same side of the river as this ashram is a path leading up to the **temple of Neelkanth Mahadev** (at 1,700 metres or 5,577 feet), 11 kilometres (seven miles) from the town, and with commanding views over it. Among the other temples to visit are the **Lakshman Temple**, three kilometres (two miles) from the town centre, and the **Rishikund and Raghunath temples** where Lord Ram is said to have bathed.

Deforestation

Deforestation is a major problem throughout India, affecting the inhabitants of both the hills and the plains. There is no one set of accepted figures for the rate of deforestation, but one impartial source is the National Remote Sensing Agency. Its satellite survey of India showed that the country lost one-sixth of its forests in the seven years between 1974-5 and 1981-2. At the beginning of the period, some 16.9 percent of the country had forest cover but at the end of it, this had been reduced to 14.1 percent, showing a loss of 1.3 million hectares (3.2 million acres) every year, eight times more than officially recognised by the Forest Department. If deforestation continues at this rate, there will be no forests left by the 21st century. An increasing proportion of forests are also getting degraded, being left without good tree cover.

Any traveller in the hills cannot fail to notice denuded hillsides at some point in their journey, often covered with lantana or cacti, sure signs of degraded slopes. With the loss of trees, the soil loses quality and becomes compacted and less able to absorb rain. Rainwater running off hillsides causes floods, while once perennial springs, vital sources of water to villagers, dry up for much of the year because rainwater is no longer absorbed. Deforested hillsides are also more prone to erosion and landslides. An estimated 5,334 tonnes of soil is eroded in India each year. Much of it ends up in river beds. Some 70 years ago a bridge was built over the Kaulgarh Nullah on the Dehra Dun-Mussoorie road, at that time clearing the river bed by 20 metres (65 feet). The catchment area of the stream has since been deforested, and by 1980 the arch of the bridge was barely visible and the river bed level was rising by 35 centimetres (a foot) every year. Silt in river beds obviously leads to more flooding in the monsoon. Landslides also cause major floods. In 1968, 1970 and 1978, for example, landslides blocked the Himalayan rivers Teesta, Alaknanda and Bhagirathi. When these 'natural dams' burst they caused flooding on a massive scale.

Where there is deforestation there has also been a change in the climate. Summers are hotter than they used to be and in many hill stations now you find ceiling fans, unheard of 40 years ago. Rainfall is also decreasing in areas where there has been widespread deforestation, for example the hill station of Ootacamund in south India, but there is a fierce debate over how much of this is due to felling. One of the most detailed studies was carried out in southwest India, which catches the full force of the monsoon. It showed that deforestation does not reduce the amount of rain but it does reduce the number of rainy days. This makes the rains more intense, more likely to cause floods and more erratic, which has an adverse effect on agriculture.

Decreasing rainfall, the drying up of springs and growing population have led to water shortages in most major hill stations during the summer. The government is having to arrange for water to be pumped up the resorts, often over long distances.

Who is to blame for this mass destruction? Commercial felling has accounted for a large proportion of it, and the high timber prices have encouraged illicit felling. Ironically, however, it is the people and the government's programmes for helping them which are often blamed the most. This is despite the fact that the forest represents 'the soul of the people' living in the hills. It provides their energy needs, and fodder for cattle which, in turn, produce manure. The forest protects the water sources, provides slates, stones and timber for houses as well as bamboo, honey and medicinal herbs.

Between 1950 and 1980, 150,000 hectares (370,650 acres) of forest were lost each year in India for development projects like dams and roads. Forest land was the easiest form of land to acquire for projects as it belonged to the government and was inexpensive. Road building in the unstable Himalayas has led to enormous soil erosion and landslides while improved access makes it easier to cut and carry away trees. There are some 44,000 kilometres (27,300 miles) of roads in the Himalayas and it is estimated that they generate over 24 million cubic metres (31 million cubic yards) of debris each year. Travelling in the mountains you can often see the ugly gashes in the hillsides caused by these roads.

The population in the hill areas has grown dramatically since Independence; in Uttar Pradesh, for example, it has almost doubled, but ways of life have remained the same. The forests are cropped and grazed, and land is cultivated on precarious hillside terraces devoid of trees. Professional foresters say this is the main cause of deforestation. However, many environmentalists argue that in Uttar Pradesh the area under cultivation and the cattle and buffalo population have remained more or less static over the last 30 years and that there can be enough forest for all if only it is properly managed. As Mahatma Gandhi put it, 'Nature has enough for everybody's need but not for everybody's greed.'

The colonial forest administration left behind by the British had a

conventional European view on forestry — that it should produce timber. This commercial system owes its origin to three German foresters. Over a century ago the Black Forest was being afforested and Germans had the highest reputation for forestry. The British called on German expertise and D Brandis, W Schlich and B Ribbentrop became the first Inspector Generals of Forests in India. But European ways often fail to meet Indian needs. The need of the hill people is fuel and fodder first and timber second. The demands of industry for timber are limited, and the demands of the people more urgent and greater.

Awareness of the need to afforest and to do so with the needs of the people in mind is growing. The voluntary organisations have done a great deal to this end. The Chipko Movement, whose members hug trees to protect them from the axe, is one of the most famous. This movement concentrates on involving women, who are the pivot of the family and also the fuel and fodder collectors. In deforested hill areas they leave home by four in the morning and spend the whole day in this latter activity. In 1974, the women of Reni village in northern Uttar Pradesh, called their forests their *mayaka*, or mother's home, and refused to allow lumberjacks to fell their trees. The movement has had numerous successes. There are now many other voluntary groups working with villagers in the hills, and there have also been marches through the Himalayas and along the length of the Western Ghats to draw national attention to the problems of deforestation.

In the case of Mussoorie, the government has addressed deforestation on what Indian bureaucrats describe as 'a war-footing'. A section of the Territorial Army is stationed in the Doon valley, forming an eco-taskforce which is planting trees with military precision and efficiency. But this is expensive, and cannot be an all-India solution.

Recent legislation has made forests, previously in the hands of the state government alone, a subject in which the central government also has powers. No forest land can be diverted for other purposes without the permission of the central government. This has led to complaints that development works are being delayed, but between 1980 and 1986 it also reduced the amount of forest land being diverted annually to a total of 33,875 hectares (83,705 acres).

At the suggestion of the central government, several states have banned felling above 1,000 metres (3,281 feet). There have also been major efforts to eliminate the middleman in the equation — the forest contractor whose interest is first and foremost. In Himachal Pradesh the state government is also doing

Forests in the foothills of Mount Nanda Kot

its best to promote apple and fruit boxes made of cardboard or plastic instead of wood, but progress has been slow.

Legislation by government is also not enough to stop deforestation. There are many worthy laws on the statute book which are rarely implemented. The government realises that it also needs 'a people's movement' but there is still no clear conclusions on how to achieve this.

Suggestions for Uttar Pradesh include changing the law to allow people to cut down trees grown on their own land. This would encourage afforestation on much privately owned degraded land which cannot support crops. Another is to reinforce and extend the powers of the village forest councils, which empower local people to control and develop forests for their needs. Certainly an urgent need is to place some controls over the use of hillsides as common land, which belong to no one and which everyone overgrazes.

Discussions also continue on which species of trees to plant. For example, the chir pine, ubiquitous in the Western Himalayan hills, produces resin but no fodder, prevents undergrowth, is particularly susceptible to fire and dries the soil. However, when people protest the forest department's reply is that the earth is too degraded to support broad-leaved trees.

Deforestation is still proceeding faster than afforestation, but the current level of awareness and debate provides hope for the future.

Deforestation at Jowai, Jaingie Hills, Meghalaya

RIVER RAFTING

The new Yuppie sport in India is river rafting, and the most accessible spot from Delhi is above Rishikesh. Tented camps on the banks of the Ganga are the bases for the rafting trips on either the Ganga, its tributary the Alaknanda, or both. Trips can last from one day to a week. On these stretches the rafts negotiate numerous Grade III and a few Grade IV rapids. Safety standards are high and young children are not allowed. Bookings are made from Delhi where there are now several companies offering the sport. Among the best is Himalayan River Runners (based at F-5, Hauz Khas Enclave, New Delhi 110 016; tel. 6852602). Its river camp has a particularly good location on a secluded river 'beach'.

From Rishikesh to the Four Dhams

North of Rishikesh the road rises steeply to **Narendra Nagar** at 1,067 metres (3,500 feet), which is the raja of Tehri's own hill station and the site of his summer palace. His capital of Tehri is 83 kilometres (52 miles) from Rishikesh and only 770 metres (2,526 feet) above sea level. It is at the bottom of a narrow valley which in summer is nearly as hot as the plains. Tehri is at the confluence of the Bhagirathi and the Bhilargana. The somewhat dilapidated palace still stands in Tehri, although, like the rest of the town, it will be submerged if the controversial Tehri Dam on the Bhagirathi is completed. From Tehri the road runs along the river valley to **Dharsu**, 120 kilometres (75 miles) away, where a road branches off to **Hanuman Chatti**, 13 kilometres' (eight miles') trek from Yamunotri, at 3,290 metres (10,794 feet).

The main road continues to **Uttarkashi**, 26 kilometres (16 miles) further on. Uttarkashi is a prosperous district town on the Bhagirathi. Among its many temples, that of **Lord Vishwanath** (Shiva) is the most important. The road from Uttarkashi takes you right up to **Gangotri Temple** at 3,140 metres (10,302 feet). The temple, over 250 years old, was built by the Gorkha commander, Aman Singh Thapa. The Gangotri glacier, the source of the River Ganga, here called the Bhagirathi, is a day's trek away beyond Gaumukh.

The road from Rishikesh to **Kedarnath** and **Badrinath** runs past the picturesque **Deoprayag**. Here the Alaknanda joins the Bhagirathi from Gangotri and the river is from this point known as the Ganga. Above the houses, with their pitched stone roofs, rises the *shikhara* of the **Raghunath Temple** established by the great Hindu philosopher, Shankaracharya. Some 35 kilometres (22 miles) further on is the valley of **Srinagar**, the ancient capital of Garhwal, rebuilt after its destruction by floods. Srinagar is now the home of the Garhwal University.

Unlike the old rajas, the British rulers of Garhwal chose to make their capital a hill station. **Pauri**, 30 kilometres (19 miles) from Srinagar and Deoprayag, is 1,823 metres (5,981 feet) above sea level and is the headquarters of Tehri district. Slightly off the main pilgrimage route, it is well worth a short visit as it looks over forests to the Himalayas. Near the town is the **Bhuvaneshwari Devi Temple** where goats and buffaloes are still occasionally sacrificed to appease the temple goddess.

Rudraprayag, at the confluence of the Mandakini from Kedarnath and the Alaknanda from Badrinath, lies 34 kilometres (21 miles) beyond Srinagar. From here the road to Kedarnath takes you to **Guptakashi**. Beyond Guptakashi is a narrow road regulated to one-way traffic by what is known as the 'gate system'. Vehicles on the route leave in convoys at certain times of the day. The motor road ends at **Gaurikund**, leaving a 14-kilometre (nine-mile) trek to Kedarnath.

The route to Badrinath runs via **Joshimath**, 110 kilometres (68 miles) from Rudraprayag. Joshimath is the main town on this road and is developing into a hill station in its own right. A few kilometres from the town are the beautiful slopes of **Auli**, which is being developed as a ski resort. For most visitors, however, Joshimath is first and foremost the seat of the great Hindu sage, the Adiguru Shankaracharya. He attained enlightenment in a cave here, above which stands a mulberry tree supposedly 2,400 years old. The Guru's monastery or *math* is known as the **Jyotirmath**. The most famous temple is that of **Narsingh Bhagwan** (Vishnu in his man-lion incarnation). It is said that one arm of the image is growing thinner and that, when it breaks, the mountains near Badrinath will collapse and close the way to the shrine. The Narsingh Bhagwan Temple is also the centre of worship of Vishnu when Badrinath is closed. Travel along the remaining 50 kilometres (31 miles) to the holy shrine is again restricted by the gate system. The road however runs right up to the shrine. The same cannot be said of the route to the Sikh temple of Hemkund, which involves a steep trek from Govindghat on this road.

GETTING AROUND

Pilgrims prefer to start their journeys from Haridwar, but for tourists Mussoorie and Dehra Dun can be equally good starting points. Buses and taxis are available as far as the roads go, except in the winter when some roads are closed. Roads are also risky during the monsoon months (June-September).

Accommodation is mainly pilgrim-orientated — very simple. There are tourist bungalows at the main overnight halts, but there are too few beds available at the peak pilgrim seasons. PWD and Forest resthouses, if you can find the official concerned, provide adequate rooms in most places. Temple *dharamsalas* also provide very basic accommodation.

Nainital

Nainital is one of the most popular hill stations in northern India, due largely to its fine setting. It is built around the shores of a mountain lake 1,940 metres (6,365 feet) above sea level and is surrounded by forested slopes. Now the headquarters of the district of Nainital, it was formerly the summer capital of the government of the United Provinces, now known as Uttar Pradesh. Although the East India Company controlled the Nainital area from 1815, it wasn't until 1839 that an Englishman in the sugar trade, P Barron, stumbled on the lake. Being a good businessman, he immediately recognised its potential and canvassed for its development by publishing articles under the name of 'Pilgrim'. He also persuaded the local headman to surrender his claim to the lake and the land around it. Barron took the headman out into the middle of the lake in his boat, and offered him the option of accepting the claims of the Company or being capsized with his property intact. As Barron himself wrote:

> He looked very blank, said the lake was very deep and agreed to waive his claim in preference to the chance or rather certainty of being drowned if the boat were upset ... Being always provided with a book and pencil when in the hills, I produced them and the poor man wrote out in it a deed by which he resigned all claim to the lake. As all the Puharees [hill people] of Kumaon, however poor, can read and write, as

soon as we returned to the shore I exhibited this document
to the assembled crowd.

Barron's house Pilgrim's Cottage, near the present Nainital
Club, was the first to be built. It was soon followed by others and it is
these bungalows, hotels and imposing civic edifices which dominate
Nainital still.

Today, Nainital is the summer residence of the governor of Uttar
Pradesh, and crocodiles of school children walking down the Mall
reveal that it is a prestigious educational centre. One of the first sights
to meet the eye on the route up to Nainital is the fort-like building of
St Joseph's School. Nainital's peak season is mercifully short (June-mid-
July and September-October). During this season, Nainital is crowded
and many hotels put their prices up by 50 percent.

GETTING THERE AND AROUND

Pantnagar airport is 71 kilometres (44 miles) away but does not have
regular flights. The nearest railway station is Kathgodam, 35 kilometres
(22 miles) away. On the metre-guage line, Kathgodam is connected by
direct services to Agra, Lucknow, and Bareilly. From Delhi you can
travel to Bareilly, 250 kilometres (155 miles) away, by rail, Bareilly to
Kathgodam by metre-guage and on to Nainital by road. Direct buses are
available from Delhi (322 kilometres or 200 miles via Hapur and 336
kilometres or 209 miles via Meerut), and surrounding areas.

Nainital is full of private companies offering bus and taxi trips. If
you want unbiased general information, speak to the Government
tourist office on the Mall (tel. 35337). Tours on offer are to the lakes,
Kausani, Ranikhet, Badrinath and Corbett National Park.

There are plenty of places to stay in Nainital, see page 275.

SIGHTS

Nainital is divided into two parts: **Tallital** at the lower end of the lake, has a crowded bazaar and the bus station; **Mallital**, at the upper end of the lake, is the main centre of the town. The two are connected by the North Mall running along one side of the lake and the South Mall, a bridle path, along the other. The lake, now rather more polluted than it was in Barron's day, is the centre of activity, and dozens of rowing boats will take you from Tallital to Mallital.

If you enjoy small-boat sailing or would simply like a drink in the best bar in Nainital, then you should visit the **Boat House Club**, originally the Nainital Yacht Club, established in 1890. The Boat House Club offers temporary membership which entitles visitors to use the spacious lounge bar with its leather armchairs, billiards room and verandah overlooking the lake, as well as to sail the club's dinghies. This club is also the centre of Nainital's very lively season society.

Also on the shores of the lake at Mallital is the red-roofed **temple of Naina Devi**, the goddess after whom the town is named. *Naina* means 'eye' and *tal* 'lake'. It is believed that the eye of the goddess Parvati fell into the lake as her spouse Shiva was carrying her back to his dwelling on Mount Kailash. The original temple was destroyed in a landslide in 1880 but the new building still attracts crowds of worshippers, especially during August/September, when there is a festival in honour of Nanda Devi (identified with Parvati), who is the patron goddess of Kumaon.

The Flats are the sporting centre of Nainital. During the season, large crowds gather to watch hockey and other matches on this stretch of grey shale at the edge of the lake. Here too is the main **pony stand**. The Flats are the remains of the 1880 landslide which left 151 dead and destroyed the Victoria Hotel, and Bell's department store as well as the original Naina Devi temple.

The car-free main **Bara Bazaar** leads up from the Flats and here there are rows of souvenir shops reminiscent of an English seaside resort. Carved walking-sticks, locally manufactured candles in the shape of Hindu gods and the celebrated local fudge known as *bal mithai*, are for sale.

Above Bara Bazaar is the **Church of St John-in-the-Wilderness**, one of the earliest buildings erected in Nainital and possibly the finest church in any Indian hill station. The church was named by the bishop of Calcutta who came to Nainital in 1844, when the place was still very much a wilderness. The impression was strengthened by the fact that the bishop was taken ill and forced to stay in a mud hut which only admitted light through the doorway. Now very much neglected, St John's is still surrounded by trees, and has some saplings growing from its walls. The interior, especially the stained-glass, is still impressive, despite the fact that thieves have stolen most of the brass plaques, except those by the altar which give the names of the landslide victims.

The other two main churches in central Nainital — the **Methodist Church** on the Mall near the Flats and the Roman Catholic **Church of St Francis,** also on the Mall — are much better preserved.

Wildlife enthusiasts can see the picturesque **Gurney House** which used to belong to the great writer and hunter of maneating tigers, Jim Corbett, after whom the famous Corbett National Park is named. This is now a private residence but still has trophies from Corbett's time and seems to be much as he had left it.

The fine buildings are the **old Government House**, former residence of the governor of the United Provinces, near **Snow View**, and the present residence, **Raj Bhavan**, of the governor of Uttar Pradesh. Its large grounds can be opened to individual members of the public on application.

Nainital is in a bowl of mountains and so, to see the surrounding countryside, you have to climb to the rim of the bowl. **The Uttar Pradesh State Astronomical Observatory** stands on **Manora Peak**, 1,950 metres (6,398 feet) above sea level on a bridle path some four and half kilometres (three miles) from Tallital bus stand. It is 11 kilometres (seven miles) by motor road and looks out towards the plains. The Observatory can be visited by prior appointment on certain days.

On the way to the Observatory is the **Hanumangarh Temple**, dedicated to the monkey god Hanuman. This is a favourite picnic place and offers sunset views.

Above the Mall is **Snow View**, at 2,270 metres (7,448 feet) above sea level, which is conveniently reached by the aerial express ropeway

Hutton Cottage, Nainital

Sailing boats on Nainital Lake

which runs from the Mallital end of the Mall to the summit. There is also a good bridle road and, on a clear day, there are excellent views of the Great Himalayas, which can also be observed more closely through a telescope.

Ayarpetta is the mountain on the opposite side of the lake to Snow View. Most of the town's prestigious schools and Raj Bhavan are on this hill. A bridle path leads up to **Tiffin Top** and **Dorothy's Seat**, at 2,292 metres (7,520 feet), which offer a limited view of the Himalayas and also views of Nainital and the plains. The seat was put there by an Englishman in memory of his wife.

Three kilometres (two miles) from the strangely formed rocks known as **Bara Patthar** (12 stones) near St John's Church, is **Land's End** which looks out over terraced fields and the lake **Khurpa Tal**. However, the most impressive views can be had from the highest vantage point, **Naina (or Cheena) Peak**, 2,610 metres (8,563 feet) high, which towers over Mallital. Six kilometres (four miles) from the Flats, a steep path leads to the summit where there is a tourist department log cabin for those who wish to stay overnight and see the sunrise. Anyone wishing to do this is advised to take his or her own bedding and food. But the view is worth it — the Great Himalayas are only just over 100 kilometres (62 miles) away and you can see from Gangotri to Nepal.

The Nainital Forest

Even if you visit Nainital in the summer, it is not difficult to retreat from the crowds and honking buses. The Cheena Peak road takes you to a forest of oak, deodar, spruce, cypress and rhododendron only a few kilometres from Mallital, and it would be a mistake to visit Nainital and not travel at least as far as **Kilbury**, an old resthouse 12 kilometres (seven and a half miles) from Nainital and at a height of 2,195 metres (7,201 feet).

This quiet road has excellent views. Two other forest resthouses lie beyond: one at **Binayak**, 22 kilometres (14 miles) from Nainital, at 2,225 metres (7,300 feet), and the other at **Kunjkharak**, 38 kilometres (24 miles) from Nainital, 16 kilometres (ten miles) from Binayak at 2,600 metres (8,530 feet). The latter has the most spectacular position, but no bedding, and the nearest water supply is a kilometre away. You can either hire a car (although the road is precarious at points) or walk to these locations. Binayak and Kunjkhrak can be used as bases for short treks. The resthouses can be booked through the Divisional Forest Officer, Nainital.

The Lake District of Kumaon

This area of the Himalayas is remarkable for its small mountain lakes which led the British to call it the Westmorland of India.

Sat Tal, at a height of 1,371 metres (4,498 feet), means, literally, seven lakes, as it consists of seven interconnected tarns. It lies 21 kilometres (13 miles) from Nainital via the fruit market of Bhowali. The land here is mainly privately owned and the forests of pine and oak have been carefully preserved. By the three main lakes, known as Ram, Sita and Lakshman (after the hero, heroine and hero's brother of the *Ramayana*), there are a couple of tea stalls and a few paddle boats. However, these do not spoil the peace of the area, which is rich in birdlife. There is also a small tourist resthouse by these lakes for overnight halts.

Bhimtal, at 1,371 metres (4,398 feet), is 22 kilometres (14 miles) from Nainital and has a larger and much cleaner lake. However, a 'pollution-free' industrial estate being built nearby doesn't add to its attractions and, apart from a few places, the hills around are sadly deforested. Boating on Bhimtal, as a day trip from Nainital, is still popular among tourists.

Naukuchia Tal, a distance of 26 kilometres (16 miles) from Nainital, is beyond Bhimtal and lies at 1,219 metres (4,000 feet). It takes its name from the fact that it had nine corners (*nau kuchia*) and is in a picturesque location.

Another popular destination from Nainital is **Ramgarh**, 26 kilometres (16 miles) on the Nainital-Mukteswar road and 1,792 metres (5,879 feet) high. This is an area famous for its orchards, and the fact that it was here that Rabindranath Tagore completed his collection of poems, *Gitanjali*, which won him the Nobel Prize.

Corbett National Park

Corbett Park is one of the finest tiger reserves in India. As well as tiger, there are other species, including elephant, leopard, crocodile and gharial. The park covers 520 square kilometres (200 square miles) of mixed deciduous *terai* forest in the Himalayan foothills. It remains open from November to June each year. The main offices of the park are at **Ramnagar** and here you can make or confirm reservations. For visitors travelling without the 'full *bandobast*' of car, cook, all kitchen utensils and food, the place to stay is the main settlement of **Dhikala**, 50 kilometres (31 miles) from Ramnagar in the heart of the park. If possible, try to reserve accommodation in advance by contacting the Field Director, Project Tiger, Corbett National Park, Ramnagar (tel. 85489) or the Chief Wildlife Warden, Uttar Pradesh, 17 Rana Pratap Marg, Lucknow (tel. 28390). The Uttar Pradesh tourist offices in Nainital and in Delhi will help with reservations. On the way from Nainital, 116 kilometres (72 miles) from Dhikala, you can visit **Kaladhungi**, where Corbett spent much of his life, and see his house which has now been converted into a museum.

Ranikhet

Ranikhet means 'Queen's Field' and is said to be named after the wife of the 12th-century raja, Sudhar Deve. The rani (queen) may have visited but she did not stay and the field remained in the hands of its farmers until the British chose to turn it into a cantonment in 1869.

Spread along a ridge at 1,830 metres (6,004 feet), Ranikhet is covered with pine and oak forests. On its northern side it offers fine snow views. The climate is especially pleasant, being protected from the southwest monsoon by a high plateau which reduces the average annual rainfall to 127 centimetres (50 inches), half that of Nainital. It is, however, slightly warmer than its more famous neighbour, and although it snows in Ranikhet the snow rarely settles. Ranikhet is still a cantonment and the army must take the credit for limiting the spread of the bazaar and maintaining the forests. The town is now the home of the Kumaon Regiment, one of the Indian army's best. Its history goes back to 1780 when a Kumaoni battalion was raised to serve Hyderabad

A Bharmanu villager enjoying a hookah *on his doorstep*

state in southern India. Many buildings in Ranikhet bear the regimental crest, and most of the vehicles driving on the Upper Mall belong to the regiment. Young recruits undergo their 36-week basic training here and can be seen drilling on the parade grounds.

The summer tourist invasion is not too much in evidence here, and Ranikhet is worth visiting in May or June.

GETTING THERE
Ranikhet is connected by bus with Delhi, 367 kilometres (228 miles) away, and Nainital, 59 kilometres (37 miles) away. Both government and privately owned buses run on the local hill routes, though often not on time. The nearest railheads are Kathgodam, at a distance of 84 kilometres (53 miles), and Ramnagar, 97 kilometres (60 miles) away. The Ramnagar-Raniket road, running along the edge of Corbett National Park, is especially attractive.

For a list of hotels in Ranikhet, see page 276.

SIGHTS
The Town and Around
Sadar Bazaar is the main shopping area, and has a number of small restaurants and hotels. It boasts two bus stations — one for the government and the other for the private buses of the KMOU (Kumaon Motor Owners Union). Just above the government bus station is the **tourist office** and nearby is the government tour company, **Parvat Tours**. The bazaar is the noisiest and most crowded part of the town.

The **Upper Mall**, in contrast, offers peaceful walks. Two roads loop through the forest to join the Mall at each end. One leaves the Mall by the Meghdoot Hotel and joins it opposite the West View. Along this road are sundry decaying bungalows with names like Rosemount. A deserted lane running through thick forest branches off the Mall opposite the West View and joins it again near the **Jhula Devi Temple**. It is said that, once a month, a leopard comes to the temple, but only the priest sees it. Certainly there are some leopards in the neighbourhood. Above Jhula Devi is a **temple of Lord Ram**.

A few kilometres further along the Upper Mall, ten kilometres (six miles) from Sadar Bazaar, is **Chaubatia**, originally a sanatorium for British troops. It now houses the **Government Fruit Garden and**

Research Station which grows 200 varieties of fruit. After wandering through the extensive woods and orchards of the garden you can also buy the produce at knockdown prices. The peak of the apple season is August-September.

A three-kilometre (two-mile) walk from Chaubatia leads to the artificial lake of **Bhaludam**.

Uphat, six kilometres (four miles) from Sadar Bazaar on Almora Road, is the site of one of the highest **golf courses** with views of the Great Himalayas. The course was originally laid out by a British cavalry officer as a cross-country race track, and the track now forms the perimeter of the nine-hole course. The golf course is run by the army, but anyone with a set of clubs is welcome to a game for a nominal charge. The course is, however, closed during the monsoon, from July to September. There is a refreshment kiosk in the centre of the golf course.

Just beyond the golf course is a small **temple to Kalika** and a government **forest nursery** which should both be avoided during the video-coach season in May and June.

Further along the same road, 13 kilometres (eight miles) from Sadar Bazaar, is **Majkhali**, recommended for its views of the snows.

One of the best viewpoints within easy walking distance of the main bazaar is the **Hera Khan Temple and Ashram**, near Chilianaula village, four kilometres (two and a half miles) from Sadar Bazaar. The Hindu saint, Hera Khan, died in 1984 and the modern marble-faced temple with a garden was constructed according to his wishes. The baba had many European followers and the ashram is inhabited mainly by them.

EXCURSIONS

Private taxis and the government's Parvat Tours will hire out taxis to local sights and places further afield like Badrinath.

Dwarahat, 38 kilometres (24 miles) from Ranikhet on the Badrinath road, was once the seat of the Katyari kings who are said to have ruled from the Great Himalayas to the plains. It is now famous for its 55 temples divided into eight groups dating from the 11th century. Many are in a ruined condition but still have some fascinating stone carvings. A five-kilometre (three-mile) walk from Dwarahat, or 15 kilometres (nine

Church, Parade and Officers' Mess Ranikhet, c 1910

miles) away by road, is **Dunagiri** with views of the Himalayas. There is also a **Durga temple** built in 1181.

Tarikhet is a village eight kilometres (five miles) from Ranikhet on the Ramnagar road. A small hut, **Gandhi Kuti**, where Mahatma Gandhi stayed during the Freedom Movement, is its main attraction.

Sitlakhet, (26 kilometres or 16 miles from Ranikhet), **Manila** (66 kilometres or 41 miles) and **Chaukutiya** (85 kilometres or 53 miles) are all beautiful picnic spots offering spectacular panoramic views of the Himalayas.

Almora

The small town of Almora is perched on a five-kilometre- (three-mile-) long horseshoe-shaped ridge, 1,650 metres (5,413 feet) above sea level. The town looks out over a fertile terraced valley and four ranges of hills — Banari Devi, Kasan Devi, Shyahi Devi and Katarmal. Beyond them you can see Trishul and Nanda Devi in the Great Himalayas.

Unlike most hill stations, Almora wasn't an empty hillside 'discovered' by the British. It was already an established town with a long history. Kashaya Hill, on which Almora is built, is mentioned in the Hindu scripture, the *Skanda Purana*. It is believed that the great god Vishnu dwelt here. The area has been inhabited since the earliest historical times, but it was only in 1560 that Raja Kalyan Chand of Kumaon decided to make it his capital. Gorkha invaders put an end to the Chand dynasty in 1790 and occupied Almora fort, but after the Gorkhas were themselves defeated by the British in 1815, Almora gained a new lease of life as a minor hill station.

Although it is below the mosquito line and was made a hill resort for strategic reasons, British medical men soon became convinced of its beneficial climate. As one wrote: 'The circulation of the air is much freer than at Naini Tal and Bhim Tal, and the place is perhaps the healthiest of the Kumaon stations.'

GETTING THERE

Frequent, though somewhat irregular, bus services link Almora with other places in the region including Nainital, a distance of 67 kilometres (42 miles), and Ranikhet, 50 kilometres (31 miles) away. The nearest railhead is Kathgodam, 90 kilometres (56 miles) from Almora via Khairua and 133 kilometres (83 miles) via Ranikhet. Almora is 335 kilometres (208 miles) from Delhi and 196 kilometres (122 miles) from Bareilly on a direct bus route.

For details of where to stay, see page 276.

SIGHTS

The Town

The main thoroughfare in Almora is the **Mall**, which has the bus stand, small restaurants and hotels. Private taxis are available near the bus stand but rates are not fixed and you will have to bargain. Almora's chequered past is reflected in the buildings along the Mall. There has been a struggle between 'wild west Swiss' and local styles of architecture. You can see indigenous hill cottages with bungalow trimmings and British bungalows half Indianised with great slabs of stone for roofs. The **post office**, built in 1905, is still very British but the main **clock tower** (opposite the **tourist office**), erected in 1886 by an Indian but constructed by a British engineer, shows a strange confusion of styles. Nowadays a third style predominates — modern concrete boxes.

Old Almora still survives in the **temple of Nanda Devi**, the patron goddess of the Chand rajas, which stands in the antechamber of a **Shiva temple**, and also in the bazaars above and adjoining the Mall.

The stone-flagged bazaars have an authentic oriental flavour especially in the evening when they are thronged with customers. Here too there is a mixture of ancient and modern. The older buildings are most attractive, with carved wooden doorways, window frames and pitched roofs. The best example of the old style is in the **Khazanchi Mohalla**, the area which once belonged to the state treasurers. The highest point of the Almora bazaars, above the Mall, is the **Collectorate**. This is in fact the old Almora fort, from where you can get a 360° view of Almora and the surrounding mountains. In the Collectorate courtyard are a group of small **temples** underneath a peepal tree and on one of the buildings nearby there is this inscription: 'Fort Nanda Devi, erected by Chand Rajas and strengthened by Gurkha government, captured by British under Col. Nicholls on 26.4.1815. The convention for the surrender of Kumaon was formed the next day.'

One of the traditional crafts of Almora is copperware and some of the best coppersmiths still work from their traditional area in the old city, **Tamta Mohalla**. Other local crafts are the weaving of traditional tweeds and shawls.

Walks
Brighton End Corner, named after England's popular seaside resort, is two kilometres (just over a mile) from the bus station on the Mall and is the most popular point for sunset and sunrise views of the Himalayas. Walking further on you can climb up to the **Durga and Khagmara temples**, on paths leading off the Mall.

Simtola, three kilometres (two miles) from Almora, on the opposite side of the horseshoe ridge, is a pine-covered picnic spot. Close by are **Hiradungi**, once a diamond mining centre and the scenic **Greynite Hill**.

Excellent views of Almora and the Himalayan peaks can be had from **Kalimath**, four and a half kilometres (three miles) from Almora, and the

The metre-gauge steam train passing through Coonoor en route to Ootacamund

Kasar Devi Temple, six kilometres (four miles) away. Kasar Devi stands on what is still known as **Crank's Ridge**, formerly a haunt of artists and writers. D H Lawrence spent two summers here, and it has also attracted Bob Dylan, Cat Stevens and Timothy Leary, the father of the hippy movement. Hippies came in their wake and rented cottages but now even they have moved on, leaving just a few drifters. Two kilometres (just over a mile) from the Kasar Devi Temple, in **Upreti Khola** district, is a second-century-BC **rock inscription** dedicated to the goddess.

Another hilltop temple stands six kilometres (four miles) from Almora at **Chital**. The god here is Lord Golla, a deified general of the Chand dynasty, and his shrine is decorated with a canopy of bells offered in thanksgiving by devotees.

OUT OF TOWN

Kumaon was the centre of great temple-building activity between AD 700 and 1300. Some 400 temples were built in Almora district alone. One of the most famous is the **sun temple** near the village of **Katarmal**, 17 kilometres (ten and a half miles) from Almora. This temple is over 800 years old. Only a kilometre (half a mile) away from it is the **Bikut forest** which looks out over Almora.

Some 30 kilometres (19 miles) from Almora is the **forest of Binsar**. The road runs along a ridge with superb views on both sides, and Binsar itself is undoubtedly one of the most beautiful places in the district. Standing 2,412 metres (7,913 feet) above sea level, it is beyond the bus route. The nearest bus stop is 11 kilometres (seven miles) from the **Binsar tourist bungalow**, which provides basic accommodation. The climb is uphill but private taxis from Almora will take you to the top for a price. Once the summer capital of the Chand rajas, all that's left of its ancient past are two **13th-century temples** to Shiva and his consort in a meadow, a kilometre and a half (a mile) below the summit.

Binsar was revived as a capital of sorts by Henry Ramsay, commissioner of Kumaon, from 1852 to 1856. Ramsay, known as the 'King of Kumaon', built his summer residence, now deserted, and his court on the hilltop. Ramsay, a pioneer in education, health and irrigation, was fluent in Kumaoni and rode from village to village dispensing justice. His memory lives on among the villages in the area who call him 'Ramji Sahib'. In 1988, after a tough fight put up by the residents of the area, they succeeded in having 102 square kilometres (39 square miles) of Himalayan oak forest declared a sanctuary. It is planned to provide guides for visitors, but for the present you are welcome to wander through the thick forest and, if lucky, catch glimpses of leopard, barking deer, goral, Himalayan black bear and Kalij pheasant. The best time to visit Binsar is in the winter when the skies are clear and clouds lie in the valleys, leaving you alone with hundreds of kilometres of the Great Himalayan snows.

Many of the forest paths around Binsar are difficult to follow for long distances, but it is possible to take the forest route to **Jageshwar**, a day's walk of about 25 kilometres (15 miles). Jageshwar is 34 kilometres (21 miles) from Almora by road and is celebrated for its magnificent cluster of **150 temples**, profusely carved and dating back to the ninth century AD. Most of these temples are dedicated to Shiva and his consort, and are surrounded by tall deodar cedars. There is a tourist bungalow for overnight halts.

Kausani, 50 kilometres (31 miles) from Almora at 1,890 metres (6,201 feet), is one of the places popularised as the Switzerland of India. From this small settlement situated on a mountain top are views of nearly 400 kilometres (250 miles) of snows. From west to east are the peaks of Kedarnath, Chaukhamba, Badrinath, Nandaghunti, Trishul (only 25 kilometres or 16 miles away as the crow fies), Nanda Devi, Panchachuli, and Api and Nampa (in Nepal). The best views are between September and May. There is a pleasant **tourist bungalow** and also the **Anashakti Yoga Ashram** where Mahatma Gandhi stayed in 1929. The Mahatma was enchanted by the beauty of Kausani. The ashram, run in true Gandhian tradition of 'plain living and high thinking', has several guesthouses in its spacious compound, and a wide, north-facing terrace where you can spend the whole day watching the snows. Reservations can be made by writing to the Manager, Anashakti Ashram, Kausani.

Baijnath, at 1,125 metres (3,691 feet), is an ancient religious centre in the **Garur Valley**, 20 kilometres (13 miles) from Kausani. It is best known for its **Parvati temple** which enshrines a beautifully sculpted, human-sized image of the goddess and is said to date from the 12th or 13th century.

Trekking in Uttarakhand

This area is rich in trekking routes which are open during the summer months. One suggestion for a longer trek is to the remote Har-ki-Dun Valley, east of Yamunotri. Here the local people are still relatively unchanged by modern society and still practise polygamy.

From Kalyani, five kilometres (three miles) beyond Uttarkashi is a two-day trek to Dodital, at an altitude of 3,024 metres (9, 921 feet), one of the most beautiful Himalayan lakes, well stocked with trout and overlooked by a forest resthouse. You can then continue to Hanuman Chatti and Yamunotri.

Gaumukh is a good base for day-long treks along the Raktwan and Gangotri glaciers, while Gangotri is the base for treks to the mountain lake of Kedar Tal, 17 kilometres (ten and a half miles) away. It is also possible to trek from Gangotri to Kedarnath via the Khatling Glacier at 3,710 metres (12,172 feet). An alternative route to Kedarnath is from the roadhead at Ghuttu beyond Tehri. From here it is a six-day trek to the Khatling Glacier, one day's hard trek from Kedarnath. Ghuttu is also a base for treks to the lake region of Sahastratal (1,000 lakes).

Another trek rapidly gaining popularity is that to Roopkund Lake, at 4,778 metres (15,676 feet) with its views of Trishul. The route from Gwaldam passes through flowering alpine meadows. This shallow lake contains the skeletons of some 300 people who perished five to six hundred years ago in an unrecorded disaster.

From Govindghat, on the way to Badrinath, is the route to the Sikh shrine of Hemkund and the popular Valley of the Flowers. The Valley, at its most colourful during the monsoon months (July-September), has now been closed to trekkers, which means that you cannot stay overnight there. There are no restrictions, however, on Hemkund which attracts streams of pilgrims. The dramatic and much more inaccessible Nanda Devi Sanctuary, is surrounded by 70 to 75 snow-capped peaks. This natural sanctuary is now a national park and has also been closed to preserve the environment.

West Bengal, Sikkim and Meghalaya

All these states on the northeast of India have sensitive borders. Foreigners require permits to go to Sikkim and Meghalaya. There are no such restrictions on Indian passport holders, although even they are not allowed into certain border areas.

Permits

Foreigners can apply for permits from Indian missions abroad. However, they should do so well in advance as their application will be forwarded to New Delhi for clearance in the Home Ministry and the reply relayed back to the mission.

DARJEELING

Until recently restricted area permits were needed to visit Darjeeling, Kalimpong and other places in the northern districts of the state of West Bengal. This is no longer true. Foreign tourists can now visit all the northern districts of the state. There is no need for any permit and visitors can stay as long as their visa to remain in India is valid.

Mount Kanchenjunga taken from Jalapahar, Darjeeling

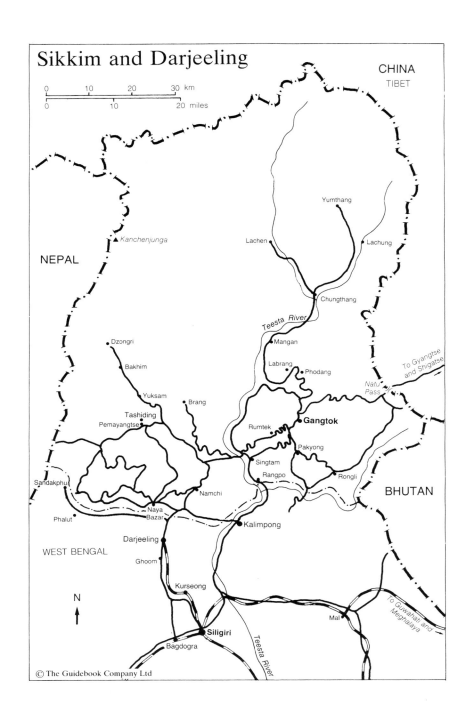

Sikkim and Darjeeling

CHINA
TIBET

0   10   20   30 km
0   10   20 miles

NEPAL

▲ Kanchenjunga

Yumthang

Lachen

Lachung

Chungthang

Teesta River

Dzongri

Mangan

Bakhim

Labrang

Phodang

To Gyangtse and Shigatse

Natu Pass

Yuksam

Brang

Tashiding

Pemayangtse

Rumtek

Gangtok

Pakyong

Sandakphu

Singtam

Rangpo

Rongli

Namchi

BHUTAN

Phalut

Naya Bazar

Kalimpong

Darjeeling

WEST BENGAL

Ghoom

N
↑

Kurseong

To Guwahati and Meghalaya

Mal

Siligiri

Bagdogra

Teesta River

SIKKIM

Individual foreign tourists can apply for a 15-day sightseeing permit, which covers Gangtok, Phodang, Rumtek and Pemayangtse either to the Foreigners' Regional Registration Offices (FRROs) in Delhi, Mumbai, Madras and Calcutta, or to the Sikkim Tourist Office, New Sikkim House, 14 Panchseel Marg, New Delhi 110021 (tel. 6115346). You can also apply at the Sikkim Tourist Information Centre, 4 C Poonam Building, 5/2 Russel Street, Calcutta 700017 (tel. 297516), or to the Sikkim Tourist Office, SNT Colony, Silliguri (tel. 432646). There is also a Sikkim Tourist Information Counter at Bagdogra airport which will direct you to the Siliguri office. Permits normally take two days to come through, and you will find the Sikkim Tourism staff very helpful. They are also responsible for issuing trekking permits. If you want to trek in the Pemayangtse area you should apply two months in advance. Trekking is limited to groups of four or more, with a government guide on certain routes. However, the Sikkim Government is trying to relax such restrictions.

SHILLONG

Individual tourists should apply for a permit to the Ministry of Home Affairs at Loknayak Bhavan in Delhi. The permit takes a minimum of ten days to come through. If you can form a group of four or more, then you can apply for a permit from the Foreigners' Registration Office in Delhi. Such visits have to be organised by a travel agency recognised by the Government of India or the state government, and the agency will send details of your tour to the state government before you arrive. You are received by a Liaison Officer who stays with you during your visit. Applications for visits to Cherrapunji can also be made from Delhi. Otherwise permission is given by the state government in Shillong. The state tourist officer at Meghalaya House, 9 Aurangzeb Road, New Delhi 110011 (tel. 3014417), offers advice and guidance.

Darjeeling

Darjeeling, centre of India's most celebrated tea-growing district, has possibly the best views of any Indian hill station. The vast bulk of Kanchenjunga, at 8,580 metres (28,150 feet), appears to sit above the

Pretty as a Picture

At one period of my Darjeeling career, I haunted the Bhootia village, or Busti, as it is called in the language of the hills, which is situated about half a mile from the station; and I may say, in strictest confidence, that I became almost part of it myself, till the very pigs began to recognise and greet me, with a contented sort of grunt, as I sketched the dearest, raggedest, dirtiest of tumble-down tenements, getting to know the dwellers, and their little black-eyed flat-faced children. At first I and my easel were regarded with the utmost suspicion — I must have the gift of the evil eye, they thought. For what other purpose could I desire to set down their ragged home-steads on paper, and carry them away with me, if it were not to weave some spell to harm them? My first appearance therefore amongst these happy simple folk ushered in a reign of terror; but as time wore on, and neither their children nor cattle died, neither did their huts topple over the precipice, they began to look upon me as an inevitable, — a grievance to be borne. Then would they come running up to meet me, as I appeared, a tiny speck on the ridge of the mountains, beneath which their village is situated, fix my easel for me, go to fetch water, sometimes even insisting on holding my colour-box, which was doubtless provoking, as were their comments upon my proceedings and presence generally; but I had no heart to repulse them. Sketching, surrounded by a crowd, even though it be an admiring one, is anything but agreeable, as all know who have tried it, and whispers are perplexing, even though they may be complimentary.

But they never really annoyed me except when, in anticipation of my arrival at their village, they attempted to tidy up the outside of their dwellings. Sometimes, whilst I was in the very act of sketching one of their huts, they could be seen all hurry and bustle, scrimmaging here and there with switches and impromptu brooms, sweeping away the delicious rubbish heaps — the accumulation of years — upon which I had set my artistic affections. Once in an incautious moment I happened to tell them I intended some day or other to make a picture of their village all in one. Their delight knew no bounds; and one morning soon after, whilst sitting at breakfast, I was told that several Lepchas and Bhootias were waiting without to see me, where I found a deputation, headed by a stately old Bhootia woman, who begged to inform me 'the village was quite ready, would I come to-day to write it down.'

Suspecting some treachery or other, but willing to gratify them, I did start, armed with easel and sandwiches for a long day of it; but what was my horror, on reaching the brow of the hill, to find the village tidied up in earnest, and decked out as for a gala day. Some of the huts were covered with little streamers, and fresh green boughs tied to bamboo stakes; wooden palisades had been mended, and their enclosures swept and garnished; and, as if this had not been enough, they had actually whitewashed the outside of the little Buddhist temple itself; the old dowager's hut had positively a new roof on, and she herself, decked out in all her finery, was standing at the door, vigorously twirling a mani (praying machine) without stopping for an instant, evidently imagining I could, amongst other wonders, even represent 'perpetual motion' in my sketch.

Nina Elizabeth Mazuchelli
The Indian Alps and How We Crossed Them, 1876

town, its twin peaks separated by a wall of granite. Kanchenjunga is flanked on its west by Kabru, at a height of 7,319 metres (24,012 feet), and on its east by Pandim, at 6,712 metres (22,021 feet), meaning 'the king's minister', so-called because it stands by the king of mountains. Nearby, Tiger Hill looks out over Mount Everest while all around the north and northeastern horizons of the town itself are range upon range of snows. One of the closest hills in the east is Tendong, at 2,645 metres (18,678 feet), which is sacred to the local Lepcha community, as it is here they are said to have retreated when a great flood covered the earth. The hill miraculously elongated itself as the flood rose and saved the Lepchas. The views cannot, however, be taken for granted. Darjeeling has a much heavier monsoon and is generally damper and more misty than the hill stations of the Western Himalayas. Clouds often veil the mountains, the best visibility being in the summer months (April-June) and at the end of the rains and beginning of the cold weather (September-November).

BACKGROUND

Until the beginning of the 19th century, Darjeeling was a sparsely inhabited, thickly forested part of the Buddhist state of Sikkim. The name 'Dorje-Ling', meaning 'place of the thunderbolt' comes from Tibetan and there was originally a Buddhist monastery on top of Observatory Hill. In the early 19th century, the Darjeeling tract, like the rest of Sikkim, was overrun by Gorkha troops from Nepal and the occupation continued until the Gorkhas were defeated by the British. Under the Treaty of Titaliya, signed in 1817, the Gorkhas ceded all Sikkimese territory to the British who in turn restored most of Sikkim to its raja. They thereby created a buffer state between Bhutan and Nepal.

Some years later, encouraged by the success of the Western Himalayan hill stations, the government began to look for suitable sites in the east. The first experiment at Cherrapunji in Assam was disastrous as it proved to be one of the wettest places in the world. The government then asked G W A Lloyd to look into a recommendation made by J W Grant, the Commercial Resident at Malda. Lloyd later claimed to have been the first European ever to have seen Darjeeling but it seems likely that Grant really deserves the credit for the discovery. Both of them inspected the 'old Gorkha station' in 1829, and their reports were so favourable that, after a survey, Lloyd was told to open discreet negotiations with the raja.

In 1834 Lloyd raised the matter with the raja who agreed to grant Darjeeling to the British but demanded in return the release of one of his revenue officers who had run off with a large sum of money, and the restoration of more of the state's former territory. The government turned this down and ordered Lloyd to cease negotiations but by this time he had already accepted the deed of grant. The situation then became very confused. The raja suggested that the deed be accepted as a free gift, and oriental etiquette forbade the taking back of a gift. Lloyd then forwarded the deed to Calcutta, but without mentioning that the raja's sense of etiquette also demanded that the British should respond with a similar gift. Instead of a gift of land, the raja was landed with a sovereign British enclave within his state which disrupted his monopoly of trade and encouraged the inflow of thousands of settlers from Nepal. Darjeeling prospered, its success due in large to its first superintendent, the energetic Dr Campbell. However, the raja and his influential subjects never forgave the British and in 1849 they went so far as to arrest Dr Campbell and Sir Joseph Hooker. They were released after a month, but by that time the damage was done and the British relieved the raja of the annual allowance they had granted him for Darjeeling, and of a sizeable chunk of territory, making Darjeeling contiguous with British Bengal. In 1861 matters again came to a head and the raja abdicated in favour of his son who seemed much more amenable to British paramouncy.

By the late 1860s, Darjeeling district had grown even further - the British had also annexed Kalimpong from Bhutan — and the hill station had become the official summer capital of the Bengal government. The tea and chichona industries were fast developing. Chichona, a tree from South America, was cultivated for its bark which contains quinine, used to treat malaria. Darjeeling was a base for the tea planters. Army cantonments were also being established at Jalapahar (overlooking the settlement), Ghoom and Lebong. However, until 1869, the journey from Calcutta to Darjeeling was still difficult, although it did not take the 98 hours it had in the 1830s. In 1869, a road which bullock carts could climb — still called the Hill Cart Road — was

Darjeeling Tea

D arjeeling tea, known as the Champagne of Teas, is grown in high-altitude estates surrounding the town. The neatly manicured gardens are planted with shade trees and their greenery contrasts with the snows of Kanchenjunga and the Great Himalayas. Early in the 19th century, tea seed was imported from China and in 1841 Dr Campbell raised the first tea bushes at his house in Darjeeling. His success led the government to set up tea nurseries whose young bushes were used to start the first commercial garden in 1852. By the 1870s, there were 113 gardens and 6,000 hectares (14,800 acres) under tea.

Darjeeling planters kept growing the original Chinese tea although their colleagues in most other parts of India dug up their Chinese bushes and replaced them with local and more robust indigenous Assamese tea bushes which did much better in plains conditions. Darjeeling tea has always been more costly to produce than other teas — the yield is low per hectare, the leaves are small and expensive to harvest. Unlike in southern India, the tea bush in Darjeeling 'hibernates' in winter. The 'first flush' of new shoots come in spring, and after these are picked there is a lull until the 'second flush' appears. This is the vintage crop of the whole year. Monsoon teas are of a lower quality. After the monsoon, until November, is the time for the autumnal crop.

Each tea garden has its own factory where the freshly picked tea is dried. The smell of a tea factory is unique but indefinable — it has the freshness of newly mown grass.

The tea is first spread on trays to 'wither' and then 'rolled' to bruise the leaves, which become curled and twisted. In China, the leaves were originally rubbed by hand, which added perspiration to the process. The effect of rolling is to bring the juices of the tea to the surface. The leaves are then left to ferment, which develops the flavour, before being dried and sifted into grades. The grades are Golden Flowery Orange Pekoe (unbroken leaves), Golden Broken Orange Pekoe, Orange Fannings, and the lowest quality of broken leaf, Dust. From the factory the tea is transported in chests down narrow mountain roads to railheads and the tea auctions. Since Independence, ownership of tea gardens has changed greatly. The periodic slumps in international tea prices, which left them below the cost of production, and recent political upheavals in the area, have led to difficulties for all tea gardens and forced some to close down. There are now some 75 gardens in the area producing an average of

10.5 million kilograms (23.2 million pounds) of tea each year from 16,500 hectares (40,770 acres). Half the population of the area is dependent on the tea industry for its living.

The planters are trying to boost the fortunes of the Champagne of Teas by improving the gardens, developing hybrid tea bushes and protecting the brand name. At present there is no control over the use of the name 'Darjeeling tea'; as a result, some 40 million kilograms (88.2 million pounds) of tea are sold as 'Darjeeling' every year, 30 million kilograms (66.2 million pounds) more than the area actually produces.

From Darjeeling you can easily visit the Happy Tea Estate, three kilometres (two miles) away, and its factory. Timings are 8 am-12 noon and 1-4.30 pm. Mondays and Sunday afternoons it is closed.

Tea from the various gardens is available from shops in Darjeeling, or directly from some gardens. It is light and best with a little sugar to taste and no milk. This is the way it is drunk in Russia and Central Asia which is one of the biggest markets for Indian tea. Darjeeling is also blended with darker, stronger teas for those who prefer their tea with milk. But however you drink it, remember its great qualities. As Hunt, Hillary and Tenzing attested in 1953, 'During our ascent of Mount Everest, Indian tea constantly gave us cheer and vigour.'

completed, and, in 1881, the opening of the Darjeeling Himalayan Railway, a narrow-gauge steam 'tramway' between Siliguri and Darjeeling, made the final leg of the journey a pleasure. Once a bridge was completed across the Ganga in 1915, Darjeeling became the most accessible of resorts, a mere 13 hours from Calcutta.

At Independence, Darjeeling ceased to be the summer capital of Bengal but it remains the premier hill station of the present state of West Bengal. The population is predominantly of Nepalese descent (now officially called Gorkhas) although there are also communities of Sikkimese Bhutias and Lepchas, refugee Tibetans, and Indians from the plains.

GETTING THERE AND AROUND

Bagdogra, 'the place of the roaring tigers', has lost its tigers but gained an airport with daily flights to and from Delhi and Calcutta. The airport is 90 kilometres (50 miles) from Darjeeling, about three hours drive by taxi. Siliguri, a confusing and unappealing town, is the point where the Himalayas begin to rise from the plains. Trains run to Siliguri, or nearby New Jalpaiguri railway station, from Calcutta, Delhi, Mumbai, Madras and Varanasi. Calcutta is a convenient overnight train journey away, and there are also long-distance buses from that city. From New Jalpaiguri or Siliguri you can take the narrow-guage railway up to Darjeeling (see box), or catch a bus. The road and railway take you up via the small satellite hill station of Kurseong, 32 kilometres (20 miles) from Darjeeling, and surrounded by tea gardens.

SIGHTS

The Town

Darjeeling is built on a long spur projecting northwards like a letter Y from the Senchal–Singalila range. The base of the letter is **Ghoom**, whose mists are known as the Ghoom Gloom and from where criminals are said to have been thrown to their deaths in pre-British times. From Ghoom the ridge rises sharply to the high point of **Katapahar** at 2,426 metres (7,959 feet) before descending to the town centre at Chaurasta. This forms the stem of the Y. Above Chaurasta is Observatory Hill, beyond which the spur divides in two (the arms of the Y), and sinks down into the valley of the **Great Rangit River**, a tributary of the Teesta, the main river in the area. On the western spur is **Birch Hill**, while the eastern is the **Lebong spur**.

The top of the spur on which the town is built is narrow and descends the hillsides in a series of landings. At the highest level is the **Mall** with the best hotels, restaurants, curio shops, the skating rink and the government-run **Manjusha Emporium**; and at the middle level are the cheaper hotels and wayside restaurants; and at the bottom the **bazaars** of the Nepalis, Tibetans, Bhutias and Lepchas, the equivalent of the Lower Bazaar in Shimla.

All roads lead to **Chaurasta**, 'the crossroads', at **Observatory Hill** which is considered a holy place by both Hindus and Buddhists. The original monastery was destroyed by the Gorkhas when they overran Sikkim. It was later rebuilt but then shifted further down the hill to the **Bhutia Basti**, the Bhutia quarter. On the way down to the monastery from Chaurasta is the house, **Step Aside**, home of the famous leader of the freedom movement, Deshbandu Chittaranjan Das. It is also the site of the unsolved Bhowal Sanyasi case. The kumar of Bhowal was discovered dead here on 16 June 1925 by a Hindu holy man and cremated. Twelve years later, on the anniversary of his death, the kumar appeared in Dacca and claimed his estate. Who died? Who was cremated? No one knows. The tourist office is also at Chaurasta.

The **Mall**, now **Bhanu Bhakta Sarani**, runs round Observatory Hill, and in British days was used for pony races. Here too is **St Andrew's Church**, built in 1870 on the site of an earlier church whose foundation stone was laid on St Andrew's Day, 1843. There is a memorial tablet to G W A Lloyd who negotiated the transfer of the Darjeeling tract. South from Chaurasta, on **Nehru Road**, as the other part by the Mall is now called, is the **Planters' Club**, in true half-timbered, hill station style, which is now the headquarters of the Darjeeling Planters Association. The nearby **Capitol cinema** is far more dilapidated than it was in the last days of the Raj. Also in this direction is Grindlays Bank, one of the better places to change money, the post office, Indian Airlines and the Foreigners' Registration Office.

Off the Cart Road is the railway station, below which is the Hindu Dhirdham Temple built in the style of the famous Pashupatinath Temple in Kathmandu.

The Darjeeling Himalayan Railway

The Darjeeling Himalayan Railway (DHR) climbs up the mountain for 88 kilometres (55 miles) from New Jalpaiguri station to Darjeeling. The bus will take less than half the time, and the tramline of the railway runs alongside the road for much of the way, and frequently crosses it. But seeing the train from the road cannot equal the pleasure of travelling first class behind the original Boyennold steam engines which have completed their century but are still not, as one driver put it, 'on their way to the pavilion'. The engines are lovingly oiled and watered by their crew at each stop.

Work on the line — founded by the agent of the Eastern Bengal Railway, Franklin Prestage — began in 1879 and was completed on 4 July 1881. The trains climb from near sea level to a maximum height of 2,222 metres (7,290 feet) at Ghoom, one of the 14 stations on the line. Indian Rail claims that this makes Ghoom the world's highest railway station. The ascent is achieved through steep gradients, sharp curves, Z-crossings and loops. There are five Z-crossings, or reverses, on the line, the first of which is some 35 kilometres (22 miles) out of New Jalpaiguri. The train reverses up the line, and then moves forward so that it makes a letter Z on the hillside and climbs a considerable amount over a short distance. The Batasia Loop between Ghoom and Darjeeling stations is the most celebrated of the four loops on the line.

The first part of the journey is across the plain from New Jalpaiguri, via Siliguri, to Sukhna, at 160 metres (525 feet), from where both road and rail begin to climb dramatically. The first major station on the line is Tindharia, at 847 metres (2,779 feet), where there is a railway workshop. The train stops long enough for passengers to take tea and snacks on the station platform. Tindharia is considered above the fever line, and you are truly in the hills. Beyond the station the line continues to rise steeply to Gayabari station from where you can see several Lepcha monuments, erected as memorials to their chiefs, on the ridge above. Beyond Gayabari the road and railway line cross the Pagla Jhora, or 'mad stream', whose monsoon excesses bring down huge boulders every year to test the initiative of road and rail engineers. Near Mahanadi station the train

passes through a rock cutting and reveals a fresh view of the plains. A large projecting rock here is known as Artillery Man's rock, as one chose to leap from here to his death. A short distance further on you come to Kurseong, at 1,459 metres (4,787 feet), a small, satellite hill station of Darjeeling with a thriving bazaar, and surrounded by tea estates. There is an excellent view of the plains from Eagle's Crag.

Beyond Kurseong is Sonada station, where roads from many tea gardens converge. Ascending gradually through dramatic scenery the train eventually reaches Ghoom, famous for its weather which can often obscure the view of Kanchenjunga and is known locally as the Ghoom Gloom. If the Gloom lifts there is a splendid view of India's highest mountain from the Batasia Loop, before the train steams into the last station on the line, Darjeeling, at 2,044 metres (6,706 feet).

Services on the DHR can be interrupted or cancelled by bad weather so check that the trains are running before you head for the railway station.

On Tenzing Norgay Road to the east is **St Paul's School**, the most famous of the many prestigious schools in Darjeeling, established here in 1864, and the **Aloobari Buddhist Monastery**.

Down the hillside, to the west of Observatory Hill and below the Market Motor Stand are the **Lloyd Botanical Gardens**, named after the proprietor of Lloyd's Bank, Darjeeling, who donated the land. It has an indigenous section containing Himalayan plants, and also has a number of hothouses for exotic species.

On Birch Hill (renamed **Jawahar Parbat**), on one arm of the Darjeeling Y, is **Raj Bhawan**, the summer residence of the governor of West Bengal.

Further north on Birch Hill is the **Padmaja Naidu Himalayan Zoological** Park, which has some high-altitude fauna, including the Himalayan black bear. Nearby is the **Himalayan Mountaineering Institute** where Sherpa Tenzing used to teach.

Around Darjeeling
Eight kilometres (five miles) from Ghoom is the **Yiga-Choling Buddhist Monastery**, the most famous in the area, which enshrines an image of the Maitreya Buddha (the Buddha to Come). A road from nearby **Jorbangalow** leads to the most celebrated viewpoint in the area, **Tiger Hill** at 2,590 metres (8,497 feet) and 11 kilometres (seven miles) from Darjeeling. On a clear day Mount Everest is visible in the distance, but again it is Kanchenjunga, the third highest mountain in the world, which dominates the scene.

Near Tiger Hill is **Senchal Lake**, 'the lake of damp mists', which is Darjeeling's water supply and is also a popular picnic spot.

Proof of the continuing success of the hill station is **Mirik**, at 1,785 metres (5,856 feet), a new resort being developed midway on the alternative route between Darjeeling and Siliguri. It has a newly dammed lake and good views of both plains and mountains.

Takdah, 26 kilometres (16 miles) from Darjeeling is famous for its **Orchid Culture Centre**.

TREKS
The two main trekking destinations in Darjeeling district are **Sandakphu** and **Phalut**. Sandakphu lies at 3,635 metres (11,926 feet)

and is 56 kilometres (35 miles) from Darjeeling. It is now connected by a jeepable road. Phalut is 21 kilometres (13 miles) from Darjeeling and lies at a height of 3,600 metres (11,811 feet). Phalut, which means 'the peeled summit' because of its treeless slopes, has excellent views of Kanchenjunga but Everest is really visible only from Sandakphu.

The best trekking months are April–May, when the rhododendron forest is in flower, and October–November. Equipment can be hired from the warden at the youth hostel, and there are also several travel agents who will provide all the essentials for a trek, including porters and guides. You should bear in mind that the trek will lead you from valley bottom to mountain top, so take clothing suitable to cope with both extremes of temperature and the occasional shower.

Kalimpong

Kalimpong, at 1,250 metres (4,100 feet), is a minor hill station of the Raj. It is 50 kilometres (31 miles) from Darjeeling by a road which descends dramatically to the Teesta River below its confluence with the Great Rangit. It is only 65 kilometres (40 miles) from Siliguri at the base of the hills. This hill station was formerly an important destination on the ancient Tibetan mule caravan route, and its main commodity used to be wool. Today the trade route is closed but the town, built on a ridge with views of Kanchenjunga, is still famous for its bazaars where villagers arrive every week to sell their farm produce and shops sell local curios and handicrafts.

There are several private hotels, one of the best being the Himalayan Hotel. The West Bengal Government runs a Tourist Lodge, but there is no separate tourist office. Local taxis are for hire from the Motor Stand, as are ponies. The Motor Stand and Chaurasta are in the centre of town and there are many cheap restaurants nearby.

Kalimpong was once Bhutanese territory. The oldest monastery in the town, the **Thongsa Gompa**, is of Bhutanese origin and was built around 1692. The **Pedong Monastery**, established in 1837, also shows Bhutanese influence and is situated within a mile of the Bhutanese **fort of Damsang**. A festival is held there each February. The **Tharpa Choling Monastery**, which belongs to the Dalai Lama's Yellow Hat Sect, was established in 1937.

Kalimpong has the ideal climate for orchid-growing and has a number of commercial nurseries which export orchids and cacti.

Gangtok

Sikkim, the smallest state in India, was not part of the British Raj and has no Raj hill station. Now, despite restrictions, the state government is doing its best to encourage visitors and make the capital, Gangtok, a latter-day hill resort.

Gangtok, at 1,574 metres (5,164 feet), was built along a ridge to one side of the Ranipool River, looking towards the Kanchenjunga range. It became the capital of Sikkim only in the 19th century and so the buildings are relatively modern.

BACKGROUND

The first settlers of Sikkim were the Lepcha foragers and small farmers whose descendants still form 18 percent of the population. They were followed by the Bhutias, caravan traders and herdsmen, from Tibet. In the 15th century, religious strife between various Buddhist sects led to more immigration. In Tibet the Dalai Lama's Yellow Hat or Sakyapa, Sect became dominant while in Sikkim the Red Hat or Nyingmapa Sect gained power. Buddhism was the religion of the raja, or *chogyal*, and the state. After the British established themselves in Darjeeling they exercised increasing influence over Sikkim, much to the annoyance of Tibet which considered it a vassal state.

In 1947, Sikkim officially became an independent state although India controlled its foreign affairs and defence. The country also relied on Indian expertise to run the administration and was dependent on India for its trade. In the 1970s there was tension between the Nepalis, now making up over 70 percent of the population, and the minority Lepchas and Bhutia communities. In 1975, after riots in the capital, the Sikkim Assembly called for a merger with India, and amid much controversy Sikkim duly became the 22nd state of the Indian Union.

Buddhism is still the most visible religion in the state, although only 30 percent of the population are now Buddhists, and Sikkim's dramatic scenery and monasteries are still its lodestones.

Hill people in Raman village near Rimbik, Darjeeling

GETTING THERE AND AROUND

The nearest airport is Bagdogra, a distance of 124 kilometres (77 miles) from Gangtok. There is a Sikkim Nationalised Transport minibus running from the airport to Gangtok, and buses and taxis also ply from the railheads of New Jalpaiguri, 125 kilometres (77 miles) from Gangtok, and Siliguri, 114 kilometres (71 miles) away. The most scenic route, however, is from Darjeeling over the Teesta River to the border town of Rangpo. Rangpo is famous for its distillery which produces, amongst other things, crème de ménthe, an innovation introduced at the suggestion of the last *chogyal's* American wife. From Rangpo the road climbs steadily to Gangtok, 40 kilometres (25 miles) away.

The transport wing of Sikkim's Tourism Department hires out cars and jeeps; private taxis are also available. Private and state buses travel to local destinations. Conducted tours run to the Tashi Viewpoint, the Orchidarium and monasteries close by. Helicopter trips are also being organised from Gangtok to the Kanchenjunga range and back from October to mid-December and late March to May.

For details of accommodation in Gangtok, see page 277.

SIGHTS

The Town

In the centre of Gangtok, near the main bazaar, are the tourist office (tel. 22064, 23425), the Foreigners' Registration Office and the bus station. To the south is the palace of the *chogyals*. Within its grounds is the **Tsuklakhang**, the royal chapel. This is the principal place of worship and assembly for the Buddhist community and in the past, coronations and royal weddings took place here. Around mid-September, the **Pang Lhabsol festival** is celebrated. This festival is unique to Sikkim and commemorates the consecration of Mount Kanchenjunga as the guardian deity of the state. The **Kagyat festival**, around the beginning of December, features a particularly impressive dance drama by Buddhist monks; it symbolises the victory of good over evil. The dance takes place prior to **Losoong, the Sikkimese New Year**, which is celebrated privately among family and friends. Around February, the royal chapel is a centre for the celebration of **Losar, the Tibetan New Year**. The chapel also has a fine collection of Buddhist scriptures.

To the south is the **Secretariat** complex, built in traditional style, and a **deer park** complete with an imposing **statue of Buddha** in a teaching pose, a replica of the original at Sarnath. Below is the **Research Institute of Tibetology** which has a collection of rare Lepcha, Tibetan and Sanskrit manuscripts, statues and *thankas*, used in Buddhist liturgy. It is open to visitors from 10 am to 4 pm on working days.

Next to the peaceful grounds of the institute is the **Orchid Sanctuary** in which you can see over 200 species of temperate and intermediate orchids. In the same area is the **Do-Drul Chorten** (or stupa) built in 1945 by the venerable Trulsi Rinpoche, head of the Nyingmapa order. Around the chorten are 108 prayer wheels and adjacent to it is a temple containing two huge images of Guru Padmasambhava, the Indian teacher who took Buddhism to Tibet.

On the outskirts of Gangtok is the **Enchey Monastery**, an important seat of the Nyingmapa order, built on the site blessed by Lama Druptab Karpo, whose mystic powers were such that he had mastered flight. This monastery is 200 years old and the annual *chaam*, or masked dance, is performed here every January.

At the opposite end of town from the palace is the **state assembly**, the **Cottage Industries Emporium** which has local handicrafts, including Lepcha shawls, for sale, and **Raj Bhawan**, formerly the British and then the Indian Residency and now the Governor's Residence.

Out of Town

Some 14 kilometres (nine miles) from the town is the **Orchidarium**, a home for Sikkim's many exotic orchids and other rare tropical and temperate plants. It is run by the Department of Forests. Only eight kilometres (five miles) to the north is the **Tashi Viewpoint** from where you can see distant monasteries and the peak of Siniolchu.

The Monasteries of Sikkim

Sikkim has nearly 70 monasteries, notable for their murals and fascinating temple images. The **Phodang Monastery**, 40 kilometres (25 miles) to the north of Gangtok is one of the six major monasteries of the state. It has been rebuilt in recent years but the **Labrang Gompa** above it is still in its original form.

The **Rumtek Monastery**, 24 kilometres (15 miles) away by road but clearly visible from Gangtok, is the seat of the Kagyu order, one of the four major Tibetan Buddhist sects. Again a modern building, it is designed in the traditional style and closely resembles the original Kargyu headquarters in Tibet. The last head of the order died in 1982 and ten years later, in 1992, his incarnation was installed as the 17th Gyalwa Karuapa.

The premier monastery of Sikkim, **Pemayangtse**, is in western Sikkim and belongs to the Nyingmapa order. The monastery, situated at 2,085 metres (6,841 feet), has panoramic views.

From Pemayangtse you can approach the **Tashiding Monastery** which is believed to be the most sacred in Sikkim. The mere sight of Tashiding is supposed to cleanse you of your sins. It is built on a hill between the Rangit and Ratong rivers at the end of a rainbow which once emanated from Mount Kanchenjunga.

Treks

All of East Sikkim beyond Rongli, and North Sikkim beyond Phodang is restricted even for Indian citizens. The main trekking routes are in West Sikkim, from Pemayangtse to Yuksam, a tableland of apple orchards and barley; through forests to Bakhim and beyond to the high point of Dzongri at 4,030 metres (13,222 feet). The best trekking months are mid-February to late-May and October to December. The state government is also encouraging the development of river rafting on the Teesta.

Shillong

Shillong, at 1,496 metres (4,908 feet), is a pleasant summer resort surrounded by rolling green hills, pine trees and waterfalls which led the British, and in particular the Scots tea planters, to dub it 'the Scotland of the East'. It is now the capital of the state of Meghalaya formed in 1971 from part of Assam state. The state consists of the Garo, Khasi and Jaintia hills whose original inhabitants are some of the most ancient peoples in India (see page 172). Shillong itself stands in the Khasi Hills. It is sufficiently far inland to be protected from the fiercest onslaught of the monsoon, although it is not as dry as the hill

Gelupa or Yellow Hat Lamas of Santhaling Gompa in Nubra on their way to morning prayers

stations of the northwest, as the name of the state, meaning 'abode of the clouds', indicates.

BACKGROUND

The hills of Meghalaya lie on the edge of the erstwhile kingdom of the Ahoms, a tribe from northern Thailand, who entered Assam in the 13th century. The Ahoms fought off Mughal armies sent to crush 'the rats of Assam' but in 1792 succumbed to Burmese invasion. After the Anglo-Burmese War of 1824–6, Burma ceded Assam to the East India Company, making it part of the British Empire. Up to this time the Garo, Jaintia and Khasi communities had maintained their independence in township kingdoms, called the *seiyams*. The British proceeded to annex these one by one and made them part of British Assam. The new rulers brought Christianity and their own form of administration. In 1848, they persuaded the Garos, who had once practised human sacrifice, to take down the human skulls on display in their houses.

GETTING THERE AND AROUND

Frequent Indian Airlines flights link Umroi airport (Shillong airport), 20 kilometres (12 and a half miles) from Shillong with Calcutta. Guwahati, 103 kilometres (64 miles) away in Assam, is the nearest railhead and airport with Indian Airlines connections. Meghalaya Tourism Development Corporation (MTDC) buses ply daily between Shillong and Guwahati railway station and Borjhar (Guwahati) airport. Taxis are also available.

The MTDC has taxis for hire which can be booked through the Pinewood or Shillong Tourist Hotel. There are yellow-top taxis which have fixed rates and there is a city bus service. There are conducted tours run by the MTDC from the Orchid Hotel (tel. 224933). There are two local sightseeing trips a day during the season (October/November–April) and four a week off season. Another tour takes you to Cherrapunji.

SIGHTS

The Town

Police Bazaar is the centre of the town and here you can find the Government of India tourist office and Sheba Travels (tel. 543280),

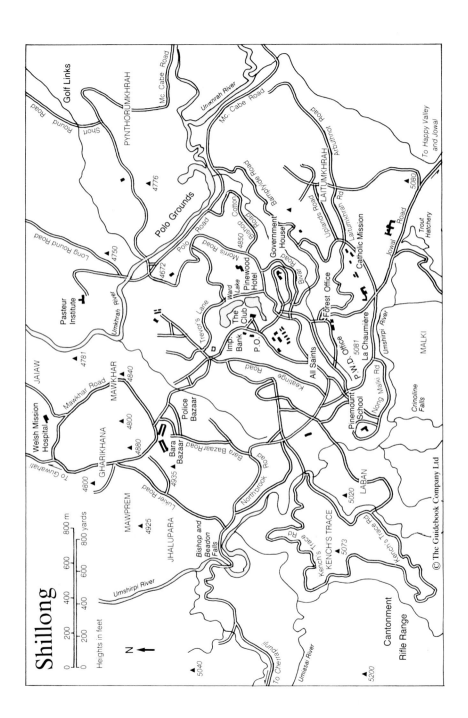

The Hill Peoples of Meghalaya

Meghalaya is the home of three ancient communities — the Khasis, the Jaintias and the Garos — who have for centuries lived in the hills to which they gave their names. The Khasis and the Jaintias are believed to be descendants of the first Mongolian influx into India and they speak a Mon-Khmer language related to those spoken in Burma and Cambodia. The Garos are a branch of the Tibeto-Burman family. Until the British consolidated their administration in this part of northeastern India, and made Shillong in the Khasi Hills the capital of Assam, these tribes succeeded in maintaining their independence. The Khasis and Jaintias came into closer contact with the British, and later Indian administration, than the Garos who, until the 1960s lived an isolated existence in the thick forests of the Garo Hills, away from the modernising influence of the 20th century.

Despite their different origins all three societies are matrilineal. In Khasi-Jaintia society, inheritance and succession pass from mother to youngest daughter. The management of property is, however, in the hands of maternal uncles. In contrast to the practice in other parts of northeastern India, there is no bride price in Meghalayan tribal society. Every child that is born belongs to the mother, thereby banishing the stigma of illegitimacy.

The indigenous faiths of these tribes centre around a supreme being who is a powerful creator and protector. They also believe in a host of spirits who have to be propitiated with offerings. It is because of this that their tribal beliefs are called animist. To some extent these beliefs survive today, although most of the tribal population of Meghalaya was converted to Christianity by missionaries, notably Presbyterians, who established themselves in the region in the 19th century.

However, several traditional festivals are still celebrated. Many are associated with events in the farming year, the majority of the population in the state still relying on agriculture for their income. Between October and November each year the Khasis celebrate Ka Ponblang Nonkrem, a five-day festival of thanksgiving to God. The festival begins with dances by the unmarried girls in full traditional costume and heavy gold bead jewellery. Shad Suk Mynsiem is held after harvest around April and also features dances by young women and men who carry swords in their hands. The Jaintias celebrate Behdeinkhlam after sowing in July, and the Garos celebrate harvest with song and dance at their own festival, Wangala.

Farmers on the flooded terraces in the 'valley of rice', Sikkim

both agents for Indian Airlines. (The other agent is **A S Sen** at the Shillong Club.) Police Bazaar is also one of the main shopping areas, the others being **Laitumkrah** and **Bara Bazaar** where you can still enjoy the atmosphere of an old market town and taste Khasi dishes. The local products on sale include pure orange honey from the Cherrapunji area, handwoven shawls and canework.

Two minutes' walk from the Police Bazaar taxi stand is **Ward Lake**, popular for its boating and garden. The town's other main garden is the **Lady Hydari Park** to the south. A species of pine (*Pinus khasia*) native to these hills has been planted here. Near the park is the **Crinoline Waterfalls** and the **Shillong Swimming Club and Health Resort**.

To the north of Lady Hydari Park is the **Meghalaya State Museum** in the **State Central Library Building**. It covers the flora, fauna and culture of the state and is open on all days except Sundays and public holidays. Some of the huge variety of Meghalaya's insect life is on display at **Wankhar and Co** in **Raitsamthiah**. They mount butterflies on wall plates but have also begun to breed them, both to conserve the species and as a commercial proposition.

To the north of the town are the **polo grounds** and a well-laid-out 18-hole **golf course**, which is a popular evening walk even for non-golfers. Its club house resembles an English manor house.

Shillong has Hindu and Buddhist temples and even a Sikh *gurudwara*, as well as prayer halls of the original Seng Khasi religion of the Khasis. However, churches outnumber the other places of worship. There is a Roman Catholic cathedral and there are Presbyterian churches in all localities.

Out of Town

On the edge of the town are the **Bishop** and **Beadon falls**, both of which plunge down the same escarpment into a dark, wooded valley. The falls are near the Shillong-Guwahati road. Some 16 kilometres (ten miles) from the town on this road is **Umiam Lake** surrounded by hills.

The drive to Cherrapunji, 56 kilometres (35 miles) from Shillong, takes you near 1,960-metre- (6,430-foot-) high **Shillong Peak**, overlooking the town, and the **Elephant Falls**. The road passes through some of the most attractive landscape of the Khasi Hills. You also pass monoliths commemorating the Khasi dead.

Deforestation (see page 124) has brought down Cherrapunji's rainfall but it is still one of the wettest places in the world, with over 1,050 centimetres (413 inches) of rain each year. The humidity produces an enormous variety of damp-loving plants, especially ferns and orchids. In the town there is a large monastery belonging to the **Ramakrishna Mission** and an **old church** built by the Khasis who first received the Christian message. From here one can see into Bangladesh. Beyond Cherrapunji, 24 kilometres (15 miles) to the south, is the barren, windswept plateau of Mawphalang, marked by innumerable monoliths.

At **Jakrem**, 64 kilometres (40 miles) from Shillong, there is a hot spring which is patronised for its health-giving qualities. At Mawsynram, 55 kilometres (33 miles) from Shillong, is the **Mawjymbuin Cave**. It has an unusual breast-shaped stalactite which drips water onto a stalagmite resembling a Shiva lingam. During recent years, Mawsynram has proved even wetter than Cherrapunji, with annual rainfall in excess of 1,200 centimetres (473 inches).

A panoramic view of Shillong from Shillong Peak

Madhya Pradesh

Pachmari

Madhya Pradesh is one of the largest, least densely populated and least known states of India. It hardly ever made the national news bulletins until the Bhopal gas disaster gave worldwide notoriety to its peaceful, lakeside capital. If you want an unusual holiday, try exploring this state which has more to offer than the famous tourist centre and temple town of Khajuraho. Bhopal is only a short flight or an eight–hour train journey from Delhi by Shatabdi. From Bhopal it is a mere 210 kilometres (131 miles) to Pachmarhi, 1,067 metres (3,501 feet) above sea level in the Mahadeo Hills of the Satpura range.

Madhya Pradesh has many hills but only one hill station — Pachmari. The plateau on which it stands may once have lain at the bottom of an ancient sea. The name means 'five dwellings' and refers to five caves

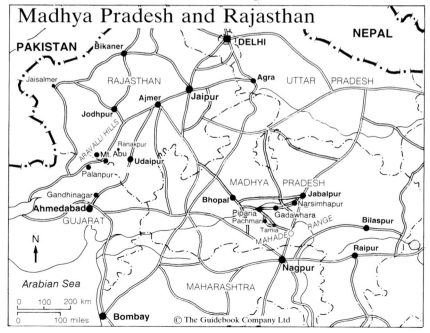

Madhya Pradesh and Rajasthan

near the centre of the hill station where the five Pandava brothers of the *Mahabharata* epic are said to have spent their exile. The settlement was created as a sanatorium and summer retreat for the British in the then Central Provinces in the 1860s. It was discovered by Captain J Forsyth, when he was sent to explore the forests of the Satpura range in 1862. Forsyth was a remarkable man; an environmental zealot, who explored the forests of central India. Despite his lack of formal training he became an expert in local natural history. Unfortunately he died young. He wrote of Pachmari: 'Everywhere the massive groups of trees and park-like scenery strikes the eye, and the greenery of glades and wild flowers, unseen at lower elevations, maintains the illusion that the scene is a bit out of our own temperate zone rather than of the tropics.'

Forsyth's memory, however, is not honoured and the spot from which he first laid eyes on Pachmari, Forsyth Point, is now called Priyadarshini after the late prime minister, Indira Priyadarshini Gandhi. As far as names are concerned, Pachmari has cast off the imperial yoke much more thoroughly than most hill stations. Bishop's Squeeze, Piccadilly Circus and Hog's Back have been Sanskritised and Irene, Helen and Kitty, not to mention Lansdowne, Malcolm and Frazer, have all been officially banished. Luckily for Saunders, he has just about survived in the renamed Sundar (Beautiful) Pool.

The Indian inhabitants of the hills during the Raj were, as they are today, ancient adivasi tribal communities of Gonds and Korkus who are outside the caste system of the Hindus. The land-owning Gonds and traditionally forest-dwelling Korkus have their own separate customs and traditions. These are a blend of Hinduism and animism in which creation myths are linked with a belief in Lord Mahadeva and every tool, implement and festival is instilled with supra-human vibration and purpose.

In the remote crags and ravines of the Mahadeo Hills there are numerous rock shelters covered with paintings. Many are a thousand and some perhaps ten thousand years old. The precise age of the paintings is unclear because older drawings are often superimposed with more recent ones. The paintings have never been scientifically listed and documented and so the determined trekker can still find undiscovered caves. The paintings show scenes of warfare with soldiers shooting bows and arrows, hunting, wild animals and domestic cattle,

Cave paintings, Pachmari, Madhya Pradesh

as well as rows of dancing women. Some figures have buns and large hoop earrings resembling the hairstyles and ornaments still current among some local tribal people.

Pachmari itself is a small, neat town, with tourist facilities and a school of oriental music at Ravi Shankar Bhavan. It is surrounded by areas of well-preserved forest consisting of wild mango trees, jamun, sal, bamboo, mahua, and the ferny-leaved *amla*, whose tart green fruit are full of vitamin C.

Part of the forest around the station has been declared a sanctuary to help preserve the wildlife of the area which includes gaur, or Indian bison, sambhar, barking deer, bear and leopard.

The edges of Pachmari plateau are crisscrossed by streams which form attractive bathing pools. The pools are particularly attractive in the hottest months of May and June when the temperatures can rise to over 30°C (86°F). Pachmari is, however, an all-year-round hill station with the thinnest tourist population during the monsoon (July–September).

GETTING THERE

The nearest airport is Bhopal, 210 kilometres (131 miles) away, connected by regular flights with Delhi, Gwalior, Indore and Mumbai. Bhopal is also a mainline railway station with trains to most major destinations. The nearest station to Pachmari, however, is Pipariya, a distance of 47 kilometres (29 miles), on the main Mumbai–Howrah line via Allahabad. Regular bus services run to and from Pipariya from Bhopal, Hoshangabad, and other towns in Madhya Pradesh.

For details of accommodation in Pachmari, see page 277.

Walks

You can spend weeks exploring the walks and points around Pachmari. Not far from the small bazaar and the solid **Christchurch** is the **Pachmari Club** from where there is a path up to **Raj Giri** (formerly Club Hill), which gives a panoramic view of the settlement.

Near the Satpura Retreat Hotel are the **Pandav caves**, which contain early relief sculptures dating from perhaps as far back as the eighth century AD, and the footpath to **Apsara Vihar** (Fairy Pool), formed by a small waterfall. It is a popular picnic spot. A ten-minute walk over rocks and boulders leads you to the top of **Raja Prapat** (Big Falls) which plunge down a precipice.

Two popular morning walks are the **Long Chakkar** (circuit) and the **Short Chakkar**. On the Long Chakkar, near the Retreat, you can approach **Handi Khoh**, the station's most impressive ravine with a 100-metre- (328-foot-) high precipice and dramatically steep sides. Bees nest in the hollow below the railings, and if you listen carefully, you can hear the sound of flowing water below.

Further down the Long Chakkar, on the Mahadeo Road, is the celebrated **Priyadarshini Point** (once Forsyth Point). This road leads to the Mahadeo Hill itself, with its **temple to Lord Shiva**, the Mahadeo (Great God). On the east side of the hill is a fine cave shelter. Four kilometres (two and half miles) beyond Mahadeo is **Chauragarh**, one of the prominent landmarks around Pachmari. The hill is surmounted by a Shiva temple (Lord Shiva is believed to have taken refuge here from the demon Bhasamasur) and a huge marble statue of the god, which had to be winched 300 metres (984 feet) up the mountainside to its position there. Leading to the temple are 1,100 steps. On Shivratri, a night sacred to Lord Shiva, thousands of devotees climb these steps carrying tridents, symbols of the god, to plant on the summit.

Lanjee Giri (Lanjee Hill), a little higher than Raj Giri, can he climbed from the east or the west. Rock climbers can practise scaling near the summit. Near the western summit is an underground passage which takes you down the northern face. Lower down the northern face is a sal forest.

Dhupgarh (Fort of the Sun), the highest peak of the Satpuras at 1,360 metres (4,462 feet), lies on the periphery of Pachmari. A steep road leads up towards the summit. From the peak, there are magnificent views of the surrounding countryside. Other points in the direction of Dhupgarh are the steep black rocks of **Pathar Chatta, Vanshri Vihar** (Pansy Pool) and **Tridhara** (Piccadilly Circus), **Sakree Gali** (White Fish Gully), **Sushma Saar** (Crump Crag), and **Denwa Darshan** (Helen's Point).

Ramya Kund (Irene Pool) is a pretty pool discovered by Irene Bose, wife of Justice Vivian Bose, both great Pachmari loyalists. You approach the pool from the car stop to **Reech Garh** (Bear Fort). From here, across a stream, is a kilometre- (half-mile-) long path to the pool. If you follow the stream up from the pool it will lead you to a cave through which it goes underground, appearing again at **Jalavataran** (Duchess Falls).

The main route to these falls is down the path from Belle View. Three kilometres (two miles) along this path, branching off from the Bhrant Neer (Dorothy Deep) milestone, is the path to the falls. It is a stiff walk and the descent is steep for almost four kilometres (two and a half miles) to the base of the falls. If you cross the stream below Duchess Falls you can take a two-and-a-half-kilometre- (one-and-a-half-mile-) long footpath to a large rocky pool called **Sundar Kund** (Saunders Pool), an excellent swimming and picnic spot.

Jata Shankar (the Locks of Shiva) is a sacred cave reached by a flight of steps at the source of the Jambu Dwip stream. Legend has it that Lord Shiva came here during his flight from the demon Bhasamasur. A rock formation is said to resemble the matted locks of the ascetic god.

Chhota Mahadeo, reached by a path two kilometres (one and a quarter miles) down the hill from the Civil Hospital, is a narrow point in the Jambu Dwip valley where rocks hang over the stream and water falls from a spring above a mango tree. This spot is also an area sacred to Shiva.

Perhaps the most accessible cave shelter is the **Maradeo Cave**, six kilometres (four miles) down the Pipariya Road from the Jai Stambh (Victory Column), in the town. On this road is an old house known as the **Begum Sahiba's Bungalow**, near the **Amba Devi Temple**. Two kilometres (one and a quarter miles) further down, northeast of the house, are the caves of the **Putli** (doll) **Lane**. Before reaching the Putli Lane, there is a fork to the right to another set of rock shelters with paintings. The best of the paintings in the Putli Lane are in the Maradeo Cave. You can reach the bottom of the cave by climbing down a short ladder from where there is a 50-metre- (55-yard-) long underground passage to a neighbouring cave.

Other shelters are at **Dhuandhar**, reached from the footpath to Apsara Vihar. The paintings here are mostly in white and show a troop of archers with buns and hooped earrings. **Bhrant Neer** (Dorothy Deep) has good rocks for climbing as well as shelters with animal paintings. It can be reached down a steep path from **Astachal Hill** on which there are four shelters with paintings. Along the northern side of the **Jambu Dwip** valley are some six shelters with a large number of paintings, including a battle scene. Near Jata Shankar is **Harper's Cave**, named after one painting showing a man playing an instrument resembling a harp.

There are other paintings in white and red on the terrace running the length of the southeast faces of **Dudrishya** (Kitty's Crag).

While in Pachmari it's also well worth visiting the surrounding areas. One supreme beauty spot is **Tamia**, 79 kilometres (49 miles) away. It has a resthouse overlooking the Narmada Valley. The view of the Dudhi Plateau from 330 metres (1,083 feet) of sheer, overhanging cliffs is one of the most spectacular anywhere south of the Vindhyas.

Rajasthan

Mount Abu

Mount Abu, 1,220 metres (4,003 feet) in the Aravalli Hills, is the sole hill station of the desert state of Rajasthan. The nearest of the great Rajasthani tourism centres, Udaipur, is 185 kilometres (115 miles) away and Abu remains slightly off the foreign tourist route. Its visitors are mainly Indians and during the season it is well patronised, especially by honeymoon couples.

The name Abu is variously described as a corruption of Arbuddha, hill of wisdom, or Arbuda, the name of a powerful serpent who rescued Lord Shiva's mount, the bull Nandi, from a chasm here. Legends surround the town. The Nakki Lake is said to have been excavated by the nails of the gods, and the great Hindu sage, Vashisht, is believed to have performed a sacrifice here which led to the birth of four Rajput warrior clans whose descendants ruled large areas of India. For centuries, Mount Abu has been a pilgrimage site and its most remarkable attractions are its beautifully carved Jain temples, nearly a thousand years old.

The British added a chapter to Mount Abu's long history by making it a hill station. They had no hill retreat in Rajputana, as Rajasthan was then called, until 1845, when the government leased Mount Abu from its Rajput owner. The station was built principally for the British Resident of Rajputana, and in 1847, for the first time, 60 Britons escaped to the hill from the plains. While the British built private bungalows, and a polo ground, the Raiput princes constructed palatial residences.

Mount Abu has a cooler climate than the plains and stands among great granite outcrops, surrounded by scrub-covered hills. It is worth visiting all year round but the peak seasons are March–June and September–November.

GETTING THERE AND AROUND
The nearest airport is Udaipur, 185 kilometres (115 miles) away; the nearest railway station, Abu Road, 27 kilometres (17 miles) away, is on

Mount Abu, Rajasthan

the main metre-gauge line between Delhi and Ahmedabad. Some superfast trains stop here. There are taxis and regular buses from the bus stand next to Abu Road station to the town.

Abu has good long-distance bus services to and from major destinations: Ajmer, 370 kilometres (230 miles) away; Ahmedabad, 222 kilometres (115 miles) via Palanpur or 250 kilometres (155 miles) via Ambaji; Delhi, 764 kilometres (474 miles); Jaipur 509 kilometres (316 miles); Jodhpur, 264 kilometres (164 miles); and Udaipur, 185 kilometres (115 miles) via Jaswantgarh, or 275 kilometres (171 miles) via Ranakpur. On your way up check that your bus stops at the town and not at Abu Road.

In Mount Abu you can choose between unmetered taxis and horse-drawn carts (*tangas*). There are also large baby prams for children. Local buses run to certain sights. The tourist office opposite the bus stand will advise you on which ones to take. Rajasthan State Tourism runs two conducted tours a day during the season, which cover the main sights in four hours.

For details of where to stay in Mount Abu, see page 278.

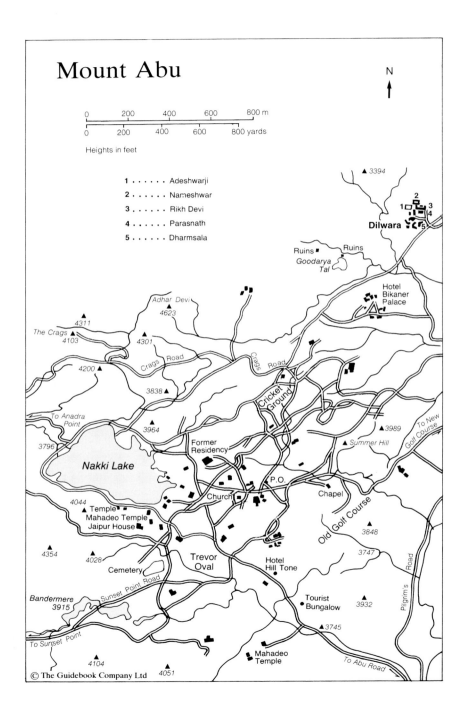

Mount Abu

N

0	200	400	600	800 m
0	200	400	600	800 yards

Heights in feet

1 . . . . . . Adeshwarji
2 . . . . . . Nameshwar
3 . . . . . . Rikh Devi
4 . . . . . . Parasnath
5 . . . . . . Dharmsala

▲ 3394

2
1 3
4
Dilwara 5

Ruins ▪ Ruins
Goodarya
Tal

Hotel
Bikaner
Palace

Adhar Devi
4623

▲
4311
The Crags ▲ ▲
4103 4301

Crags Road
Crags Road

4200 ▲

3838 ▲

To Anadra
Point
3964

Cricket
Ground

3796

Nakki Lake

Former
Residency

P.O.

▲3989

To New
Golf Course

▲ Summer Hill

Church

Chapel

4044
▲ Temple ▪
Mahadeo Temple
Jaipur House ▪

Old Golf Course

3848

▲
4354
4028

Trevor
Oval

Cemetery

Hotel
Hill Tone

3747

Pilgrim's Road

Bandermere
3915

Sunset Point Road

Tourist
Bungalow 3932

To Sunset Point

▲3745

Mahadeo
Temple

To Abu Road

© The Guidebook Company Ltd   4051

▲
4104

SIGHTS

Mount Abu is a curiously elongated hill station. The bus stand has become the town's centre, and here you will find the main hotels. Roads to the northeast and southwest lead to the **Guru Shikhar Peak** and the **Gaumukh Temple**, respectively.

In the central part of Mount Abu is **Nakki Lake**, which can contract dramatically in a rainless year. Take a walk around it or hire a rowing boat or a motor launch. Overhanging the lake is the **Toad Rock** clearly resembling a gigantic toad. Other rocks are supposed to resemble a camel and the bull Nandi. There are a number of shrines and cave-dwellings of ascetics on the shores of the lake. The most outstanding temple is that of Lord Raghunath (Ram) founded in the 14th century. At the bus stand end of the lake is the bazaar selling Rajasthani fabrics and crafts. Nearby is the reliable Rajasthan State Emporium. In the same area is the **St Lawrence Church** and a small **Museum and Art Gallery** (closed on Fridays) on Bhawan Road, opposite the post office.

Popular viewpoints are **Sunset Point** to the southwest, which overlooks the plains, and **Honeymoon (or Anadra) Point**. On the footpath between the latter and Subhash Road to the north of the bazaar is another path which leads to the **Crag's Viewpoint**. Three kilometres (almost two miles) north from the town centre, down a path at the end of Subhash Road, is the **Adhar Devi Temple** from where you get a fine view of Mount Abu. The temple to the goddess is carved out of a huge rock and is reached by an ascent of 200 steps.

To the north of Adhar Devi Temple is **Trevor's Tank**, the area around which has been declared a wildlife sanctuary.

The **Dilwara Jain Temples** stand on the road to the Guru Shikar Peak, under an hour's gentle walk from the centre of town going northwest. There are several shrines on the site but the most important are the **Vimal Vasahi and Tejpal temples**. Both were built during the rule of the stable Solanki dynasty of Gujarat (11th–13th centuries) whose territory included parts of Rajasthan. The period of Solanki rule saw one of the most prolific developments in architecture in north India. Gujarat was a centre of commerce and the arts. It was an age of opulence and spiritual devotion. Senior ministers, many of them Jains, used their great wealth to build both Hindu and Jain temples, and the general public contributed small amounts on a large scale.

The **Vimal Vasahi Temple**, constructed of white marble from the mine at Makrana, was built in 1031 in the village of Dilwara by Vimal Shah, a minister of the first Solanki ruler. The temple is dedicated to Adinath, or Rishabh Deo, the first *Tirthankara* or sage of the Jain religion. It was the Jain custom to build on summits of mountains as they consider high places sacred. The temple is surrounded by a high enclosure wall of 52 cells which contain seated figures of Adinath. Facing the entrance is a six pillared pavilion with a representation of the holy mountain of the Jains in the centre. It is surrounded by ten statues of the founder and his family, each member seated on an elephant. The temple interior is a profusion of rich carving. There is a columned hall before the main shrine. The dome at the centre is built of 11 concentric rings, five depicting patterns of figures and animals. Superimposed on the rings of carvings are 16 female figures of *vidya-devis* or goddesses of knowledge. A passage between two sets of pillars leads to the main shrine and its figure of Adinath.

The **Tejpal**, or Luna Vasahi, Temple was built two centuries later under the patronage of Vastupal and Tejpal, two brothers who were the powerful ministers of a later Solanki ruler. Rewards of silver and gold were offered to the masons. The temple, dedicated to the 22nd Jain *Tirthankara*, Neminath, whose symbol is the conch shell, is very similar to the Vimal temple, showing how little building styles had changed over 200 years. In this temple, however, there is a deeper attention to detail. The excellence of the workmanship can be seen in the lotus-flower pendant at the centre of the dome which is so finely carved as to be almost transparent. The porticos of the 39 cells surrounding the sanctuary are ornamented with carvings depicting various episodes in Neminath's life. One shows his decision to renounce the world after seeing a procession of animals being led to the slaughter for his wedding feast. Jains do not believe in violence and show respect for all forms of life.

Both temples are still used for worship and open to non-Jains daily from 12 noon to 7 pm. No leather is allowed inside.

Eleven kilometres (seven miles) from the centre of town is **Achalgarh**, the site of a 14th-century fort. Outside the 15th-century Shiva **temple of Achaleshwar Mahadev** there are three large granite buffaloes and the figure of a king shooting at them with bow and arrows. The tank here was said to have been full of *ghee* (clarified butter) but demons, in buffalo form, came to drink it each night until the king shot them. The temple has a brass Nandi or bull of Shiva, and instead of the usual lingam in the central shrine, there is a deep hole which is believed to descend to the underworld. From here there is a path up to a group of Jain temples with good views of the plains.

The highest peak in the area, **Guru Shikhar**, 15 kilometres (a little over nine miles) from the town centre, at 1,722 metres (5,650 feet), is at the end of the Mount Abu plateau, surmounted by the **Atri Rishi Temple**. It is an unequalled viewpoint.

To the south of the hill station a road leads to the **temple of Hanuman**, the monkey god, four kilometres (two and a half miles) away and the **Gaumukh** (cow's mouth), eight kilometres (five miles) away. A flight of 700 steps leads to Gaumukh, where a spring flows from the mouth of a marble cow. It was here that the four clans of Rajputs were said to have appeared from the sacrificial fire. The **hill temple of Arbuda** is also reached by a flight of several hundred steps. The serpent Arbuda is believed to house the rescued bull Nandi there. The temple is five kilometres (three miles) on from the end of the jeep track.

Interior of the Dilwara Temple, Mount Abu

Maharashtra

Matheran

Matheran is situated 800 metres (2,625 feet) above sea level amid dark green jambol forest. Its eight square kilometres (three square miles) cover a hilltop in the Sahyadris, or Western Ghats and is the closest hill station to Mumbai. It is unique in that no motor transport is allowed within its area.

Matheran was 'discovered' by Hugh Poyntz Malet, the collector of Thane district in 1850. He was camping below in the village of Chowk and climbed up via the spot now known as One Tree Hill. He returned by Rambagh, and on the way down, took some water from a spring on the hilltop. The hilltop still bears his name. He later built the first house at Matheran, The Byke.

Lord Elphinstone, the governor of Bombay, visited Matheran in 1855 and chose a site for the bungalow still known as Elphinstone Lodge. His patronage made Matheran a popular resort. A *kuccha* (rough) road up to the resort was completed in 1855 but it was the mountain railway, opened in 1907, which made it easily accessible. The British built two churches here. The Anglican church of St Paul's is, like the Matheran Club, no longer in use. The Roman Catholic church, however, is still active and the most popular school in the station is St Xavier's.

By the turn of the century, the British were moving further afield for their holidays and the resort was dominated by affluent Parsis and Bohra Muslims from Bombay. Their hold began to weaken at Independence, although the Parsis still own some of the best hotels. Their clients, however, are mainly Mumbai-based Gujaratis.

The climate of Matheran has changed since 1947. Deforestation (see page 124) in the surrounding hills means that summer is warm though not quite as hot as Mumbai. And sweltering Mumbai-*wallahs* still make their way up the mountains between October and May each year. The station is at its litter-free best outside the peak seasons of Christmas, Diwali (October–November) and May–June. The heaviest rain (the Sahyadris take the full force of the monsoon) is over by the end of July and the tail end of the rains is when the station is at its most attractive, the mountains streaked white with waterfalls.

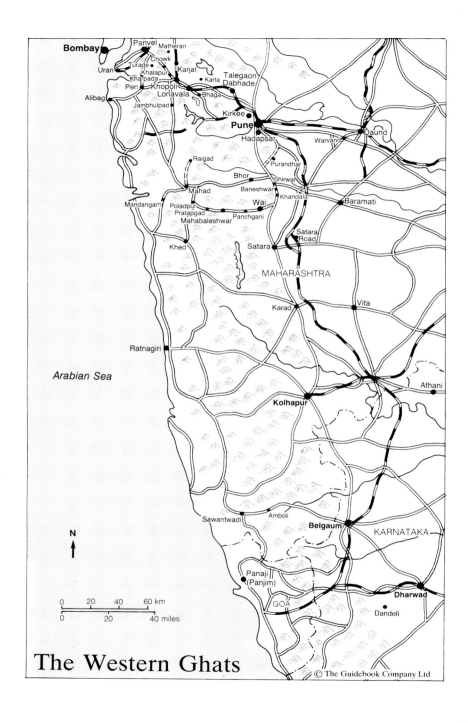

Bombay
Panvel
Matheran
Chowk
Uran
Turade
Khalapur
Karjat
Khalpada
Talegaon
Dabhade
Pen
Khopoli
Karla
Lonavala
Alibag
Bhaga
Jambhulpad
Kirkee
Pune
Hadapsar
Warvand
Daund
Raigad
Purandhar
Bhor
Shirwal
Mahad
Baneshwar
Mandangarh
Poladpur
Khandala
Baramati
Pratapgad
Wai
Mahabaleshwar
Panchgani
Khed
Satara
Road
Satara
MAHARASHTRA
Karad
Vita
Ratnagiri

Arabian Sea

Athani

Kolhapur

KARNATAKA

N

Sawantwadi
Amboli
Belgaum

Panaji
(Panjim)

GOA

Dharwad

Dandeli

0	20	40	60 km
0		20	40 miles

The Western Ghats

Simple Prejudice

*L*ater, we had lunch, and they talked. I was merely the kid brother, and nobody expected me to do much else but listen. They talked of school and the school library, of all the books that the library badly needed; and of the ghatis who were flooding the school of late.

In the particular version of reality we inherited, ghatis were always flooding places, they never just went there. Ghatis were flooding the banks, desecrating the sanctity of institutions, and taking up all the coveted jobs. Ghatis were even flooding the colleges and universities, a thing unheard of. Wherever you turned, the bloody ghatis were flooding the place.

With much shame I remember this word ghati. A suppurating sore of a word, oozing the stench of bigotry. It consigned a whole race to the mute roles of coolies and menials, forever unredeemable.

During one of our rare vacations to Matheran, as a child, I watched with detachment while a straining coolie loaded the family's baggage on his person. The big metal trunk was placed flat on his head, with the leather suitcase over it. The enormous hold-all was slung on his left arm, which he raised to steady the load on his head, and the remaining suitcase went in the right hand. It was all accomplished with much the same approach and consideration used in loading a cart or barrow — the main thing was balance, to avoid tipping over. The skeletal man then tottered off towards the train that would transport us to the little hill station. There, similar skeletal beings would be waiting with rickshaws. Automobiles were prohibited in Matheran, to preserve the pastoral purity of the place and the livelihood of the rickshawallas.

Many years later I found myself at the same hill station, a member of my college hikers' club, labouring up its slopes with a knapsack. Automobiles were still not permitted in Matheran,

and every time a rickshaw sped by in a flurry of legs and
wheels, we'd yell at the occupant ensconced within: "Capitalist
pig! You bastard! Stop riding on your brother's back!" The
bewildered passenger would lean forward for a moment, not
quite understanding, then fall back into the cushioned comfort of
the rickshaw.

But this kind of smug socialism did not come till much later.
First we had to reckon with school, school uniforms, brown
paper covers for textbooks and exercise books, and the mad
morning rush for the school bus. I remember how Percy used to
rage and shout at our scrawny ghaton if the pathetic creature
ever got in his way as she swept and mopped the floors.
Mummy would proudly observe, "He has a temper just like
Grandpa's." She would also discreetly admonish Percy, since
this was in the days when it was becoming quite difficult to
find a new ghaton, especially if the first one quit due to abuse
from the scion of the family and established her reasons for
quitting among her colleagues.

I was never sure why some people called them ghatons and
others, gungas. I supposed the latter was intended to placate —
the collective conferment of the name of India's sacred river
balanced the occasions of harshness and ill-treatment. But the
good old days, when you could scream at a ghaton that you
would kick her and hurl her down the steps, and expect her to
show up for work the next morning, had definitely passed.

Rohinton Mistry, Tales from Firozsha Baag

Getting There and Around

Matheran is still most easily reached by rail. The railway tourist guide opposite platform nine at Mumbai's magnificent Victoria Terminus (VT) will advise you on the best train to take. Many trains leave VT for the small mainline station of Neral, from where you can connect with the narrow-gauge train to Matheran. Except during the monsoon (June-September), there are several trains a day on the mountain railway which take two hours to cover the 20-kilometre (12-and-a-half-mile) climb to their destination. The speed of the train allows locals to jump off near their homes without endangering their lives, while soft drink and snack vendors make their way up and down hanging on to the outside of the carriages. The journey shows off the ghats to their best advantage — grassy hillsides, great spurs reaching down to the plains, sheer cliffs, flat-topped hills and, finally, thick jambul forest. Stations on the way have quaint names like Water Pipe and there is also the famous One Kiss Tunnel. During the monsoon, the service is restricted to one train a day and during heavy rain even this can be cancelled due to landslides.

The old foot-trail is now a road to Matheran. For a small price you can share a taxi to the car park. The drive takes 20 minutes but the car park is a good four-kilometre (two-and-half-mile) forest walk from the centre of the resort.

Transport in the town is restricted to ponies, foot, and hand-pulled rickshaws (one man pulls and two push).

For details of where to stay, see page 279.

Sights

The Bazaar

The main Mahatma Gandhi Road is lined with shops selling the famous *chikki* sweets and local honey. *Chikki* is a softer version of peanut brittle made from jaggery and there are seemingly endless varieties — peanut, sesame seed, coconut, ginger and mango. Decorative grasses are also dried locally. Another speciality is footwear. Local craftsmen will make you a pair of sandals, shoes or riding boots to order in just a few days. Among the best shoe shops are **New Prabhat** and **Rajan's Footwear**. There are walking-stick shops, snack shops and even a video games parlour. The **Kapadia Market**, set up by Mr P N Kapadia in

1919 in memory of his wife, is the main bazaar. Another reminder of the station's history is the small **Karsondas Mulji Library** founded in 1897 at the far end of Mahatma Gandhi Road. A sign on the wall reads 'No one ever really paid the price of a book, only the price of printing it.' The post office and the only bank in Matheran, the Union Bank of India, are also in the bazaar. The bank offers very unfavourable rates of exchange, so bring your rupees with you.

Points
The hill stations of this region specialise in points from where you look down to the plains or across to more ghats. There are 33 points in Matheran. The western areas look down towards Mumbai which is visible on a clear day. Well-marked paths run through the woodland. There are also short hikes along paths made by the local people down into the valleys. Here are some of the main points with distances from the post office; north to south on the western side.

Panorama Point, five kilometres (three miles) north of the post office, has the most spectacular views. Below lies Neral, to the west Mumbai and to the north are the ghats. It's a popular place to watch the sun rise. To the south are **Hart Point** and **Monkey Point** which look down over the plains. Between the two is a path down to **Dhodani Lake** and village. **Porcupine Point**, further to the southwest, is the popular sunset view. If you want to avoid crowds during the season, it's generally best to come here at sunrise and go to Panorama Point at sunset. **Coronation Point**, to the south, commemorates the coronation of King Edward VII in 1903. From nearby **Malang Point** you can walk to **Hashya Cha Patti** village which has a small temple dedicated to the monkey god, Hanuman. The return journey will take you about two and a half hours. **Louisa Point**, three kilometres (two miles) west of the post office, is on a plateau with views of the ruined forts **Prabal** and **Vishalgarh**. One of the nearby rocks is called **Lion's Head** because of its supposed resemblance to one. Further on **Echo Point**, really does have an echo. **Charlotte Lake**, away from the edge of the hilltop, is the main source of drinking water for the town, and is dammed at one end. The lake looks splendid in the monsoon, with swirling coffee brown water, but dries up in the summer. Near the dam are some food stalls and the main Hindu temple, the **Pisarnath Mandir**. From the dam you look over the solitary jambal tree at **One Tree Point**, three kilometres

Tribal girl at the tailors, Matheran

(two miles) south of the post office, from which it gets its name. The point overlooks the main Mumbai–Pune highway and Chowk village. From here a steep path called **Shivaji's Ladder** descends to the valley but there is no evidence that the hero ever used it. **Chowk Point**, four kilometres (two and a half miles) from the post office, is at the extreme southern end of Matheran.

The chief points on the eastern side of Matheran, from south to north, and again with distances from the post office, are as follows. **Rambagh** lies two kilometres (a mile and a quarter) away looking towards Khandala and Karjat. There is a path to the foot of the hill here. A pleasant short trek is from Rambagh to Bhorgaon returning to One Tree Point via Shivaji's Ladder. From **Alexander Point**, one kilometre (just over half a mile) to the north, you can see Garbut Point, the Chowk Valley and the Ulhas River. To the north of this is the bazaar and **Khandala Point**. The easternmost and somewhat lesser frequented point is **Garbut Point**, five kilometres (three miles) from the post office. **Mount Barry**, further north, is one of the highest spots in Matheran, with splendid views. Between Mount Barry and Panorama Point is **Governor's Hill**, another viewpoint.

Lonavala, Khandala and Karla

Lonavala, 625 metres (2,000 feet) above sea level, and neighbouring Khandala are not as close to Mumbai as Matheran, but are far more accessible. As long ago as the 1850s they had become favourite retreats for the wealthy inhabitants of Bombay. Lying on the busy Mumbai-Pune highway, every hotel is packed most weekends most of the year. Even in the monsoon, when other hill stations are deserted, Lonavala and Khandala are full of holidaymakers from Mumbai, soaked to the skin and enjoying the rain. So if you want to go to these towns, visit during weekdays. Between January and March, however, the crowds are slightly reduced. Both towns, but Lonavala in particular, are being transformed by an enormous amount of construction — mainly weekend bungalows for the rich of Mumbai. Despite all this, the surrounding ghats are still comparatively untouched and these with the Buddhist caves of Karla, Bhaja and Bedsa, are the main attractions.

Shrine at the foot of the climb to the Karla Caves

GETTING THERE AND AROUND

There are many trains from Mumbai's Victoria Terminus to Lonavala and fewer to the small Khandala station. The ghat section of line before Lonavala makes the journey worthwhile in itself, especially during and immediately after the monsoon when the ghats are their greenest. Regular buses also ply from Mumbai to Lonavala, a distance of 100 kilometres (63 miles), and Khandala, a distance of 96 kilometres (60 miles). There is a frequent local train service between Lonavala and Pune, a distance of 64 kilometres (40 miles), as well as a bus service.

The Maharashtra Tourist Development Corporation (MTDC) runs buses from the station to their holiday resort near Karla and the caves. They also arrange conducted tours of the area from the station, but rather than wait for one you may prefer to take an (unmetered) taxi or a three-wheeler.

For a list of hotels, see page 279.

SIGHTS

Points and Walks

Lonavala is another paradise for *chikki* lovers and also does a roaring trade in rather soft but very tasty fudge. There are plenty of small restaurants for hungry trippers. The **Khandala Bazaar** is smaller but also provides cheap Indian snacks.

The most famous points of Khandala are **Rajmachi Point**, six and a half kilometres (four miles) from Lonavala station, looking out over the ruined fort of the same name, and the **Duke's Nose**, 12 kilometres (eight miles) away. The hill was named after its remarkable resemblance to the nose of the Duke of Wellington! Halfway between Lonavala and Khandala, on the highway, is **Kune Point**. **Tiger's Leap** is the name given to a 650-metre (2,133-foot) cliff with superb views from the top. You can get a bus up to a stop called **INS Shivaji** and the remaining kilometre and a half (one mile) can be covered on foot. The **Valvan Dam**, one and a half kilometres (one mile) from the station, is a popular evening strolling destination, with a garden and views. Lakes in the area include **Tungarli**, three kilometres (two miles) away and **Lonavala**, a kilometre and a half (one mile) away.

Caves

The most remarkable feature of this area are the Buddhist caves which are carved out of solid rock. Almost 2,000 years ago, obviously very determined craftsmen carefully copied in stone contemporary shrines made of wood, none of which now survive. There are three groups of caves, each with a main *chaitya* for worship. *Chaitya* is another word for stupa or dome containing sacred relics. In worship, the *chaitya* would have been circumambulated in a clockwise direction. The other caves form *viharas* (monasteries) where mendicant monks would gather during the rainy season for contemplation. The caves are built in the Hinayana Buddhist style which does not depict the Buddha himself. The caves at Bhaja are the oldest, dating from the second century BC while those at Karla and Bedsa date from about the first century AD. All were built in the time of the Satavahanas, the earliest known western Indian rulers, whose capital was in the present Aurangabad district.

Karla's 45-metre- (148-foot-) long Chaitya Hall is possibly the finest of its kind in the country. The caves are 12 kilometres (seven and a half miles) from Lonavala and a kilometre and a half (a mile) to the left of the Mumbai–Pune highway. A road runs to the bottom of a flight of some 350 steps which climb up the hill to the entrance. Outside is a modern **Hindu temple** and a **pillar** of the Buddhist period surmounted by four lions. An inscription on the shaft shows that it was presented to the monastery by one Maharathi, probably an ancestor of the present-day Marathas. The lion symbolises Buddha's birth. On the facade of the cave are carved temple screens, railing ornaments and human couples.

An outer and inner screen form a vestibule to the main cave. On top of the inner screen is a gallery above which the whole of the cave is open and forms a great horseshoe window which throws soft light onto the stupa. There are three doorways in the inner screen — one opening onto the nave and the others onto the two aisles of the cave. The original decoration was simple: a rail pattern copied from wood and, to the side of the doorways, finely sculptured panels of embracing couples. Around the seventh century AD, additions were made in the style of the later Mahayana sect which did not reject representations of the Buddha. One of these additions, by the central doorway, shows the Buddha seated on a lion-supported throne with his hands in the gesture of teaching. In the vestibule there are also carvings of the fronts of three magnificent elephants.

On each side, 15 pillars separate the narrow, flat-roofed aisles from the vaulted nave. Each pillar has a pot-based octagonal shaft. This again is in imitation of the pillars in early wooden temples which were made to stand in pots to protect them from white ants. On the capital of each column are two elephants, each with a man and a woman, or sometimes two women, riding them. On the sides of the capitals, facing the aisles, are horses with a single rider on each. The columns behind the *chaitya* are plain. Inscriptions show that many of the pillars were donated by devotees.

The vaulted roof is lined with teak beams, most of them original. The *chaitya* itself is cut from solid rock and surmounted by a stepped capital and umbrella.

The caves of the *viharas* are somewhat ruinous but worth exploring. Several have been converted into Hindu places of worship. One thing to remember at Karla — it can be crowded and noisy at weekends and on holidays.

The **Bhaja caves** are diametrically opposite the Karla groups on the other side of the highway and three kilometres (two miles) from Malavali station, a regular stop for local trains running between Lonavala and Pune. There is a motorable road up to a kilometre and a half (a mile) from the caves. The remaining distance has to be covered on foot. The largest cave is a *chaitya* similar to that at Karla. Cave One is the house of the master architect. Several more are *viharas* and there are some fine carvings. To the south of the *chaitya* hall is a group of burial stupas of the monks.

The most remote group of Buddhist caves are those at **Bedsa**. These are found to the south of the Bhaja caves, down a road opposite Kamset station, the next station down from Malavali. You can either walk or take a bus to Bedsa village from where it is a further three and a half kilometres (two miles) to the caves. These fine caves, especially the *chaitya* hall, well reward the trouble taken in reaching them.

Forts

There are two ruined forts west of the Bhaja and Bedsa caves. The largest, **Lohagad**, the Iron Fort, was twice captured by Shivaji. It was garrisoned after 1818 by British troops until at least 1845. The neighbouring and smaller fort of **Visapur** is of much later origin and was built by the first Peshwa. It too was occupied in 1818 when its northern and southern gateways were blown up. Lohagad has splendid views, but it is an arduous 11-kilometre (seven-mile) trek from Malavali station.

Pune University

Betting at the Pune Races

Pune

Pune, known to the British as Poona, is the nearest city and railhead for the hill stations of Panchgani and Mahabaleswar. Now a fast-expanding city with a population of more than a million, Pune retains the atmosphere and some of the architecture that made it a favourite hill station of the Raj. At 598 metres (1,962 feet), it hardly had the height to justify this position, but the surrounding hills and a pleasant climate helped to make it the western military capital of the Deccan. The government of the Bombay Presidency made Pune one of its two summer headquarters.

The city has the distinction of not being 'discovered' by the British. It was the main town of the Maratha hero Shivaji's original estates. When he came to Pune as a teenager the town was in ruins.

Although Pune can no longer be considered a hill station it is still worth a stopover, for it has several interesting sights. The ruined **Shanwarwada Palace** of the Peshwas was built in 1736 and, although destroyed by fire in 1827, it still maintains a certain dignity. At the eccentric **Raja Kelkar Museum** you can see the recreated bedroom of the legendary Maratha lovers, Peshwa Bajirao I and his sweetheart, Mastani. The hilltop **Parvati Temple**, built in 1749, is where the last Peshwa is said to have stood to watch his troops being defeated by the British. The **Pataleshwar Cave**, an early rock-cut temple, is also worth seeing. The **Aga Khan's Palace** in Yeravda is where Mahatma Gandhi and his wife were imprisoned during the Quit India Movement; his wife, Kasturba, and his secretary, Mahadev Desai, died there and the simple marble memorials mark the spots where they were cremated. Other sights include **Shinde Chhatri**, the memorial of the Maratha Mahadji Shinde; the **Sarasbag** and **Bund Gardens**, the latter on the River Mula-Mutha on the way to Yeravda; and the **ashram** of the late controversial godman, Osho Rajneesh. Pune also has one of the finest turf clubs in the country with regular race meetings.

There are many good, reasonable hotels. The most convenient for the railway station, and one of the best and biggest in town, is Hotel Amir on Connaught Road (tel. 621840, fax. 0212-623094). The Blue Diamond (tel. 625555, fax. 0212-627755) on Koregaon Road offers five-star luxury.

Panchgani

Some 100 kilometres (62 miles) from Pune and 277 kilometres (172 miles) from Mumbai, Panchgani is a small hill station 1,335 metres (4,380 feet) above sea level on a ridge of the steep Parasni Ghat. On the hillsides stand tall trees, known locally as 'silver oaks' but completely different from the silver oaks of the Himalayas. Below lies the Krishna Valley and the huge reservoir formed by the Dhome Dam.

Panchgani takes its name from the five (*panch*) hills, or alternatively villages, surrounding it. It was 'discovered' by John Chesson in the early 1850s, and developed into a small civic station with a large Parsi community. It was from the beginning a satellite station for the larger and more prestigious Mahabaleshwar, and remains so today. This is resented by proud modern residents who campaign against the step-motherly treatment meted out to the station. Panchgani generally only fills up when Mahabaleshwar is full, which happens quite often during the peak months. However, Panchgani is in one respect much better than its neighbour — it is in the rain shadow and only has a fraction of Mahabaleshwar's monsoon. Hotels are therefore open throughout the year. The climate has made Panchgani an educational centre with almost as many boarding schools as hotels. It also attracts the moneyed classes of Mumbai who are beginning to build second homes on a scale which has made Lonavala into a glorified suburbia. There are signs that such construction may be controlled in Panchgani.

GETTING THERE

Frequent buses run from Pune and there are regular Maharashtra Tourist Development Corporation buses from Mumbai. You can also hire cars and taxis from Pune. Locally, ponies are also available for hire.

THE TOWN

The small, old-fashioned bazaar has a number of small restaurants like the Paradise Superstar Cafe, and Purohit's Lunch Home. If you are planning to stay a few days you can become a temporary member of the **Panchgani Club**, which offers table tennis and cards and is the most popular meeting place during the season.

Jeweller and brassband on the streets of Pune

There is also a Tourist Information Centre which passes on information in the time-honoured oral tradition; in other words, don't expect maps or leaflets.

SIGHTS

The most unusual feature of Panchgani is the **Table Land** or plateau, claimed to be the second highest in the country. This huge, flat expanse of rock tops the Panchgani ghat. It has superb sunrise and sunset views and is covered by springy turf. There is a lake and schoolchildren play hockey and football around one corner during term time. There are many pleasant walks over the ghats and down into the valleys. Two popular points are **Parsi Point**, a kilometre (half a mile) from the bus stand in the direction of Mahabaleshwar, and **Sidney Point**, the same distance in the opposite direction. From the latter, there is a path leading down to the **Dhome Dam**. There are two sets of caves: the **Meherbaba** and **Rajpuri** caves, one not far from the bus stand and the other six kilometres (four miles) away. Other viewpoints include **Kachbawdi Point**, one kilometre from the bus stand, and **Harrison Folly**, four kilometres (two and a half miles) away from it.

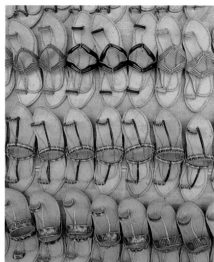

Walking sticks and chappals for sale in the main bazaar in Mahabaleshwar

Wai, 12 kilometres (seven and a half miles) away, is also suggested as a walk, although a taxi ride might be an easier way of getting to this small town, little more than a village, on the banks of the Krishna River. Wai has a number of old stone, brick and stucco temples on the river's edge. The most famous contains a huge image of the elephant god Ganesh, known here as Ganpati. A large and architecturally more interesting temple opposite is dedicated to Lord Shiva. Wai is a seat of Sanskrit learning. Seven kilometres (four miles) away are the **Buddhist caves at Lonara.**

Mahabaleshwar

Mahabaleshwar is the largest and most popular hill station in western India. At 1,372 metres (4,501 feet) above sea level, it also has the most spectacular views.

The name is a combination of three Sanskrit words: *maha, bala* and *ishwar*, meaning 'God of Great Power'. For centuries it has been considered a holy place. The hill is the source of many rivers including the Krishna, one of the main rivers of the Deccan. From at least as early as the 13th century, local rulers contributed to the building of temples in Old Mahabaleshwar, around the source of the Krishna. Shivaji and his mother visited them in 1653 to seek advice from a learned Brahmin. The hill was also one of the first territories he acquired and nearby on the Par Ghat, which the British called Corkscrew Pass, he built the Pratapgad Fort. After the British defeated the last Peshwa in 1818 they restored the hill and the fort to the 24-year-old Raja Pratapsingh of Satara, a descendant of Shivaji.

The first Briton to set foot in Mahabaleshwar was Sir Charles Malet in 1791. However, General Peter Lodwick, who arrived in 1824, was the first to try to popularise the hill as a sanatorium. The raja of Satara, encouraged by a series of British residents, began to develop the site and invited the governor of Bombay, Sir John Malcolm, there. Malcolm visited the hill in 1828 and in the same year it was officially announced that a sanatorium would be built. The next year a treaty transferred the hill to British territory. The raja insisted that the new station be named after the governor and for some years it was known as Malcolm Peth, a name now restricted to the bazaar.

Malcolm built the first government house, still known as Mount Malcolm. The raja himself constructed a palatial bungalow but pulled it down when he fell out with the British and was deposed by them in 1837.

Malcolm was Mahabaleshwar's greatest enthusiast. In June 1830 he wrote to his friend Sir Walter Scott, 'the air in these hottest of our months is such as to give a spring to both body and soul, and were it not for my occupation and absence from those 1 love, I could be content to dwell amid such scenes as those by which I am surrounded, for the remainder of my existence.'

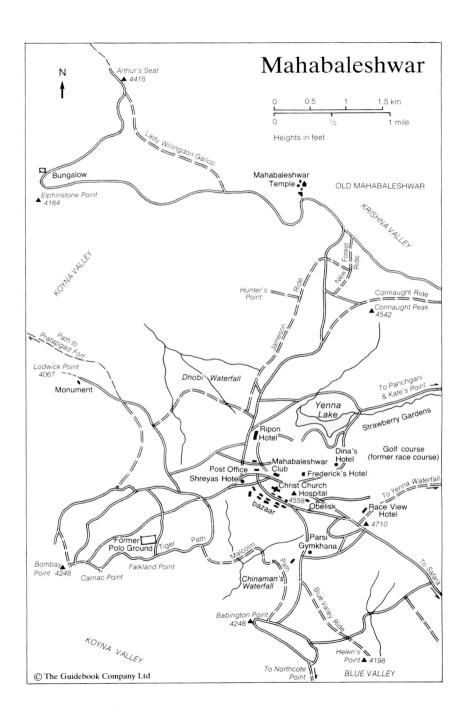

Mahabaleshwar

N

Arthur's Seat ▲ 4418

0   0.5   1   1.5 km

0   ½   1 mile

Heights in feet

Lady Willingdon Gallop

Bungalow

Mahabaleshwar Temple

OLD MAHABALESHWAR

Elphinstone Point ▲ 4184

KRISHNA VALLEY

KOYNA VALLEY

New Forest Ride

Hunter's Point

Ride

Connaught Ride

Connaught Peak ▲ 4542

Jameson

Path to Pratapgad Fort

Lodwick Point 4067

Dhobi Waterfall

To Panchgani & Kate's Point

Monument

Yenna Lake

Strawberry Gardens

Ripon Hotel

Dina's Hotel

Golf course (former race course)

Post Office
Shreyas Hotel

Mahabaleshwar Club

Frederick's Hotel

To Yenna Waterfall

Christ Church
▲ Hospital
4558 Obelisk

bazaar

Race View Hotel
▲ 4710

Former Polo Ground

Tiger Path

Malcolm

Parsi Gymkhana

Path

To Satara

Bombay ▲ Point 4248

Falkland Point

Carnac Point

Chinaman's Waterfall

Blue Valley Ride

Babington Point 4248

KOYNA VALLEY

Helen's Point ▲ 4198

© The Guidebook Company Ltd

To Northcote Point

BLUE VALLEY

Roads were built, and the resort developed quickly. Many bungalows were constructed, with names like Lily Cottage, Dingly Dell and Barchester. There was a well-stocked bazaar, several churches and the Mahabaleshwar Club as well as a polo ground (now no longer used for polo) and a race course (where the golf course now is).

Apart from the British, a community of Chinese convicts had a large part to play in the station's development. A jail for 120 Chinese and Malay convicts, whose crimes included murder, piracy and robbery, was established here soon after the sanatorium was founded. It was a rare reformatory experiment, a sort of 19th century open prison. The convicts built roads and ground cornflour during the day and were allowed to go to the bazaar in the evening for provisions. They used their spare time to introduce the cultivation of potatoes and other English vegetables, and greatly improved the resort's gardens. When the jail was abolished in 1864, some were allowed to remain on the hill. There are none left now although their name lives on in Chinaman's Waterfall. The Public Works Department bungalow stands on the site of their prison.

Among Indians, the Parsi community was again dominant, and the Parsi Gymkhana, now almost defunct, was one of the liveliest institutions in the settlement.

Mahabaleshwar's drawback was always the monsoon. As soon as it struck, Bombay's summer capital was evacuated — hotels shut, bazaars closed and officials and invalids headed for Pune. Even today, though the rainfall is less than it used to be, only a few hotels stay open. Most buildings, made of a local porous stone, are swaddled in grass to protect them from the rain. There are also a growing number of concrete buildings which require no such protection.

The season is from October to June, the most crowded times being Christmas, Diwali and the school summer holidays around May.

GETTING THERE AND AROUND

During the season, the Maharashtra Tourist Development Corporation runs direct buses from Mumbai, 290 kilometres (181 miles) via Pune and 247 kilometres (154 miles) via Mahad. There are also slower State Transport buses. The nearest railhead is Pune, 120 kilometres (75

View from Mahabaleshwar over the valley of the Gayatri and Savitri rivers

Lily Cottage, Mahabaleshwar

miles) away, from where there is also a good bus service. The drive from Pune through the ghats is very attractive.

Unlike Matheran, Mahabaleshwar has miles of motorable roads to the points and taxis are available near the bus stand. There are no meters, so you can practise your bargaining. The Tourist Information Bureau at the bus stand will tell you the going rates, and also give details of its conducted tours of Mahabaleshwar.

Ponies are available and recommended for the bridle paths and gallops. Whichever way you travel, it's useful to refer to a map of all the main points and paths. The alternative is to hire one of the guides who will approach you.

For details of where to stay in Mahabaleshwar, see page 280.

SIGHTS
Bazaars, Clubs and Churches
The **Main Street**, next to the bus stand, and **Malcolm Peth** are the main bazaars, full of snack shops and the occasional 'permit room'. The best general stores are **Treacher and Co** (which publishes a map of the area) and **Imperial** at the opposite ends of Main Street. Treacher's has its own beehives, but by far the biggest producer of the famous Mahabaleshwar honey is the state government's **Madhu Sagar Company**. Many shops in the bazaar sell the various types of honey made from seasonal flowers. Honey is collected from the jambul flowers in March, hirda in April, gella in May. Every four years the akhra plant flowers and brings akhra honey, whilst every seven years karvi and whayty honey are produced. You can buy Madhu Sagar products directly from their own centre on Mahad Road, not far from the bazaar. Besides honey, local shelves are full of strawberry crushes (the station's strawberry fields produce fruit from late February to May) and locally made jams.

Above the bazaar is the Civil Hospital, near to which stands an obelisk in memory of Sir Sidney Beckwith who succeeded Malcolm as governor of Bombay Presidency in 1830 and died at the hill station in January 1831. Its climate could work wonders but not miracles.

Near the bus station is the **Roman Catholic Holy Cross Church** which holds regular services. The more impressive Anglican **Christchurch**, behind the Makharia Garden, is now deserted. It is looked after by a Hindu family. Another memento of the Raj is the messy graveyard next to Madhu Sagar on Mahad Road.

The **Mahabaleshwar Club**, however, still flourishes. Unfortunately, you can only stay there if you are a member, but it is still worth seeing. The devotion of its members at Christmas is such that they book their rooms one whole year in advance. The Club was founded in 1881 and amongst its buildings is the original station sanatorium. The first ladies were allowed into the club in 1883, though Indians (except for princes and the Aga Khan) were kept out until after the First World War. One club facility open to all is the 18-hole golf course which you can use for a daily fee. Caddies with clubs tout for business at the entrance to the course.

Another club, the **Hindu Gymkhana**, accepts temporary members more easily and has facilities for tennis, badminton and indoor games.

Points

Around the edge of the plateau are numerous ridges and viewpoints looking out over the flat-topped ghats, forests and valleys below. Most of the roads to the points have signposts; they are also safe, despite the disconcerting red and white skull-and-crossbones warning signs on bends. Much of the plateau is covered by jambul forest, more windswept than at Matheran, with dense undergrowth — excellent habitat for forest birds. Towards Panchgani, orange-flowering lantana bushes are common.

Distances given for the following points are from the post office. On the west of the plateau is **Lodwick Point**, at a height of 1,240 metres (4,067 feet) and five kilometres (three miles) from the post office. There is a monument here to the general, erected by his son. A nearby footpath leads to **Pratapgad Fort** (see page 215). **Dhobi Waterfall** is on the bridle path from Lodwick to Elphinstone Point and is a scenic spot overlooking the Koyna River valley. Northeast of the waterfall and five kilometres (three miles) north of the post office, is **Connaught Peak** formerly known as Mount Olympia. The Duke of Connaught was impressed by the beauty of the 1,385-metre (4,544-foot) peak and its

views of Yenna Lake and the Krishna Valley. **Elphinstone Point**, named after a former governor of Bombay, is on the extreme west of the plateau ten kilometres (six miles) from the post office.

Northwards lies the valley of the Gayatri and Savitri rivers. Across the valley is the celebrated **Arthur's Seat**, named after Sir George Arthur, another governor of Bombay. At 1,348 metres (4,421 feet), it is one of the highest vantage points in the area. About a kilometre (just over half a mile) from here, a small path leads down to a spring 60 metres (197 feet) below, known as **Tiger's Spring**. The path follows the line of cliffs and joins another path going down to a small ledge known as **The Window** from where there is a magnificent view of the drop into the valley below. From Arthur's Seat you can take the **Lady Willingdon Gallop** part of the way to **Old Mahabaleshwar**, five kilometres (three miles) from the post office.

The village has a number of temples and looks out over the Krishna Valley. The old, and now tin-roofed **Mahabaleshwar Temple** dedicated to Shiva, gave the settlement its name. A **Krishna temple** with two cisterns is said to mark the source of seven rivers which rise on the plateau. Two, the Saraswati and the Bhagirathi, are there only in spirit. The others are the Krishna, the Yenna, the Koyna, the Gayatri and the Savitri. The springs gush into two cisterns from the mouth of a stone cow; the local villagers take their drinking water from here. A small image of Krishna stands to the right of the spring. Another interesting **temple of black stone** is a little distance from the others with fine views. Now a Krishna temple, the original Shiva lingam is still in place and this temple too has a tank with a spring flowing from a cow's mouth. There is a large carved Nandi, or bull of Shiva, and the carvings on the pillars include demons' heads. Guides stand ready to show you the temples but their information (for example, that the temples are 5,000 years old) is sometimes wildly inaccurate. A ride eastwards along Duchess Road will take you to **Kate's Point**, 1,290 metres (4,231 feet) up. Also on the northern edge of the plateau, this is named after one of Malcolm's daughters.

The **Lingmala Waterfall**, at the top of the Yenna Valley, six kilometres (four miles) from the post office, is the most impressive in

Lingmala Falls, Mahabaleshwar

the station, although it tends to dry up at the height of summer. A 19th-century account describes it at its best:

> The river is here precipitated over the face of the cliffs, a sheer descent of five or six hundred feet, in a nearly uninterrupted fall when its stream is swollen by rain, but in its ordinary condition, divided by rocks one third down, and scattered below into thin white streaks and spray, which the oblique rays of the morning sun may often be seen circling with rainbows.

From the Lingmala Waterfall it's a short walk to Wilson Point, which stands at 1,435 metres (4,710 feet). It is the highest point in the hill station and named after Sir Leslie Wilson, governor of Bombay from 1923 to 1928. This point is just two kilometres (one and a half miles) from the post office. Southeast of Wilson Point, on the eastern edge of the plateau, is **Helen's Point** which stands at the head of the Blue Valley of the River Solshi. Overlooking the Blue Valley from the south are **Panchgani** and **Gaolani points**.

On the southern edge of the plateau is **Babington Point** overlooking the Koyna Valley. It is 1,295 metres (4,248 feet) high and three kilometres (two miles) from the post office. From here a path leads southwards to **Makrandgad** or **Saddle-back Hill**, 20 kilometres (12 and a half miles) from the post office. From Babington Point, the Malcolm Path Ride takes you around the edge of the plateau to the **Chinaman's Waterfall** and from there, heading southwards along the beautiful Chinaman's Ride and Tiger Path Ride you reach **Falkland Point**. Nearby is **Carnac Point** named in honour of Sir James Rivett Carnac, the governor who deposed the raja of Satara, and installed his brother Shahji in his place. From here the Tiger Path leads to **Bombay Point** at a height of 1,295 metres (4,249 feet). On the Old Bombay Road, it has the most extensive views of any point and looks over to Pratapgad Fort. It is five kilometres (three miles) from the post office. During the Raj a space was cleared here large enough to accommodate several carriages and a band played from a bandstand. As the most popular sunset point, it is, for that very reason, best avoided on summer evenings.

If you enjoy boating you will find boats for hire on the central Yenna Lake next to the golf course.

Shivaji and His Forts

Shivaji (1627–80) was a great ruler who rose from the ranks of the Marathas, the dominant caste of the modern state of Maharashtra. He was known to fellow Marathas as Chatrapati (the Lord Protector) Shivaji, as 'the great rebel' to his biographers, as 'our neighbour Shivaji' to the British in Bombay, and as 'the mountain rat' to the Mughal emperor, Aurangzeb. Shivaji is a national hero, a local chieftain who took on the mighty Mughal Empire, and won. He is even today the most potent figure in the popular imagination of the Maharashtrian people and an aggressively parochial and Hindu party has taken advantage of this and called itself the Shiv Sena, 'the army of Shivaji'.

Shivaji's family land lay at the southern edge of the Mughal Empire at Pune, west of the independent sultanate of Bijapur. His early years were spent in the Western Ghats, hiding from Mughal forces. In his early teens, he was summoned as a subsidiary chieftain to the court at Bijapur where he showed his audacious and independent spirit by refusing to make the orthodox ceremonial obeisance to the sultan. He was sent back to his family lands, but was not content with this confinement for very long. At the age of 19, he first challenged the Mughal Empire by capturing a fort when the garrison, weary of the monsoon, had moved down from the mountain pass. From then on, Shivaji used his sharp wits and sense of strategy to harrass the vastly more powerful Mughal Empire and eventually to wrest a kingdom for himself. His strengths were his hardy hill warriors, his lightly armoured, swiftly mobile cavalry and his brilliant guerilla tactics; and his hill-forts were the main bastions of his power. The typical, hat-topped hills of the Sahyadris, surrounded by steep and often overhanging cliffs, provided natural defences which could be made almost invincible with minimum fortification.

The last Great Mughal, Aurangzeb (1618-1707), was the Maratha leader's main adversary. Aurangzeb's general, Jai Singh — the maharaja of Amber and founder of Jaipur — realised the importance of the forts to Shivaji. By concentrating his attacks on them, he forced Shivaji to capitulate and brought him captive to the Mughal court at Agra. Insulted by the emperor, Shivaji was placed under house arrest until, with characteristic élan, he escaped in a basket supposedly full of fruit and made his way to his capital disguised as a mendicant Brahmin.

He was never forced to submit again, although he fought many more battles. He consolidated his territory, organising a humane tax system for his lands and exacted *chauth* (a fourth of the land revenue) as the price for not attacking other peoples' lands. He remained a fort builder *par excellence*. It is said that he conquered 130 forts, built 111 and, at the time of his death, possessed some 240.

Shivaji died in his early fifties and his successors could not equal him. Control of the Maratha territories fell into the hands of the Peshwas: Brahmins who were originally chief ministers to the Maratha rulers. After Aurangzeb died, the Marathas under the Peshwas came to dominate even the Delhi durbar, but inner dissension paved the way for the defeat of the last Peshwa by the British in 1818.

Shivaji had always regarded the British with generosity. On both occasions when he had looted the Mughal port of Surat, the British traders had defended their factory bravely and he had not harmed or looted them. He had also bought guns from them, although perhaps unaware that he was receiving shoddy goods. Those sent to him in 1671 were described as 'very bad within, yet they may last a while' and those sold in 1672 as 'old defective guns with great holes in them'. Despite this sharp practice, the British did respect Shivaji. The English chaplain of Bombay described him as, 'erect, and of excellent proportion, active in exercise, and whenever he speaks he seems to smile. He has a quick and piercing eye.'

The British dismantled Shivajis forts in order to remove the threat of rebellion from their control of Maratha territory. Despite their efforts, there is still a great deal of romance in the ruined forts of the Chatrapati and there are several worth visiting around the hill stations of the Sahyadris.

Sinhabad, the Lion Fort, is 25 kilometres (15 and a half miles) from Pune. You can still see the ruins of the four-kilometre- (two-and-a-half-mile-) long walls with their 73 bastions and two main gates. In a daring night attack, Shivaji's general, Tanaji, scaled the cliffs of this 1,270-metre- (4,166-foot-) high fort and captured it from the Mughals. He was killed in the assault and a monument marks the spot where he fell. Shivaji's remark was, '*Garh ala, Sinh gela*' -- 'I have won the Lion Fort but lost my Lion.'

The memorial of Shivaji's son and successor, Rajaram, is also nearby.

Purandhar, 40 kilometres (25 miles) from Pune and ten kilometres (six miles) off the Pune–Panchgani Road, is a large and comparatively well-preserved fort, 1,350 metres (4,428 feet) above sea level. The upper part contains the citadel and the lower, called the *machi* or terrace, the outer fortifications which originally stretched over 40 kilometres (25 miles). Purandhar is overlooked by the neighbouring **Vajragad Fort** which proved its undoing both under Mughal and British attack.

Raigad, 67 kilometres (42 miles) from Mahabaleshwar and 126 kilometres (79 miles) from Pune, was Shivaji's splendid fort and capital from 1664 to 1680. Even today you get an impression of its former grandeur. Here, in 1674, Shivaji held his coronation; the elaborate ceremonies and celebrations lasted nearly a month. The Maharashtra Tourist Development Corporation provides some accommodation here but it also makes a very pleasant day trip.

Pratapgad, 20 kilometres (12 and a half miles) from Mahabaleshwar, was built from scratch by Shivaji in 1656. Three years later the Maratha leader was besieged here by the Bijapur general, Afzal Khan. Agreeing to a parley, both warriors met near the fort. According to the Maratha version, Afzal Khan tried to kill Shivaji and the Maratha responded by stabbing the general with a set of 'tiger's claws' — sharp metal talons worn in the palm of the hand. In the following scuffle, Khan was killed; his simple grave is nearby. In the battle which ensued, his troops were routed and Shivaji won a famous victory. Inside the fort is a temple of Bhawani, Shivaji's family goddess. On the west and north of the fort are cliffs which in places drop vertically for 300 metres (980 feet).

Ajinkyatara Fort, at the small town of Satara, became the capital of the Maratha empire in 1699. It lies 50 kilometres (31 miles) from Mahabaleshwar, and 106 kilometres (66 miles) from Pune. After their victory, the British made a descendant of Shivaji the raja of Satara, and he granted them the site of Mahabaleshwar.

Pandavgarh is a minor fort seven kilometres (four miles) northwest of the temple town of Wai. **Lohagad**, **Visapur** and **Rajmachi** are near Lonavala.

Amboli

Amboli, the closest hill station to Goa, is a small settlement perched 690 metres (2,264 feet) up in the Western Ghats. It was developed as a hill station by the British political agent, Colonel Westrop, after the opening of the Ghat Road from the coastal town of Vengurla, now in southern Maharashtra, to Belgaum. Of Amboli in the 1880s it was said, 'the ghats ... swarm with wild beasts, but the jungle is so dense that it is almost impossible to drive them from their lairs.' Even today, there is some forest around Amboli. Amboli is on record as the wettest place in Maharashtra, with an average of nearly 750 centimetres (296 inches) of rainfall a year, falling between June and October. At this time, the hill station is wrapped in mist. In other seasons there are fine views of the Konkan coastal belt. Because of its size and distance from Mumbai, it is quiet and peaceful.

Getting There

Panaji, the main town of Goa, is only around 90 kilometres (56 miles) away. There is one bus a day from Panaji to Amboli, but several from Panaji to Sawantwadi on the way to Amboli. From Sawantwadi, there are frequent buses to Amboli between 6 am and 6 pm every day. The nearest airport and railhead is Belgaum, 67 kilometres (42 miles) away in neighbouring Karnataka state. Regular buses also run from Belgaum and Kolhapur, Pune, 390 kilometres (242 miles) away and Mumbai, 549 kilometres (341 miles) away in Maharashtra.

For details of where to stay in Amboli, see page 281.

Sights

You can either walk or take a scooter-rickshaw to explore the area around Amboli. Among the main viewpoints are **Mahadeo Gad**, a natural fort, and **Temple View**, **Shirgaonkar**, **Sunset** and **Sea View points**. Amboli is one of the few hill stations from where you can really see the sea. Excursions include another former fortress — **Narayan Gad** — a distance of ten kilometres (six miles), and **Nagattas Falls**, also ten kilometres (six miles) away.

Karnataka

If you want to explore an area as yet undeveloped for tourism, Kodagu or Coorg is ideal, and its capital Madikeri, or Mercara, 1,220 metres (4,003 feet) above sea level, is a good place to start. Arriving in the district from the dusty countryside of Mysore is like entering an enchanted land. Range upon range of forested hills stretch into the distance. There are rosewood and sandalwood trees, and deep in the shade are thousands of hectares of coffee bushes, black pepper vines, the celebrated Coorg orange trees and near the beds of streams, cardamom plants. The valleys are brilliant green with paddy which produces small-grained aromatic rice that is the staple diet of the Kodavas. The best time to visit Kodagu is in April or early May, before the monsoons, or in late November or December when the temperature drops to 10°C (50°F).

BACKGROUND

The Kodavas, or Coorgs, have been the majority population in Kodagu since at least the ninth century AD, the first time the area is mentioned in historical records. The 1870 *Gazetteer of Coorg* describes the Coorgs as 'tall, muscular, broad-chested, strong-limbed and swift-footed. Men of six feet and above are not uncommon. Their features are regular, often distinguished by an aquiline nose and finely chiselled lips set off by a well-trimmed moustache.'

The Coorgs of today still fit that description, and they preserve a separate identity from other Hindus. They are enterprising and well educated and maintain the ancient martial traditions they have had since the earliest days. Practically every family has one man serving in the armed forces. Until recently the Coorgs were exempted from the operations of the Indian Firearms Act, a privilege which goes back to the British Raj. Hunting is a favourite and fitting pastime for a warrior race, and traditionally both men and women would take part. Venison and wild boar are considered delicacies, and alcohol and meat are essential ingredients for a Kodava feast. The importance of arms is clear in the ancient festival of Keilpodhu in September when guns, knives and hunting implements are cleaned, polished and offered for worship.

Traditional Kodava society was based on the *okka* or joint family, and the *nad* or village. These emphasised the importance of family ties, working together on the land, love of and loyalty to one's village and deep respect for elders — especially ancestors. The most extreme punishment for a Kodava was to be ostracised by his *okka*. Although the joint families no longer exist as they once did, the traditions of Kodava society live on in folk songs, ceremonial occasions and festivals. A simple example of this is the dress worn at ceremonies such as weddings. The Coorg sari is worn in a unique style, with the pleats at the back and the end of the sari drawn under the left shoulder and fastened over the right. A long headscarf or *vastra*, the symbol of a married woman, covers the head and is tied at the nape of the neck with the two ends draped over the shoulders. The men wear *kupya*, a black half-sleeved cotton robe which comes down below the knees, and which is secured around the waist with a maroon and gold cummerbund known as a *chale*. They carry an ornate silver dagger tucked into the cummerbund.

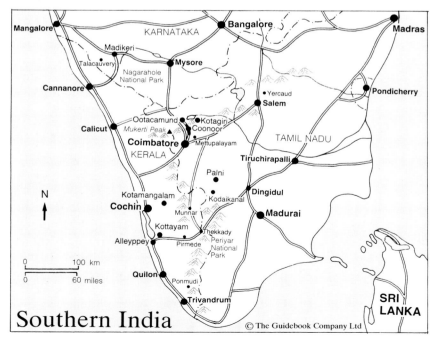

Southern India

© The Guidebook Company Ltd

Despite the martial traditions of the Coorgs, and their chieftains or *nayaks* who controlled well fortified hill defences ringed by ditches, they came under the rule of several dynasties and finally the British. The last Indian dynasty to rule Coorg was that of the Lingayat kings from Bednur in Karnataka, one of whom made Madikeri his capital in the late 17th century. The Lingayats are a distinct community of Shaivites with their own customs. They are strict vegetarians and bury, rather than burn, their dead. The Coorg soldiers served their rajas loyally despite the atrocities which, according to British accounts, the last rajas committed.

The British and the rajas never saw eye-to-eye and the bad relationship culminated in a proclamation by the last ruler, Vira Raja (1820–34), calling on all natives to overthrow the British. He claimed they were trying to convert all Hindus and Muslims to Christianity. The British reply was to recommend he be deposed for the sake of good government. The raja then proclaimed that the British were the sons of whores and should be completely destroyed. Not surprisingly, in 1834, 6,000 British troops marched into Mercara and hoisted the British flag. The raja decamped without a fight, but he had not played his last card.

In 1852 Vira Raja obtained leave from the British governor–general to visit England and took with him his favourite child Gauramma, then ten years old. In England he said he would like Gauramma to become a Christian and was able to have her baptised by the Archbishop of Canterbury. Queen Victoria herself stood sponsor at her baptism. Gauramma was baptised Victoria and brought up in England. Her father, now basking in royal favour, immediately launched a suit against the East India Company for the recovery of Rs680,000. Unfortunately, India was brought under the Crown in 1858 and his suit fell through. Never laying eyes on India again, he died in London and was buried as a heathen in Kensal Green graveyard. His ill-fated daughter fared no better. She died in 1864 after an unhappy marriage to an English officer.

After Independence, Coorg remained a separate entity with its own assembly until 1956, when it was merged with the former Mysore state.

Madikeri

GETTING THERE AND AROUND

Madikeri (Mercara) is only 120 kilometres (74 miles) from Mysore from where there are regular but slow buses. The town may also be approached from the Kerala side, the coastal town of Cannanore being 110 kilometres (68 miles) away. There is no convenient railway station or airport.

Taxis, jeeps and scooter-rickshaws are available from near the bus stand one stop before the bus terminal. The transport from the bus terminal itself is not so varied. If you don't know a local language, communication with drivers can be a problem, so be patient.

For details of where to stay, see page 281.

SIGHTS

The Town

Madikeri has a population of some 25,000 people, and as you approach the town you see streets of low, red-tiled houses. The most notable building is the **fort of the former Lingayat rajas**. The construction of the **palace** inside was commenced in 1735 and follows the ground plan of a traditional Coorg house with a superstructure in European fashion. In British times the palace was occupied by a 'native' regiment and now it is occupied by offices of the state government. You can still step through the great studded doors and see the enclosed courtyard, with its pillared verandahs and carved stone tortoise in the middle. Outside the palace stand two life-size black stone elephants with startlingly white eyes and tusks. They are replicas of two beasts devoted to Coorg's Vira Raja. Also in the compound is a former **Anglican church** which was erected in 1856. The stained–glass window shows Christ as a shepherd. Underneath are the words: 'Come unto me all ye that labour and are hearily laden and I will give you rest.' This church is now a museum (closed on Mondays) with some fine Jain statues dating from the 11th or 12th centuries when the Changalvas, who were Jains, ruled Kodagu. There is also a portrait of Field Marshal K M Cariappa, the first Indian commander-in-chief of the army, who was Coorg's most famous son and revered almost as a god. Outside the museum are a number of hero stones recalling the martial traditions of old Coorg.

Near the fort is a modern memorial dedicated to soldiers who gave their lives in the Second World War and for an independent India. There is a branch of the invaluable **Spencer's department store**, and next to the **Kodava Samaj building**, used for marriages, there is the **Janatha Bazaar** which includes a small honey emporium belonging to the Coorg Honey Progressive Co-operative Society. Coorg honey is very good, especially the honey produced after the bees have fed on nectar from the coffee flowers in March. Good quality cardamom is for sale from the **Coorg Cardamom Co-operative Marketing Society** opposite, the post office. The town has branches of all the main nationalised banks. The small tourist office is located in the Public Works Department (PWD) Traveller's Bungalow not far from the fort.

Temples are few in Coorg as the Kodava people are basically ancestor worshippers, but there is one notable temple built by Linga Raja II in 1820. The **Onkareswara Temple** stands below a ridge at the end of a street whose houses still belong to members of the Lingayat community. The temple complex consists of brick buildings in the Indo-Saracenic style set within courtyards surrounded by pillared verandahs with tiled roofs. The outer courtyard contains a water tank. The doorway to the inner courtyard is flanked by two yellow lions and in the main sanctuary there is a lingam, the symbol of Shiva, which was brought from the holy city of Varanasi. To the side of the central shrine are smaller ones dedicated to Shiva's sons: Ganesh, the elephant god, and Subramanya.

The other notable monuments of Madikeri are built in similar onion-domed fashion, with minarets at the four corners of the roof. These are the **mausoleums of Doddaviraraja** (who ruled 1780-1809), his son Linga Raja II (1809-20) and their wives. The third smaller tomb belongs to their guru, Rudramuni, and was built in 1834, the, final year of the reign of the last raja. The tombs are generally kept locked except in the early morning when the old caretaker-priest worships the Shiva lingams in the tombs and offers fresh flowers. This priest, who speaks no English, lives in a cottage adjoining the tomb compound and is prepared to unlock the monuments for visitors.

The most popular viewpoint in the town is **Raja's Seat**, which is on the way to the Hotel Mayura Valley View.

Out of Town

From Madikeri you can make your own explorations of the district. Eight kilometres (five miles) away are the **Abbi Falls**, previously named the Jessy Falls after a daughter of the first chaplain of Madikeri. There is no public transport to this spot.

The **Igguthappa Temple**, several kilometres out of town, is dedicated to Ayyappa, a particular deity of the Kodavas. Pilgrims here offer *tulabhara* or their weight in gold, silver or rice to the Lord.

But the most important shrine in the district is that at the source of the Cauvery River. **Talacauvery**, at an altitude of 1,276 metres (4,186 feet), is the birthplace of the Cauvery, widely worshipped as a goddess. It stands in the **Brahmagiri Hills**, 45 kilometres (28 miles) from Madikeri. On a clear day you can see the Malabar coast. Every year in October the shrine becomes the centre of a great festival bringing pilgrims from all over the country. On 17 or 18 October the goddess appears, her presence indicated by a gurgling sound in a small, enclosed square within a pool of water at the source. During the festival special buses run from Madikeri, otherwise there is only one a day and it is more convenient to go by car.

After making its appearance at Talacauvery, the river runs underground, coming to the surface again at **Bhagamandala**. Here it is joined by the stream of the Kannika; tradition also has it that a subterranean river called the Sujyothy also flows into it. The place is therefore called the **Triveni Sangam** (confluence of three rivers) and there are major temples dedicated to Ishwara, Vishnu, Subramanya and Ganesh (or Ganapati). Bhagamandala is also the main honey-producing centre and there is a **Research and Training Centre** which employs modern methods of bee-keeping and which it is possible to visit.

From Madikeri you can move on to **Nagarahole National Park**, some 80 kilometres (50 miles) away, which is home to elephant, bison, leopard and tiger. It is also very rich in birdlife. The **Kabini River**, which flows through the 573-square-kilometre (221-square-mile) park, has been dammed to form a large and attractive reservoir which separates the park from Bandipur Tiger Reserve to the southeast. Game viewing is well organised by the Kabini River Lodge, an attractive small hotel on the banks of the lake. The lodge is run by Karnataka state government. For reservations contact Jungle Lodges and Resorts Ltd, second floor, Shrungar Shopping Centre, Mahatma Gandhi Road, Bangalore 560001, tel. 5597021, 5586163. There are also some **forest resthouses** within the park, although obviously these do not offer the same facilities. The booking authorities are the Range Forest Officer, Nagarahole, and the Assistant Conservator of Forests, Wildlife Preservation, Vanivilas Road, KR Mohalla, Mysore.

Himalayan Pied Woodpecker

Blue-throated Barbet

Coffee

According to legend, coffee was first introduced into southern India by a Muslim saint called Bababudin in the early 17th century and was well established as a crop before the British set up a plantation in Mysore in 1823. The first British superintendent of Kodagu encouraged Kodavas to plant coffee in their compounds. Perhaps he guessed what is known today — that the land is so rich that it can grow four times more coffee per hectare than the neighbouring district of Chikamagalur. The first plantation was opened near Madikeri in 1854. Various disasters hit the new industry: in the 1870s it was pests and disease; at the turn of the century, the arrival of Brazilian coffee in the market; and in the 1930s, the Great Depression in the United States. However, the plantations survived and today there are around 33,000 hectares under coffee, mostly divided among small estates. Both the larger *robusta* and the more delicate *arabica* bushes are grown in these plantations.

At any time of year, the thick plantations are a joy to see, especially when the flowering trees are in blossom. The most spectacular of these is the tulip tree. However, there is no scent which sends the head reeling more than that of hundreds of thousands of white, star-like coffee blossoms. The coffee bushes flower a few days after the 'blossom showers' which should come around March. This is also the season for harvesting pepper from the vines which wind up the shade trees. The plantation workers climb up the most rudimentary bamboo ladders to pick the long pepper pods and the seeds are extracted by rolling the pods under foot until they burst. The green-coloured 'black' pepper is then left out to dry. A Coorg speciality is green pepper pickle which should not be missed when available from the shops. A few months later, the cardamom pods are ready to be picked from the plants growing in damp stream beds.

By the end of the year the coffee berries are ripe and are harvested over a period of two months by pickers with bags over their shoulders. The berries are dried, cured and all sold to the Coffee Board; under an Act of Parliament coffee has to be pooled. It is then up to the Board to sell Indian coffee, which it does on both the domestic and London markets. This is why on a coffee estate you find most planters don't drink their own coffee. There is no such restriction, however, on the little Coorg oranges which grow amid the coffee and also ripen in the winter.

Tamil Nadu

Ootacamund

Wotkymund, Whatakaymund, Wootacamund, Wuttasamund, Ootacamund, or nowadays the official Udagamandalam are some of the names which over the last two centuries have been given to the Queen of the Southern Hill Stations. The name that has stuck, however, is the short form of Ootacamund — Ooty. Ooty stands 2,240 metres (7,349 feet) above sea level in the Nilgiri or Blue Mountains which unite the Western and the Eastern Ghats. The Nilgiris are the highest of the southern ranges, but are much less precipitous than the Himalayas, the characteristic landscape around Ooty being expanses of rolling downs with deep green woodland or *sholas* in the folds of the hills. Nowadays the open grassland of the downs has been planted with large areas of eucalyptus and exotic conifers.

The undulating countryside allows Ooty to spread over 36 square kilometres (14 square miles), and maintain a population of some 80,000 people. The climate ranges from 25°C (77°F) in the summer to near freezing in the winter, although it never suffers the severe cold of Himalayan stations. The only season to avoid is the monsoon, when you can often see nothing but rain and mist. The peak tourist season is between April and June, both in Ooty and her sister hill stations of Coonoor and Kotagiri.

Background

Ooty was once the pasture land of the Toda community who believe that they have been on the heights of the Nilgiris since their gods placed them there in the distant past (see page 242). The Indian rulers of the Nilgiris did not try to subdue them and the new European settlers knew nothing of them or their land until the beginning of the 17th century. It was then that Fr Jacome Ferreiri set off to explore the mountains which reports said were the homeland of a lost tribe of Christians. These Christians were said to be descended from the Syrian followers of St Thomas the Doubter, who brought the Gospel to India and is buried in Madras. After a perilous journey, exhausted and half-frozen with cold, he reached a spot not far from the site of Ooty, to be met by 1,000 Todas wrapped in shawls, anointed with *ghee* and blissfully ignorant of St Thomas or Christianity. The priest distributed pieces of looking glass to the 'amiable but vague' tribes people and left never to return.

The East India Company annexed the Nilgiris from the territory of Tipu Sultan, the Muslim ruler of Mysore, whom the company's troops defeated in 1799 at Seringapatnam. The hills were incorporated into the Madras Presidency and in 1818 Messrs Whish and Kindersley, young assistants of John Sullivan, the collector of Coimbatore, 'discovered' the high pastures. The two assistants had been dispatched to round up a gang of tobacco smugglers who had taken refuge in the hills. One smuggler was eventually caught but escaped on the pretext of fetching milk for the thirsty and somewhat naive officials. They set off in pursuit, but instead of catching smugglers they discovered to their delight a remote plateau over 80 kilometres (50 miles) across, teeming with game and with an English climate. Back in Coimbatore, they poured out their adventures to John Sullivan.

A solid Victorian figure with side-whiskers and a stern gaze, Sullivan was shrewd, energetic and enterprising. The next year, he visited the high pastures with M Leschenault de la Tour, the naturalist to the king of France, and an assistant surgeon. The surgeon was included in the party to help look after the naturalist who had recently been brought 'to the portals of the tomb' by Indian microbes. Two days in the Nilgiris and he was completely recovered and hard at work collecting over 200 species of flora, many of which were unknown to science. Sullivan was no less thrilled than the naturalist and was determined to establish a hill station.

His enthusiastic report was accepted by the government in Madras which approved plans for constructing a bridle path to the site of the new station. Convicts from Coimbatore were employed for this task — the countryside being so wild that escape was considered impossible — and the path was completed in 1823.

In the same year, Sullivan completed the first house in Ooty, the Stone House, which still survives as part of government buildings, on Stone House Hill. His wife took up residence here and Sullivan, too, endeavoured to spend more and more time in the hills and less and less on his official 'seat' at Coimbatore.

The District and Sessions Court   *Raj Bhawan, the governor's residence, Ooty*

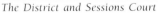

The European population increased, and Sullivan introduced English fruits, vegetables and trees, which grew enormously and well. Ooty became a land of strawberries and cream, especially for the collector who had by 1829 acquired from the Todas five times as much land as the rest of the Europeans put together. Another of his achievements was the enlargement of a natural lake, ostensibly for irrigation, which became one of the main ornamental features of the hill station. He also threw his weight behind the introduction of Australian eucalyptus and wattle, grown from seed brought by officers of the Madras Army, to replace the indigenous woodland which was quickly depleted by the demands of the new settlement.

The governors of the Madras Presidency also began to patronise Ooty. Stephen Lushington, governor from 1827 to 1832, was particularly active in promoting the station's development, and founded St Stephen's Church. As one officer reported with some justification: 'It will be the glory of Mr Lushington's government, without any extravagant hyperbole, that he has introduced Europe into Asia, for such are his improvements in the Neilghirries.'

The glory was also Sullivan's, but his amassed fortune, his absence from his office and his self-expressed high opinion of his achievements gained him enemies in Madras and even the governor was provoked to write that 'the excess of the local affection which they [the Nilgiris] inspire in those whose public duties require their presence elsewhere is the only public evil that has arisen from their discovery, and of this Mr Sullivan, the "first settler", has been the first and most enduring example.'

Despite this censure, Sullivan was promoted to be a member of the Madras Council in 1835 and retired to England a wealthy man in 1810. He left behind in St Stephen's churchyard his wife Henrietta Cecilia, and his young daughter Harriet Anne. The memorial to them still stands there.

After Sullivan's departure the hill station continued to flourish and gained its reputation as Snooty Ooty when it was made the summer capital of the Madras Presidency. Governors, governor–generals and princes flocked to the station and its active club life rivalled any centre on the plains. Satellite hill stations grew up around it — Coonoor, Kotagiri and Wellington for the army. Tea became the leading cash crop of the area after the first bushes were introduced at an experimental farm in nearby Kettu by a French botanist, M Perrotett. The best Nilgiri teas still rival Darjeeling tea for flavour. Chichona, for quinine, and coffee were also introduced. The hill station's popularity increased still further after Independence and it is now the favourite hill station for southern Indian holidaymakers.

Getting There and Around

By Bus

The buses in the south are much better than the buses in northern India. This is a statement often made by south Indians and it contains some truth. There are around four buses a day to Ooty from Bangalore, 300 kilometres (186 miles) to the north, via Mysore and the tea growing area of Gudalur. From Mysore itself, 170 kilometres (106 miles) away and one of the most attractive of Indian cities, there are five services a day. There are also buses from Coimbatore in the south, 105 kilometres (65 miles) away, Calicut, 187 kilometres (116 miles) away, and Cochin, 281 kilometres (175 miles) away on the west coast in Kerala.

By Air

The nearest airport is at Coimbatore which has daily flights to and from Madras, Mumbai, Bangalore, Cochin and Trivandrum.

By Rail

No bus or plane can compare with the train journey on the only metre-gauge mountain railway in India, and one of the last two mountain railways still using steam locomotives. (The other mountain railway is in Darjeeling, see page 160). The first sod of this impressive piece of engineering was cut by Lord Wenlock, the governor of Madras, on 3 August 1891. The lower portion of the line was opened for traffic in 1898 and the section up to Ooty — completed under the supervision of engineers C F Sykes and H Gales — carried its first passenger train in 1908.

The metre-gauge line starts from the railway junction in the small town of Mettupallayam at the foot of the mountains. The Nilgiri Express leaves Madras at night, reaching Coimbatore the next morning and continues to Mettupalayam to connect with the morning train to Ooty.

Coimbatore, proudly proclaimed as 'The Manchester of South India', is a convenient place to pass the night on the way up to the hills. It is an industrial town with a number of reasonable hotels; for example, the Hotel Murugan opposite the railway station. The devoted rail traveller has, however, no need to step outside the station itself for accommodation. There are several large retiring rooms and a matron who will wake you up in time for your train, for a small tip. You can take your evening meal at the platform restaurant, and wash it down with hot milk from the milk bar.

The Nilgiri Express departs at dawn and skirts the Blue Mountains, which *do* live up to the name and look blue in the morning light. At Mettupalayam be quick to occupy a place in the waiting Nilgiri Passenger if you want a window seat. First class is worth the extra money. The seats with the best views are in the first carriage facing forwards. Once you have arranged your luggage on a seat to 'save' it you are at liberty to walk up and down the platform and take a southern Indian breakfast of *iddli* and *vada* wrapped in a banana leaf, and coffee.

The hillsides here are covered with forest and the mountains appear at their best. The Swiss-made engine works itself to a frenzy and needs to take a breather at Hill Grove Station, at 1,092 metres (3,583 feet). The small station painted blue and green like the train has a combined Fruit and Vegetarian Light Refreshment Stall with bananas, *vadas*, and coffee for sale. Bonnet macaques also take vegetarian light refreshment here as passengers throw banana skins in their direction. The view of the escarpment opposite resembles Sir Arthur Conan Doyle's *Lost World*.

From Hill Grove, the train toils through rough-hewn, smoke-blackened tunnels up to the first tea gardens, past a painted slogan asking you to 'Sing and be merry in the train, be jolly and without strain'.

At Coonoor, at first sight an unimpressive town with a pretty station, the steepest part of the journey is over and the engine, exhausted of water and coal, is uncoupled. The main locomotive shed on the railway is at Coonoor and while a new engine, driver and brakeman are installed, there is time to visit the assembled locomotives, each emblazoned with the letters SR (Southern Railway) and the image of a leaping stag.

From Coonoor the track is level and the landscape more tame. You can see and smell blue-gum. Stations passed include Wellington, Aravankadu (site of a cordite factory), Ketti (needle factory) and Lovedale, which houses a celebrated school. Between Ketti and Lovedale you see the wide bowl of gentle hills which form the Ketti Valley, fields of red earth and small villages. Steaming into Ooty there are yellow flowering gorse and broom, plants of British moors. The last stretch of the track takes you along the bank of Ooty Lake into the station, 48 kilometres (30 miles) from Mettupalayam, well in time for lunch, having completed the journey in around four and a quarter hours.

Local Transport

Running taxis in the hills is a seasonal business and drivers therefore charge more than their colleagues in the plains. Ooty has taxis, three-wheeler scooter-rickshaws, local buses and, during the season, guided tours. It is often less irksome to deal with a car hire company — there are several near Charing Cross — than to deal with the often surly individual drivers. Fixed prices for standard tourist sights are listed at the Charing Cross taxi stand.

For details of where to stay in Ooty, see page 281.

St Stephen's Church, Ooty

St Thomas's Church, Ooty

SIGHTS

The Town

The main sweep of the bazaars lies between the lake and the Botanical Gardens, two of Ooty's most popular attractions.

The **lake** covers an area of four square kilometres (one and a half square miles), with the railway running along one bank. Steam enthusiasts can watch the trains puffing into the station from the paddle boats or rowing boats on hire from the boat-houses, or from the large graveyard of **St Thomas's Church**, built in 1870, which overlooks the lake and the railway line. This cemetery has the tallest memorial in Ooty, a huge **pillar** surmounted by a cross over the grave of William Patrick Adam, the governor of Madras Presidency who died in Ooty in 1881. Many memorials to Europeans were paid for by their friends and colleagues as their families were far away, but poor Mr Adam's tomb bears only the cold inscription, 'Erected by order of the Government'·

Both the bus stand, opposite the racecourse, and the railway station are at the lake end of town. Crowded bazaars run along one side of the racecourse, past the **Municipal Market** which sells all kinds of fruits and vegetables, towards Charing Cross. The closer you come to Charing Cross the classier the shops become. On sale are Ooty's specialities — tea (including *masala* varieties like cardamom, and chocolate), honey and eucalyptus oil. Signs advertise that 'tiffin' is ready, for instance at the **Irani Restaurant** opened in 1956 by a family of Bahais. It has old-fashioned coffee house furniture and the precepts of the Bahai faith on the walls, and offers Spencer's traditional ginger beer. There are small shops selling home-made chocolate of very reasonable quality. A Raj-style department store is **Kishan Chand Chellaram**, while modernity is represented by the **Nilgiris Co-operative Supermarket** and the new look **Higginbotham's bookshop**. Although an old company, this branch has electronic tills and security officers.

Near Higginbotham's is the **tourist office**, where the staff are helpful but not well informed. They can help you get on guided tours but may offer misinformation with the best intentions if you ask any difficult questions. For example, if you want to know bus timings you had better inquire at the bus stand.

Charing Cross itself is a road junction with, in its centre, a fountain of questionable taste decorated with naked pink cherubs. Next to the fountain is the taxi stand and opposite is the post office. The concretisation of Ooty is evident here. The small Raj-period **Wesleyan Church**, for example, is dwarfed by large, ugly, modern buildings.

A short walk from Charing Cross will take you to **Spencer's departmental store** which still sells its own 'Planter's Special' cigars made from Indian tobacco. Nearby are the library, unfortunately open to members only, and the **State Bank of India**, part of which is an attractive Raj building with a sizeable garden. An impressive array of cups won at the annual flower show adorn a corner of the entrance hall and the legend 'customers' satisfaction is our motto' is hung on a wall. The service is much better than at an average nationalised bank.

Ooty is far from being an epicurian's delight, but there is one restaurant that residents recommend — **Shinkow's Chinese Restaurant** which is opposite the State Bank at 42 Commissioner's Road. The part of Ooty town which most retains its old-world atmosphere is in the same area, around the crossroads on which stand **St Stephen's church**, the red-tiled **Collectorate** and **Holy Trinity Church**. Both the churches belong to the Protestant Church of South India, but the services at St Stephen's are in English and at Holy Trinity in Tamil. St Stephen's was consecrated in 1830 by the bishop of Calcutta, and named in honour of its founder Stephen Lushington, governor of Madras. It was designed by Captain John James Underwood of the Madras Engineers and the timber for the building was removed from Tipu Sultan's Lal Bagh palace at Seringapatnam. With its crenellated parapets and buttresses, it resembles an English parish church, but its fascination lies in its cemetery which climbs up the hill behind the church and tells sad tales of the Raj. John Sullivan's wife and daughter are both buried here, as are many officers of the Madras and Bombay armies, a 26-year-old deputy conservator of forests and a 36-year-old Wesleyan minister. William Graham Mclvor, superintendent of the government chichona plantation, also died in Ooty in 1876, leaving 'his little wife' to erect his monument. Many of the graves belong to children. Lieutenant-Colonel K H Havelock of HM 14th Light Dragoons remembered his daughter Isabella Frances Etheldred who died in 1851, aged 17, with this verse: 'Forgive blest soul the tributary tear that mourns thy exit from a world like this. Forgive the wish that would have kept thee there, and stayed thy progress to the realms of bliss.'

The twin towers of the **Roman Catholic Cathedral**, recently enlarged, can be seen on the road from Charing Cross to the **Botanical Gardens**. The gardens were established in 1848 by the Marquis of Tweeddale, who arranged for Mr MacIvor of Kew to come from England to supervise the work. Pink candyfloss is sold at the gates of the 22-hectare (54-acre) gardens which lie on the lower slopes of **Dodabetta Peak**, the highest point in Ooty. Inside the park, local photographers patrol the paths in search of tourists who want a permanent record of their visit. Their best clients are the honeymooners, and they direct the couples as if they were making a Tamil feature film. 'Hold her hand', 'Adjust your sari', 'Look into his eyes', they command.

The gardens are formally laid out with lily ponds and there are clipped bushes in the form of elephants with raised trunks. Here you can find over a thousand different species of plants, including some 30 types of eucalyptus. At the top of the garden is the half-timbered gateway to the governor's house, **Raj Bhawan**, which is unfortunately not open to the public. This mansion was built in 1877 by the Duke of Buckingham when he was governor of Madras. Not far from the gate, at the top of a flight of steps, is a small **temple** enshrining a gleaming brass image of the goddess Ambika Bhadrakali. A few minutes' climb up from the garden is a **Toda Mund** (village) — now merely a tourist attraction.

The gardens open from 7 am to 7 pm and the glasshouses from 8.30 am to 4.30 pm. The biggest events of the Ooty season held here are the impressive Annual Flower Show of the Nilgiris Agri-Horticultural Society and the Dog Show of the South of India Kennel Club.

Clubs

Of all the former British clubs here, the **Ootacamund Club** is the most exclusive and the best preserved. A drive lined with conifers and arum lilies leads to the Club which, despite various additions, is still recognisably the building erected in 1830 by Sir William Rumbold, a man who came to India with the intention of building on his 8,000-pound-a-year fortune and was not too scrupulous about how he did it. He bought his land in Ooty, reportedly at gunpoint, from the Todas, for whom it was particularly sacred, for the insignificant sum of 400 rupees. This transaction attracted the wrath of his compatriots. The

The Ootacamund Club

'native' official who helped him was sacked, and he was ordered by a court to pay compensation to the Todas.

However, his was by far the most comfortable house in Ooty and two of the greatest figures of the Raj, the Governor–General Lord William Bentinck, who suppressed the practice of *sati*, and Thomas Babington Macaulay, who wrote the Indian Penal Code, first met when they stayed there in 1834.

The Club was convened in 1843 and maintains its British traditions. The walls are hung with magnificent hunting trophies and there are portraits of Mahatma Gandhi, Indira Gandhi and Winston Churchill. Punishments for breaking club rules do not appear to have been increased since Independence and members removing periodicals from the public rooms risk a fine of only one rupee.

Club members are still proud to say that the game of snooker was invented in their billiards room. Its inventor was Colonel Sir Neville Chamberlain, who had first varied the game of Black Pool by placing coloured balls on the table in 1875 when he was stationed at Jabalpur. In those days, a first-year cadet at the Royal Military Academy at

Woolwich was known derisively as a 'snooker'. When one of his co-players missed a shot the colonel exclaimed, 'Why, you're a regular snooker.' As he recorded, 'To soothe the feelings of the culprit, I added that we were all, so to speak snookers at the game, so it would be very appropriate to call the game snooker.' The name was adopted but it wasn't until the colonel accompanied the Madras Army's commander-in-chief to Ooty in 1881 that the rules were worked out and posted, as they remain today, on the wall of the billiards room.

The **Ooty Hunt**, which still rides to hounds in pursuit of jackals, and which, it is claimed, is the only hunt left between Italy and Australia, is the club's other major claim to fame. The undulating landscape around Ooty makes hunting with hounds possible. The first pack was brought out in 1844, but was sold off soon after. In 1859 the 60th Rifles hunted with a 'bobbery pack' of four and a half couples of crossbred hounds. Ten years later, the hunt was revived by the commissioner of the Nilgiris and it was then that Major 'Bob' Jago, the father and mother of the Ooty Hunt, made his first appearance. As one local poet put it: 'Oh, it's jolly to hunt with the Nilgiri Pack, Major Bob with the horn and a straight-going jack.' There is a special bar dedicated to Major Bob at the Club. His portrait and riding crop hang on the wall and his forbidding countenance can be considered from the depths of polished 100-year-old leather armchairs.

Photographs of the masters of the hunt from the late-1870s line the magnificent panelled dining room, and boards of honour record their names in the mixed bar. The hunt survives today thanks to the patronage of the army at Wellington, which maintains the horses. Seventeen and a half couples of foxhounds are kept in kennels near the golf course. There is no shortage of jackals, 'the first cousin of the fox', many of which escape their pursuers, but the afforestation of the downs with eucalyptus and conifers means the huntsmen have to travel over 20 kilometres (12 and a half miles) outside Ooty to reach suitable country. The hunting season is during the monsoon and between January and March. The **Fernhill Meet**, named after the palace of the maharaja of Mysore, is still the first of the season and is followed by a breakfast hosted by the present head of the royal family. There is a well-attended Hunt Ball every year when the army officers arrive in full dress uniform and a band plays. The traditional Hunt Dinner is held at the Ooty Club.

The most notable survivor of the hill station's many other clubs is the **Ooty Gymkhana Golf Club** established over a hundred years ago, which is more accessible to visitors than the Ooty Club. For a small green-fee you can have a game of golf on the **Wenlock Downs**. Golf clubs and caddies are available. The course is open all year but the recommended golfing months are April and May. The Club is a descendant of the ABC Club which stood for Archery, Badminton and Croquet — or alternatively Asthma, Bronchitis and Coughs. This was merged with the Cricket Club to form the Blue Mountains Lawn Tennis and Cricket Club, which in turn fused with the Gymkhana Club in 1892. The site of the first links (now the racecourse) was chosen in 1890.

The Races

The Ooty Races were born out of the equestrian enthusiasm of members of the hunt. The first meeting under Turf Club rules was run on 18 May 1894. In the early 1980s the government of Tamil Nadu banned racing in the state, but in 1988 the ban was lifted and, it is hoped, will not be reimposed as the races are one of the great attractions of Ooty.

The race track is near the bus stand and looks out over the bazaars of Commercial Street and the surrounding hills. The average racegoers, however, are too engrossed in their race cards to notice the view. The earnest concentration of the punters, in their *lungis* and shirts, many with the handles of their umbrellas tucked into the back of their collars, is remarkable. They crowd the tote and the bookies (which boast names like M/s Mehta Associates, and Vinaayaga Enterprise) and stand transfixed in front of the colour television screens which replay the races, roaring with protest if they think any race has been unfairly won. A small, liveried band plays hits from old Hindi movies in between races, and in the members' stand you can see more westernised and sophisticated enthusiasts. The Ootacamund Derby is the climax of the season, and many of the meets attract the top Indian jockeys. But the races are also worth attending for any student of human character.

Another equestrian event to look out for is the point-to-point held on the downs, a popular entertainment for residents and visitors alike.

The Ooty Hunt

Out of Town

Ooty is spread out among a number of hills, many of which are now built up. However, **Dodabetta**, literally 'big mountain' standing at 2,623 metres (8,606 feet) is still comparatively bare. A motor road takes you to the top, and from here you can see as far as Coonoor and Wellington and down to the plains.

Three kilometres (two miles) from the railway station towards Fingerpost is the Roman Catholic shrine of **Kandal Cross**, which has a full-size crucifix secured on a huge boulder and a fragment of the true cross.

The valleys of the Nilgiris contain a large number of lakes and reservoirs. One of the closest to the town is **Marlimund Lake**, about five kilometres (three miles) from the railway station, which provides part of the town's water supply. Further out of town, down a turning off the main road to Coonoor, is a road which leads to **Tiger Hill**. A walk of about a kilometre (half a mile) will take you to the **Tiger Hill Reservoir**, a picnic spot, above which is the hill itself. A viewpoint has been built at **Valley View**, near Tiger Hill, looking out over the magnificent Ketti Valley.

The **Kalhatti Falls**, which drop some 40 metres (131 feet) down the mountainside, are about 12 kilometres (seven and a half miles) from Ooty down a turning to the right off the Ooty–Gudalur Road at **Talaikundha**, eight kilometres (five miles) from the town. If you don't hire a car, you can take a bus to the village of Kalhatti, from where you can walk to the falls. They are particularly spectacular during the rains, when they are also deserted by tourists.

A worthwhile excursion is to **Pykara Lake**, some 20 kilometres (12 and a half miles) northeast of Ooty, and the **falls** which lie to the north further up on the Moyar River. The views of the Western Ghats sharply descending to the plains in this area are magnificent.

In 1823 there was an avalanche at a spot 26 kilometres (16 miles) from Ooty. After this, the area became known as **Avalanche**. The road there is extremely attractive, but the bus service is almost non-existent, so hire a car if you wish to see it and are not prepared to trek and camp. This is one of the finest spots for trout fishing and rods can be hired here from the trout hatchery. However, if you want to fish, it's best to first contact the Assistant Director of Fisheries for advice on licences and the up-to-date position on rod availability. From Avalanche you can walk the seven kilometres (four miles) to **MacIvor's Bund**, or to **Avalanche Top**, another four kilometres (two and a half miles) away.

If you are adventurous, you can head for **Mukerti Peak**, at an altitude of 2,448 metres (8,031 feet), from where the souls of Todas and their funeral sacrificial buffaloes are supposed to leap together into the afterlife. *Murray's Guide* of 1897 described it thus:

> The W. side mountain is a terrific and perfectly perpendicular precipice of at least 7000 ft. The mountain seems to have been cut sheer through the centre, leaving not the slightest shelve or ledge between the pinnacle on which the traveller stands and the level of the plains below. To add to the terror of this sublime view, the spot on which the gazer places his feet is as crumbling as precipitous, the ground being so insecure

that with almost a touch large masses can be hurled down
the prodigious height into the barrier forest at the foot of
the hills, which at such a distance looks like moss.

Mukerti Peak is on the eastern edge of the Nilgiris, looking down into
Kerala, and is also part of the **Nilgiri Tahr Sanctuary** which has been
created in this most remote part of the mountains. The weather is
particularly cold and windy here in the winter months, when the lakes
are full and the mountains greenest.

Another hazard are 'ferocious' buffalo, originally domesticated by the
Todas but now completely wild. A road will take you as far as **Mukerti
Lake**, a beautiful reservoir surrounded by high hills with the peak
towards its western end. Here there are two bungalows which offer
basic accommodation (take provisions with you). If you want to visit
this area contact the Divisional Forest Officer (North Division Office,
also the headquarters of the Wildlife and Environment Association of
the Nilgiris) for further information.

Coonoor

Coonoor, 1,858 metres (6,096 feet) above sea level, is the second largest hill station in the Nilgiris, with a population of 45,000. It lies on the eastern side of the Dodabetta Range at the head of the Hulikal Ravine. It has a climate which is slightly warmer and less wet than that of Ooty, and has its share of period churches and boarding schools, its own branch of Spencer's and a golf course.

The town, much of it having grown in an unkempt fashion, is divided into two parts. **Sim's Park** is in upper Coonoor and was named after the Honorary J D Sim, a member of the Governor–General's Council in the 1870s. Many plants that cannot thrive in Ooty's climate do so here. The park is also the location of the prestigious **Coonoor Fruit and Vegetable Show** which follows the Flower Show at Ooty.

Picnic spots around the station include **Lady Canning's Seat**, about three kilometres (two miles) away, named after Countess Charlotte Canning. **Lamb's Rock**, five and a half kilometres (three and a half miles) away, looks down a precipice onto the railway line below and the surrounding forest. In the distance you can see the town of Mettupalayam, from where the steep climb to the Nilgiris begins. Further along the road to Lamb's Rock is the path to **Dolphin's Nose**, a distance of 12 kilometres (seven and a half miles). The climb to this rock is worth it for the view of the **Katherine Falls** and the **Coonoor Stream**. Another picnic spot is **Law's Falls**, named after the man who constructed the Coonoor Ghat Road. It lies about five kilometres (three miles) from Coonoor on the Mettupalayam Road where the Coonoor and Kateri rivers meet.

The **Droog**, or **Pakkasuran Kottai**, is a peak which can be reached after a three-kilometre (two-mile) trek from the nearest road. It's said that the great opponent of the British, Haider Ali of Mysore, built a fort here. It is also said that you can see the sea from its heights. There is little evidence remaining of the fort, and even if you can't see the sea, the view of the plains is exhilarating.

For details of accommodation in Coonoor, see page 282.

The Todas

Before Mr Sullivan opened up the high pastures to the doubtful benefits of western civilisation, they were the preserve of four tribes: the Kotas, who gave their name to Kotagiri, made tools and music; the Badagas, who cultivated the land; the forest-dwelling Kurumbas who collected honey and wood and also performed feats of sorcery; and the Todas who, with their herds of sacred buffalo, provided milk and *ghee*.

The Todas have unique traditions revolving around their buffalo and their temples, which are dairies. They themselves believe they were placed on the Nilgiris by their gods and are of a superior race, but some scholars suggest that they moved from the plains of Kerala up to the hills at the beginning of the Christian era. They claim that the strangely sibilant Toda language, which has no script of its own, is distantly related to the Dravidian languages of south India.

Lieutenant Evan Macpherson, an early visitor to the Nilgiris, described the average Toda in the 1820s as 'fair and handsome, with a fine expressive countenance, an intelligent eye and aquiline nose; his appearance is manly, being tall, strong-built, and well set up, his limbs muscular and finely proportioned.' The pastoral Todas had to be hardy to live on the cold heights, their only protection being homespun cotton wraps or *putkuli*, finely embroidered by the women with black and red designs. For ceremonies and festive occasions traditional dress is still worn, and older women anoint their hair with *ghee* and twist it into long ringlets. Some Todas also maintain old views of feminine beauty, judging a woman by the narrowness of the feet, or the amount of facial hair (the more the better).

The Todas live in small villages called *munds*, and even where the *munds* no longer exist the name lives on — as in Ootacamund. The old houses were barrel-shaped, thatched structures; new houses are less distinguished concrete huts.

The dairy-temples retain the traditional design. These dairies are the preserve of the Todas alone and visitors are considered to pollute them. Each dairy belongs to one of the 16 Toda clans, and the men of each clan become priests in turn. During the time a man is a priest he maintains ritual purity, lives alone in the dairy, does not cut his hair or shave. His tasks include milking the sacred buffalo, which belong to a particular bloodline, and churning the milk. The temple is a male preserve, the traditional symbols of women's work being the broom, the winnowing tray and a long pestle for pounding grain.

A Toda temple

The Toda buffalo, like the Todas themselves, are unique. Plains buffalo are mostly black and hairless; Toda buffalo are pale brown, with a thicker coat to resist the cold. They are also more ferocious and in the 19th century were noted to be 'exceedingly savage when Europeans come near'. To the Todas however, the buffalo is a gentle beast. Each female has her own personal name and the herds are so tractable that even a small child can control them.

The major landmarks of Toda life revolve around the dairy-temple and the buffalo. A new-born child is ceremonially shown the temple's holy objects; at funerals the buffalo are sacrificed before the cremation. It is believed that their souls will accompany those of the deceased into the afterlife.

Until recently it was the custom for men and women to be married at a young age and for the wife of one brother to automatically be considered the wife of all the brothers in a family — a system known as Adelphic polyandry. A woman was also given the freedom to take a lover, and the paternity of her first child was decided at a ceremony when one of her husbands, generally the eldest brother, presented her with a symbolic bow and arrow. He was thereafter considered the father of all her children, the actual biological father being of no importance in Toda eyes.

The system of polyandry became prevalent partly because of an imbalance in the population of men and women. The Todas were never numerous and new diseases like influenza, an import from the plains, threatened to wipe out the entire tribe. In 1952, Prince Peter of Greece and Denmark, an anthropologist, published a report on the desperate problems of the community and the Madras government set up a medical unit specifically for them.

In 1955, the medical unit was joined by the Todas' own Florence Nightingale, Evam Piljain. Evam had qualified as a nurse in Ireland, an unparalleled achievement for any Toda which was due partly to the fact that she was a Christian and had had a Western education. Various missionaries had attempted to convert the Todas; most, however, had failed completely to understand a people who had no words for adultery, sin or forgiveness, and who maintained a proud culture and strong beliefs in their own gods. Only one missionary, Miss Ling, made any noticeable headway. However, she had to spend 50 years with the Todas to achieve this, learning their language and translating St Mark's Gospel into highly eccentric Toda.

Evam — her name means 'gift' — heard of Prince Peter's report when she was in England. For several days she could neither eat nor sleep. Within two weeks she resigned her position and set out for India, where she began work as a voluntary assistant. As a Christian and a woman advocating a foreign system of medicine, she had to struggle to win over the majority of her tribe. This she did when one of her cousins became seriously ill as she was about to give birth. Evam took her to hospital and was later visited by the cousin's irate husband who smashed the windows of her house in his fury and demanded that his wife be returned home, where at least she could die in dignity. Evam stood up to the husband who returned home. Later that night she walked miles over the downs to bring the same man to the hospital to give permission for an operation. Her courage in walking the dark paths, which for Todas hold animal and supernatural dangers, gained her the respect of her community.

Evam also stood up for the Todas against outsiders. Once she was asked by the former Prime Minister, Jawaharlal Nehru, whether she was doing anything 'to change their marriage customs'. She replied, 'I am doing nothing about that'. 'Why?' he asked. 'Because they are only doing openly what many so-called civilised people do in secret. They are more honest. Why should I try to make them dishonest?'

Medical care has now brought down an almost 50 percent infant mortality rate to near zero, and the growing population, which now has more women than men, feels no need to practice polyandry and only one or two such families are left.

Evam Piljain lives at 19 Shedden Road (on the way to St Hilda's School) and keeps for sale traditional embroidery, of superior quality to that found in the bazaar. The prices are expensive by Indian standards, and cheap by European ones, and the profit goes to the Toda women who do the embroidery and towards a fund which is used for health and educational work.

The Todas' way of life is changing. Many have given over their land to cultivation, although they generally employ labourers for this. The interdependence of the various tribes of the Nilgiris has broken down. Many Todas appear to be accepting Hindu beliefs. But the herds of buffalo are still preserved and while Todas are quite happy to take from other faiths, they maintain their own temple exclusively for themselves.

Visitors can see the *mund* near the Botanical Garden with ease, although this is now a regular 'tourist *mund*'. Others are spread over the high pastures, the highest concentration being on the Wenlock Downs. There is a 12-metre-(39-foot-) high domed temple or *poh* known as the Toda Cathedral at Mutanad Mund (Nosh). It is a few kilometres outside Ooty on the Mysore Road after Tallakunda, although you can only admire the thatched exterior. There is also a block of land, typical of what the downs used to be like, at Pagalkode Mund on the Windy Gap Road about two kilometres (a mile and quarter) before you reach the viewpoint of Glen Morgan, and about 23 kilometres (14 miles) north of Ooty. Here you can see the buffalo in the early morning and evening on their way to and from their pastures, in a routine that has been unbroken for centuries.

Yercaud

Yercaud, at an altitude of 1,500 metres (4,920 feet), stands in the Servaroyan (Shevaroy) Hills above the city of Salem in Tamil Nadu. The first proper hotel in the station only opened in 1971. Until then Yercaud had not been a tourist resort but a town famous for its schools and surrounding coffee estates. Yercaud is still comparatively more peaceful and cheaper than the major southern resorts of Ooty and Kodaikanal, but every year the influx from the plains is growing larger. For the time being, its population of 35,000 gives it the atmosphere of a large village. The climate is also particularly pleasant; residents say with pride that they never need to use a fan. The most popular seasons are February–June and September–November, while late November and December tend to be cold and misty. Around April there are the pleasant showers which bring the coffee bushes into blossom.

BACKGROUND

The name Yercaud comes from two Tamil words: *yeri* or lake and *kadu* or forest. The spot was discovered by the British in the 19th century. Coffee was introduced into the Servaroyan Hills in the 1820s but the first house in Yercaud wasn't built until some 20 years after that. The first motorable road to the settlement was completed as late as 1900. The economy of the area is dependent on coffee and there are 17,000 estates, mostly small. The majority of the estates are owned by local people, although before Independence they belonged to English, Scots, Welsh, French and German, as well as Indian planters. One West Indian planter is still remembered by locals. He was an ex-boxing champion by the name of Mr Terry. The mixture of nationalities in the community led to an exceptional camaraderie. Everyone could be a member of the club where tennis, bridge and other games were and, to a lesser extent, are still played.

The cool climate attracted a number of Christian denominations and the sight of nuns and priests is not uncommon. They run the two prestigious schools — the Sacred Heart Convent for girls and the Montfort School for boys.

GETTING THERE AND AROUND

Yercaud is 40 kilometres (25 miles) from Salem, which locals call 'our Paris'. You can make the ascent by taxi or bus. The drive takes about an hour as you climb through scrub-covered hills, forest and coffee plantations, and around 20 hairpin bends. Between two of the last bends is Salem View. Salem is 335 kilometres (208 miles) from Madras and is on the main railway line from that city. Among the most convenient trains to and from Madras are the overnight Yercaud Express and the daytime Koval Express. There are also trains from Cochin, Trivandrum, Mangalore and, less conveniently timed, from Bangalore. The nearest airport is at Tiruchirapalli with connections to Madras and Madurai, but it's too far from Salem, a distance of 188 kilometres (117 miles), to be convenient.

There are a number of extremely ramshackle taxis near the bus stand which have a set rate to take passengers to viewpoints like Lady's Seat.

For details of where to stay in Yercaud, see page 283.

Holy Trinity Church, Yercaud

SIGHTS

The Town

The town with its whitewashed, red-tiled houses, stands to the south of the lake which gave the hill station its name. The **bazaar** has a number of shops catering to the plantation workers, and small coffee shops and restaurants selling cheap and tasty meals, where the residents exchange gossip. Some of the eating houses advertise themselves by playing Tamil film songs at full volume over loudspeakers. The owner of the **Padma Stores** caters more for the planters and keeps many items which are difficult to find even in Salem. There are several banks which accept travellers cheques. Most of the buildings in the bazaar are relatively new but the beautifully maintained **Holy Trinity Church** still overlooks the bazaar square, surrounded by its cemetery, much as it did a century ago. It is one of several churches in Yercaud, and is a reminder of British rule. Below the church is the **club** where planters still meet, particularly on Thursdays.

Kodaikanal

Kodaikanal is the second of south India's major hill resorts and is variously known as the 'Princess of Hill Stations' and the 'Switzerland of the East'. It is also the sole hill station in India to have been founded during the British Raj by Americans. The Palni Hills in which it stands form part of the southernmost part of the Western Ghats and rise to over 2,000 metres (6,562 feet), with steep escarpments to the north and southwest. Kodaikanal itself lies in a shallow basin, and from its southern rim are dramatic views of the mountains descending to the plains. Until recently, Kodaikanal, which has a population only one quarter the size of Ooty's, was a haven of quiet surrounded by eucalyptus, conifers and *shola* forest, with neatly terraced hillsides providing all the fresh fruit and vegetables the inhabitants could eat. As at other resorts, the last few years have seen a tourist boom, bringing throngs of Indian tourists in the peak season between April and June. That means an excess of buses at the most popular points and crowded bazaars. Even so, Kodaikanal retains its character and on Sunday mornings the valley resounds with peals of church bells, a sound you will not perhaps hear in any other hill station in India. The climate is milder than that of Ootacamund and the best months for avoiding tourists and walking the hills are January to March. From June to November the station is subject to the two monsoons which hit it one after another.

BACKGROUND

Kodaikanal might never have become a hill station were it not for the American Madura Mission, which was founded in 1834 in the temple city of Madurai. Within ten years of its founding, six missionaries had died and, in 1844, those remaining were afflicted with 'a fearful attack of cholera'. To preserve the lives of their staff, the Mission considered sending them on sea voyages to Jaffna in Sri Lanka, where the mission had originally begun its work. But taking note of the fashion of the Raj they decided instead to send missionaries to the hills. The mission members at first visited the closest hills to Madurai, the Sirumalais, and several of them never returned. They died because the hills were not high enough to safeguard them from disease. So the Americans turned to the Palnis, which had been surveyed by the British in 1821 and thereafter more or less ignored. One man who had been to Kodaikanal was an Englishman, Mr Fane. He had built godowns (storage sheds) there in 1844. On his advice, the Mission chose Kodaikanal for their retreat from the plains, and he helped them with materials to build their first houses.

By 1850, there were 20 members of the Madura Mission in Kodaikanal and as many British civil servants from Madurai district. The journey from Madurai was not far but arduous, part of the journey being spent in unsprung bullock-drawn 'transits' down roads infested with bandits. A bridle path, known as the Coolie Ghat, and now mostly overgrown, was the first route to be made passable for the annual exodus from Madras. In 1879 *Murray 's Guide* wrote that Kodaikanal 'consists of ten or fifteen small, ugly houses and a few huts for servants'.

The writer had obviously not seen the church, a remarkable building which had Tamil and English services and had been built with funds raised by subscriptions from Anglicans and American congregationalists.

Opened in 1856, its roof was made entirely of flattened Huntley and Palmer biscuit tins. In any case, Murray's information was soon out of date as improved rail and road services brought the permanent population of Kodaikanal to nearly 2,000 by the early 1890s. The new European houses were also far from ugly. You can still see the picturesque stone cottages, with roses around the door, standing in their spacious compounds. The biscuit-tin church was demolished to be replaced by sundry others belonging to individual denominations whose members followed the example of the Madura Mission and lifted their eyes unto the hills.

Recreation in the new settlement was much the same as in any other hill station, except for the popular bicycle parties (the bicycles were carried up the Coolie Ghat on porters' heads) and fern and butterfly collecting. In the 1870s, fern-decorated dresses became the rage at parties. The menfolk would scramble down gullies and retrieve from their depths a species of silver fern. The ladies would then press the leaves on to dark woollen dresses, and the fern's silvery pollen would form images of the leaves on the cloth.

With the growing population came the clubs. The first to be established was the English Club in 1887. The American Madura Mission donated the land for the club on the condition that there would never be a bar and that no games would be played on Sunday. For some time, rules about keeping the Sabbath were strictly enforced. Two members of the club were forbidden entry for six weeks because their wives and some others were found guilty of dancing on a Sunday. However, not every official in Kodaikanal had the missionary spirit, as the *Pioneer* newspaper recorded, 'During the months of April and May - the missionary season — black-coated padres fill the air with the odour of sanctity. When Kodai Spiritual departs, the Kodai Carnal season commences with the first rains.' Somehow or other, the club managed to gain a bar, a victory for the carnal faction.

The most influential club was the Kodaikanal Missionary Union (KMU), which encouraged missionaries of all denominations to meet together, rather than remain in mutually exclusive groups. Few members of modern Kodaikanal have even heard of the KMU. All that now remains of its past is the library, near the International School, still a meeting place for the few retired missionaries who live in the hill

The volcano-shaped Perumal Malai looms behind Kodaikanal

Kodaikanal Boat Club

station. It was once the centre of social activity, arranging parties, sales and theatricals — even pianos were carried up the Coolie Ghat for concerts!

At the turn of the century, a golf club was formed with mainly English membership. More popular, because it was cheaper to join, was the boat club on the lake. The lake had been created by damming a small stream at the bottom of the Kodaikanal Basin. This club was a great attraction, particularly for Indian visitors, and during the 20 years leading up to Independence many of the executive members were Indians.

The first of Kodaikanal's schools was a Jesuit Seminary set up in 1894 especially for Indian students at the Sacred Heart College. As one former missionary of the station put it, 'The Catholics came here not to holiday, but to work.' The would-be Jesuits studied at the college for eight years before completing their training in Kurseong or Pune. The Presentation Convent was another prestigious Roman Catholic School for girls. The Americans, however, founded their own Kodaikanal International School to avoid having to send their children all the way back to Oberlin, Ohio, where other mission children studied. The school opened in 1901 with 13 pupils; it still flourishes.

A municipality was set up in 1899 to look after the settlement, which consisted of the spacious compounds of the Europeans and some Indian elite, a thriving Indian bazaar and, on the outskirts, terraced fields. The members of the municipality were far-sighted and looked on in alarm when the first motor vehicles drove up the newly opened Law's Ghat Road in 1916. They feared a motor invasion and they were right. The curse of Kodaikanal is the combustion engine and the motor horn, which echoes around the hill station. The Coolie Ghat was not altogether forgotten for the station's *dhobis* or washermen still preferred to live on the plains at the bottom of the Ghat road and climb laboriously up it once a week to deliver and collect laundry.

Today, what the missionaries and the officials built — churches and cottages remain, but the missionaries themselves are lacking. At Independence, many who had planned to retire to Kodaikanal returned instead to the countries of their birth. Many of those who decided to stay on over 50 years ago, have since died. In modern India, conversion has become a politically sensitive issue, and foreign missionaries are no longer encouraged. 'In those days', a former missionary said, 'people would come to devote their whole lives here. In these changing times, there's no impetus any more.'

GETTING THERE AND AROUND

The nearest airport is Madurai, 120 kilometres (75 miles) to the southeast, famous for its fabulous temples, and connected by daily flights with Madras, 620 kilometres (385 miles) away; Tiruchirapalli, 197 kilometres (122 miles) away; and Bangalore, 600 kilometres (373 miles) away.

The nearest train will deposit you at Kodai Road. The extra word 'road' indicates that the station is nowhere near Kodaikanal, but somewhere close to the Palnis. In fact, it's 80 kilometres (50 miles) from Kodai Road to Kodaikanal. The railway station is on the line between Madras Egmore, Madurai and Quilon. There are buses from Kodai Road to Kodaikanal, and frequent services from Madurai.

If you are heading towards Kodaikanal from Kerala to the south, you can get direct buses. If, however, there's any difficulty in this, take a Dindigul-bound bus and get off at Batlagundu, from where there are almost half-hourly services during the day to your destination. There are plenty of sights to see along the way to Kodaikanal.

The best way to get around Kodaikanal is to walk, but if you despise this form of locomotion you will find a large supply of taxis. The drivers generally know little English but are quite fluent when it comes to discussing money. There are bicycles and ponies for hire near the lake. During the season guided tours of the major beauty spots are arranged; contact the tourist office in the main bazaar for details.

For details of where to stay here, see page 283.

SIGHTS

On the Way There

The 53 kilometres (33 miles) of hill road on the Batlagundu side of the Palnis, known as **Law's Ghat Road**, are exceptionally attractive, passing through plantations of citrus fruits, coffee, black pepper vines and tapioca, and overlooking waterfalls and reservoirs. On the way there is a sign 'To the dolmens' pointing down a path to the left. If you are travelling by taxi it's worth stopping to see these now overgrown remains of the first inhabitants of the Palnis to leave behind any tangible signs of their presence. The Palnis are scattered with stone cists, circles and dolmens built by these unknown people, but the dolmens near the roadside are the most easily accessible.

The buses toiling up the hill stop at **Oothu** 'for coffee', 28 kilometres (18 miles) from Kodaikanal. There is a Tamil Nadu Tourism snack bar here and some 'wayside amenities' (toilets). However, 'cheap and best' are the wayside coffee shops, and not so cheap when they see a foreigner, are numerous fruit stalls selling local produce like oranges and avocado pears. Not so much relished in southern India as in the West, avocados are often fed to pigs. Eight kilometres (five miles) before Kodaikanal you pass the **Silver Cascade**, a spectacular waterfall in the rains, and one of the sights of the hill station.

Another road to Kodaikanal starts from **Palni**, 65 kilometres (40 miles) away, where there is a famous **temple to Lord Subramanya**, a son of Shiva, situated on a small hill and illuminated at night. This road is more convenient if you are coming from the direction of Coimbatore, and the Palnis on this route have the bare grandeur of Scottish highlands.

The first six captains of the Kodaikanal Golf Club

The Town

Several concentric roads ring the lake, to one side of which is the bus stand and the small main bazaar, mainly consisting of ugly, modern buildings. At the bus stand is a manned STD phone — a convenient and easy way to make STD calls. The phone booth is just at the back of the tourist office although the tourist officer himself is often 'not on his seat'. In the same bazaar is the Canara Bank, very co-operative with travellers cheques, while the post office is also nearby. The main bookshop, in a typical stone house, not surprisingly belongs to the Christian Literature Society. Almost opposite is the Corsock (Co-ordinating Council for Social Concerns in Kodaikanal) shop which sells soft toys and all kinds of hand-embroidered items, the profits from which go towards health care, education, rural development and running a Mercy Home for the destitute. Provisions shops specialise in locally produced eucalyptus oil and honey from the Kodai Hills Beekeepers' Co–operative.

If you walk down this bazaar past lines of taxis towards the lake, you arrive at a crossroads called **Charing Cross**. Straight on is the Carlton Hotel and the lake. A road runs around the lake shore to the **Boat Club** where you can hire rowing or paddle boats and observe the English-style cottages and the hills. Further along the lake is a tiny rustic, stone **post office** and a **memorial to Sir Vere Henry Levinge**, Baronet of Knockdrin Castle, Westmeath, Ireland. He retired from the Madras Civil Service in 1867 but preferred Kodaikanal to his castle in Ireland. As the inscription reads 'to him are due nearly all the improvements the settlement possesses'. Near the memorial is the dam Levinge built, which is responsible for the lake. Above the lake post office is **Spencer's department store**, selling its own brand of lemonade.

A left turn at the crossroads brings you to the **English Club**, which accepts temporary members if nominated by a full member. It reflects the spirit of competition between the United Kingdom and the United States in pre-Independence days. On the wall are hung group photographs of tennis teams labelled 'British Empire vs America'. A right turn at Charing Cross takes you to the **Zion Lutheran Church** which, with its grey stone tower, would not be out of place in an English village. Devotees leave their shoes outside the door in respectful

Indian fashion. The church is faced by more of the grey stone cottages which give the station its charm.

Around the Town

A one-kilometre (half-a-mile) climb from the main bazaar will bring you to **Coaker's Walk**, cut from the hillside in 1867 by Lieutenant Coaker of the Royal Engineers. The footpath offers glorious views of the tallest mountain in the area, the volcano–shaped **Perumal Malai** standing at 2,440 metres (8,005 feet). You can also see over the southern rim of Kodaikanal Basin to the plains below and the huge Wagai reservoir, beyond which another range of hills rises steeply. On the way up you will pass the **Union Church of Christ the King**, previously the American church that was built to accommodate the growing congregation, and replaced the biscuit-tin church. It is now part of the unified Church of South India. At one end of Coaker's Walk is a concrete **telescope house**, above which is the little Anglican **Church of St Peter** (now Church of South India) built by Bishop Robert Caldwell, another leading citizen of the station. His house, Roslyn, is a few minutes' walk away. A stained–glass window in the church depicting the risen Christ is dedicated to his memory with the legend 'Death is swallowed up in victory'. The 'Hinduisation' of St Peter's is under way. For some reason, both Hindus and Christians come to drink from the tap in the church compound in the belief that it cures diseases.

Following the road past St Peter's up the hill surmounted by the television tower (for whose sake the last monkey puzzle tree in Kodai was sacrificed), you reach the blue and white icing-like Roman Catholic **Church of Our Lady of La Salette**. Inside there are no pews; the 150 or so congregation sit on the floor facing lifesize statues of Mary and Joseph. Opposite is **La Providence**, residence for the priesthood, from where a path called **Priest's Walk** leads down to the **Sacred Heart College** in the area of Kodai known as Shembaganur. This path is now partly overgrown, but it's still possible to descend the hillside by several others. One leads to **Levin's stream and waterfall**, and you can look over the 200-metre- (656-foot-) high **Snake Falls**. With some guidance you can walk eight kilometres (five miles) downhill from La Providence to the village of **Vellagavi** via **Dolphin's Nose**, a flat rock projecting over a chasm, and **Echo Valley**.

The **Sacred Heart College** is now reached by metalled road and the **Anglade Institute of Natural History** there has a small museum with collections of butterflies, moths, stuffed animals and, most fascinating of all, relics of the dolmen-builders of the Palni Hills. It was Jesuit priests who documented and excavated the megalithic structures built by these people. The institute also has a **Herbarium** and a **Fernery**. In its grounds are more of the tall eucalyptus trees so common in Kodai. Bonnet macaques can be seen shinning up them like steeple jacks. The college preserves the **Jesuit Madurai Province Archives** dating from 1542 when St Francis Xavier first landed in India.

A shorter walk from the town is to the **biscuit-tin church**, by the south of the lake among woodland. The deserted cemetery stands to the side of an unmade road between the main road to the golf course and the lake. The house next door is called Endhaw in Amarvil, and a rusty gate marks the entrance to the churchyard. Inside is a tall monument marking the site of the first American Mission Church where the missionaries worshipped from 1854 to 1904. British as well as American graves lie half overgrown. Notable is the memorial which reads, 'Dudley Linnell Sedgwick, third son of the late Fellow Sedgwick of Cashio Bridge, Watford in the country of Hertford, England, who was killed by a bison whilst shooting in the Palney Hills on 29th March 1875 aged 31.' Life in the Palni Hills was obviously more dangerous than in Watford. The woodland in this area is full of birdlife, and a quiet visitor may well spot black bulbuls in the branches overhead.

The Europeans established two circular routes for excursions — the 'ten-mile round' and the '40-mile round'. On both routes lies the golf course to the southwest of the town. Also on the way are the barrack-like holiday homes which were used to intern German nationals during both world wars. Kodaikanal has quite a history of political imprisonment. At the turn of the century the wazir of Chitral and the two Afghan princes, Akram and Azam, were kept here while the ex-maharaja of Nabha (in Punjab) enjoyed 20 years of imprisonment in the hill station.

The 18-hole course offers visitors a game of golf on payment of a small amount for green fees, hire of clubs, caddies and purchase of golf balls. The Palni Hills Open Championship, the big match of the season, is held in May. The clubhouse dates from 1927 and amongst other mementos of the past is a photograph of the first six captains of the club team. Only one was an Indian, the raja of Pudokotah, who was captain from 1929 to 1930.

The path to **Green Valley View**, formerly known as **Suicide Point**, is near the entrance to the club.

Beyond the club are the **Pillar Rocks**, some eight kilometres (five miles) from the town. The Pillars are three great towers of granite some 120 metres (394 feet) tall which overlook the plains to the south and can be observed from a formal 'viewpoint' at the roadside. A cave between the Pillars, known as the **Devil's Kitchen**, can be approached by a steep path.

The 'ten-mile round' ends near Pillar Rocks and a road takes you back to the northern side of the station. If you press on along the **Goschen Road**, or '40-mile round', past viewpoints like **Doctor's Delight**, ten kilometres (six miles) from town, you reach **Berijam Lake**, 21 kilometres (13 miles) away. This is a delightful route and from Berijam, another and only jeepable road continues to **Top Station** and **Munnar** in Kerala.

The round continues to the north through **Mannavanur** and **Poombari** villages until finally you return to the opposite side of Kodaikanal and the **Indian Institute of Astrophysics** where an observatory was first established at the end of the 19th century. Visiting time at the observatory, where there are optical and radio telescopes, tends to vary but it's generally between 10 am and 12 noon. There is a small museum displaying pictures of the sun and planets.

On the same side of town are the **Bear Shola Falls** about two kilometres (just over a mile) from the bus stand. They are relatively unimpressive except in the monsoon months. A better viewpoint is the **Kurunji Andavar Temple**, three kilometres (two miles) from the town beyond the main bazaar and past the small but well-tended **Chettiyar Park**. The modern rectangular temple compound stands on a hill overlooking terraced fields and more distant peaks. There is a **telescope house** nearby for closer views.

An energetic day out is to climb **Perumal Malai**, the volcano-topped mountain which dominates Kodaikanal's skyline. You can take the main ghat road down to a spot called **Neutral Saddle** where the climb begins.

Kerala

Most visitors come to Kerala for its magnificent beaches and backwaters. But less well known are the Southern Ghats, hills rich in cardamom, pepper and tea plantations, and which have the highest peak south of the Himalayas — Anaimudi — standing at 2,694 metres (8,839 feet). The main tourist offices will tell you that there are three hill stations in these hills — Munnnar, Pirmede and Ponmudi — as well as the hill wildlife sanctuary at Thekkady. In fact all but Thekkady are small settlements offering little in the way of tourist facilities. However, the views of the ghats and the plantations are a reward in themselves and especially worth seeing if you prefer to keep off the well-beaten tourist track. The hills are accessible throughout the year although very wet and misty during Kerala's two monsoons, the southwest and the northeast (late May–early November).

Munnar

Munnar, at 1,652 metres (5,420 feet), is a small town surrounded by the Annamalai Hills (or elephant mountains) and tea estates. It stands at the confluence of three rivers — the Muthirappuzh, Nallathanni and Kundala. *Moonu* in Tamil means 'three', and *aar* 'river'. The town serves the needs of the tea planters and plantation workers. It has little to recommend it architecturally. There's no 'wild west Swiss' style architecture, simply shack-like shops and low, red tin-roofed bungalows. Neither is there a tourist office nor any restaurant worth mentioning. The three most conspicuous buildings are the airy Mount Carmel Church, the multi-coloured Subramanya Temple and the green concrete Munnar Mosque. Their high position and proximity makes Munnar an advertisement for communal harmony. For the planters the most important building is the regional offices of Tata Tea, a large, yellow building which previously served as the company's railway station.

A Military Assessment

*L*et us, then, begin as we hope to end, with the enemy. In the examination of a people it is always best to take their virtues first. This clears the ground and leaves sufficient time for the investigation of the predominant characteristics. The Swatis, Bonerwals, Mohamands and other frontier tribes with whom the Malakand Field Force is at present engaged are brave and warlike. Their courage has been abundantly displayed in the present campaign. They charge home, and nothing but a bullet stops their career. Their swordsmanship — neglecting guards — concerns itself only with cuts and, careless of what injury they may receive, they devote themselves to the destruction of their opponents. In the selection of positions they exhibit considerable military skill, and as skirmishers their use of cover and preservation of order entitle them to much praise. It is mournful to be compelled to close the catalogue of their virtues thus early, but the closest scrutiny of the facts which have been placed before me has resulted in no further discovery in this direction. From year to year their life is one of feud and strife. They plough with a sword at their sides. Every field has its protecting tower, to which the agriculturist can hurry at the approach of a stranger. Successful murder — whether by open force or treachery — is the surest road to distinction among them. A recent writer has ascribed to these people those high family virtues which simple races so often possess. The consideration of one pregnant fact compels me reluctantly to abandon even this hope. Their principal article of commerce is their women — wives and daughters — who are exchanged for rifles. This degradation of mind is unrelieved by a single elevated sentiment. Their religion is the most miserable fanaticism, in which cruelty, credulity and immorality are equally represented. Their holy men — the Mullahs — prize as their chief privilege a sort of 'droit de seigneur'. It is impossible to imagine a lower type of beings or a more dreadful state of barbarism.

I am aware of the powerful influence of climate upon character. But the hill men cannot even plead the excuse of a cold and barren land for their barbarism. The valleys they inhabit are fertile and often beautiful. Once the spots where their squalid huts now stand were occupied by thriving cities, and the stone 'sangars' from which they defy their foes are built on the terraces which nourished the crops of a long forgotten civilisation. Everywhere are the relics of the old Buddhists on whom these fierce tribes, thrown out of that birthplace of nations, Central Asia, descended. Their roads, their temples, and their ruins have alone survived. All else has been destroyed in that darkness which surrounds those races whose type is hardly on the fringe of humanity. But it may be urged, 'However degraded and barbarous these people may be, they have a right to live unmolested on the soil that their fathers conquered'. 'They have attacked your posts,' says the Little Englander, carefully disassociating himself from anything British, 'but why did you ever put your posts there?' To answer this question it is necessary to consider the whole matter from a wider point of view than the Swat Valley affords.

Starting with the assumption that our Empire in India is worth holding, and admitting the possibility that others besides ourselves might wish to possess it, it obviously becomes our duty to adopt measures for its safety. It is a question of a line of defence. The Indus is now recognised by all strategists as being useless for this purpose. The most natural way of preventing an enemy from entering a house is to hold the door and windows; and the general consensus of opinion is that to secure India it is necessary to hold the passes of the mountains. With this view small military posts have been built along the frontier. The tribes whose territories adjoin have not been interfered with. Their independence has been respected, and their degradation undisturbed. More than this, the influence of the flag that flies from the fort on the hill has stimulated the trade of the valley, and increased the wealth of its inhabitants. Were the latter amenable to logical reasoning, the improvement in their condition and the strength of their adversaries would have convinced them of the folly of an outbreak. But in the land of fanatics common sense does not exist.

Winston S Churchill
Young Winston's Wars, *edited by Frederick Woods*

BACKGROUND

Until the second half of the 19th century, Munnar was part of an inhospitable and inaccessible area of thickly forested mountains. Its sole inhabitants were a tribal community called the Mudhuvans, expert hunters and gatherers, who practised slash-and-burn cultivation. They still retain their customs although the pressures of modern life are eroding them. Officially Munnar belonged to the Poonjar chiefs, the rajas of the state of Travancore, which together with Malabar and Cochin forms the present-day state of Kerala. The first European to venture into the area appears to have been the Duke of Wellington when, as Colonel Arthur Wellesly, he marched across the ghats to fight Tipu Sultan, the ruler of Mysore, in 1790. With Tipu's defeat, though not at the hands of Wellington's column, British influence in Kerala became supreme. Malabar was annexed from Mysore and the rajas of Travancore and Cochin were subject to British interference.

The year 1887 marked the beginning of the opening up of the High Range. John Daniel Munro of Pimmede, an officer of Travancore state and superintendent of the Cardamom Hills leased the hill tract from the government. Munro explored the area by following elephant paths and began to bring pioneer planters, mainly Scots, to join him in clearing the jungle. Life for pioneers was hard. In the 1880s, C Donovan camped on what is now Munnar's KDH Club.

> He had to dig a deep trench around it [the camp] to keep off the elephants. One night he awoke to find a young tusker on his side of the trench ... the frightened beast trampled everything down ... Mr Donovan and his Indian servant escaped only by jumping the trench, but the fright so affected the servant that he had to be taken to a lunatic asylum in Madras.

In the 1890s, the Finlay Muir company moved into the hills and persuaded some of the proprietary planters to work for them. The company came to control almost all the estates in the area and its name is preserved in the Indian company, Tata Finlay Ltd, which now owns them. The company's Kanan Devan tea is the most popular in south India.

Finlay Muir's arrival did not make life any easier on the plantations. The hills were still inaccessible, except from the Tamil Nadu side and so Tamil labourers were brought up to man the estates. Their descendants still work there, but in more comfortable conditions than those of the 19th century when the problem of 'coolies bolting' was common and dealt with severely. Life for the assistant managers could also be harsh as they were given long stints of duty under the supervision of the managers, who could be very strict. One young assistant who didn't ride was obliged, on his first *chakkar* of the estates, to maintain a trot on foot behind his mounted manager. Every manager rode his estate, and horses were considered more expensive than wives. Even in 1971, a planter was allowed Rs300 a month for his horse and Rs150 a month dearness allowance upon marriage.

Planters experimented with rubber and chichona (for quinine) before settling for tea which was transported by ropeway from Top Station outside Munnar to Bottom Station where it was packed in Imperial Chests shipped out from Britain and despatched to Tuticorin harbour. In 1908 a light railway was opened to take the tea from Munnar to Top Station, but it was destroyed by floods in 1924.

In 1931, the ghat road from the Cochin side of Munnar was finally opened and Top Station was no longer needed to transport tea. The horse was replaced by the Indian-made Enfield motorcycles which are now used to tour the estates. Another sign of changing times is the disappearance of the Scots planter. There is only one left, Len Latham of Surianelle Estate who has spent nearly 30 years on the plantations of Harrisons Malayalam. He joined the company by accident after being demobbed from National Service and became a manager in only five years, compared with the 15 it would take today. Latham speaks fluent Malayalam (the language of Kerala) and Tamil; when he returns to Scotland no compatriot will replace him.

GETTING THERE AND AROUND

There are roads to Munnar from Cochin, 224 kilometres (139 miles) to the west, and Thekaddy, 117 kilometres (73 miles) away. Since Munnar is not a major holiday centre you could travel Cochin–Munnar–Thekkady, a journey through extensive tea and cardamom plantations, ending at the gateway of the Periyar National Park.

Up-to-date bus timetables are on sale at the Cochin bus station but otherwise there is generally someone there earning an income by guiding tourists to the right bus. The four and a half-hour journey takes you through typical Kerala countryside — paddy fields, palm groves, banana plantations and rows of low, tiled houses. Hundreds of smartly turned-out children make their way to school, proof of the 70 percent literacy rate here. At Kothamangalam there is a brief halt where vendors try to sell you cashew nuts and lottery tickets. Two hours out of Cochin the ghats suddenly rise out of the plains, with rounded, elephant-grey summits. The road passes through luxuriant forest hung with creepers and then through a more cultivated area where black pepper vines entwine areca (betel nut) palms. You can also see coffee, cardamom and some small rubber plantations. Crosses and toddy shops mark the roadside which is overrun with the orange and pink flowers of lantana. When you see the steep slopes of the tea gardens you know you are at the threshold of Munnar.

At least one direct bus runs from Munnar to Kumily, four kilometres (two and a half miles) from Thekkady, every day. A taxi is more convenient. The narrow winding road runs entirely through the hills and mainly in the shade of the tree cover required by the long, point-leaved cardamom plants which carpet the damp ground on the forest floor. These are the Cardamom Hills and the pods are produced on sprays at the base of the plant from delicate pink and white flowers. Kerala produces 70 percent of the country's cardamom and most of that is from Idukki district in which Munnar and Thekaddy are found.

There is also a mountain road which links Munnar with Kodaikanal only 92 kilometres (57 miles) to the east. This road is extremely beautiful and lonely. Generally it is jeepable but before embarking on the journey check with locals to make sure it is passable.

There are a few buses on local routes and any number of taxis and jeeps for hire in the main bazaar. Rates are more or less fixed by the kilometre and some taxis are much more roadworthy than others. English is little understood.

For details of where to stay, see page 284.

SIGHTS

Recreational life for the planters centres on the **High Range Club** which preserves its original traditions with pride. The Men's Bar is decorated with hunting trophies including huge bison heads and elephant tusks. On the wall are the hats of planters who chalked up a continuous 30-year membership. The modern generation are less addicted to sports and club life than their predecessors. As a result, the members were forced to wind up the High Range Rugby Football Club. On 12 August 1972, a grand wake was held in its memory, 'a modicum of spiritual refreshment' being supplied 'to enable members to assuage their grief'. The nine-hole golf course is still used and the rivers around are well stocked with rainbow trout. If you have a tackle and want to see if you can catch some, contact the Chairman or Honorary Secretary of the High Range Angling Association, c/o the HR Club. Other clubs in the town are the **KDH Club** — formerly the Indian Club — which is much less formal.

On a hill above the main road near the KDH Club is the old **Protestant church** built in 1911. The hillside cemetery above it was

The Manager's Bungalow on a Tata tea estate, Munnar

Tea estates in the Annamalai Hills surrounding Munnar

established long before the church itself. The first person to be buried there was Mrs Eleanor Knight, who came to Munnar from Sri Lanka in 1894 aged 24. Shortly after their arrival, Eleanor and her husband walked across the hills to admire the view and she said, rather morbidly, 'If I die I should like to be buried here.' Two days later she *was* dead from cholera and her grave was dug exactly on the spot where they had stood together.

The roads through the estates are enormously attractive, with the sun shining on the bright green tea shoots being picked by the women plantation workers, who throw the shoots into the wicker baskets on their backs. There are streams of clear water and the occasional wild elephant can be glimpsed on a far hilltop. A particularly picturesque walk runs from the Munnar dam to the High Range Club. This, like most of the roads in the area, is the private property of the estate. However, as long as you bear this in mind and do not in any way disturb the work of the tea garden, and as long as only a few tourists come to Munnar, no one is likely to object to your presence. Fine views can be had from government roads too; for example, the **Lockhart Gap**, 20 kilometres (12 and a half miles) from town, on the way to Thekkady, and the huge **Mattupetty Reservoir**, 15 kilometres (nine miles) away, next to the Indo-Swiss cattle breeding project.

For hardy wildlife enthusiasts, a big attraction is a wild goat, the Nilgiri tahr. About a third of the world population of the tahr — 750 animals — lives in the rolling grassland and *shola* forest in the folds of the hills in the **Eravikulam National Park**. The park also shelters sambar, gaur or bison, Nilgiri langur and leopard in its 98 square kilometres (38 square miles). Visitors have a reasonable chance of seeing the tahr by driving out towards Rajamallay Tea Estate to the north of Munnar. The road passes close to salt licks on the edge of the park, where the tahr often gather. If you want to trek into the park, the road lies through the Vagavurrai Estate where the government's assistant wildlife officer is based. It's best to contact the Wildlife Office in advance to arrange the trip. The wildlife officer can give you a guide or porter to the bridle path which takes you seven kilometres (four miles) into the park. He can, at his discretion, also arrange for treks to the summit of Anaimudi. At 2,694 metres (8,839 feet), it is the highest peak in southern India. The return journey can be accomplished in one day.

The Periyar Tiger Reserve at Thekkady

Periyar Tiger Reserve functions partly as a sanctuary and partly as a hill station for the plainspeople of both Kerala and Tamil Nadu. In Periyar they find hills and boat trips on the 26-square-kilometre (ten-square-mile) reservoir on the Periyar River in the centre of the park. The sanctuary, founded in 1934 by Shri Chithira Thirunal, maharaja of the former Travancore state, is one of the oldest in India. It was enlarged after Independence and in 1978 declared a reserve under the successful Project Tiger. Most tourists who visit Periyar, however, would be very lucky to see one. The park covers 777 square kilometres (300 square miles) at altitudes of between 900 and 2,000 metres (2,950 to 6,560 feet). Nearly 40 percent of the area is tropical rainforest and much of this is out of bounds to tourists. Around the tourist area in the vicinity of the lake there is moist deciduous forest with grassland on the lake shores. The grass attracts gaur or bison, elephant, wild boar and the largest Indian deer, the sambar, to the shores. Black Nilgiri langurs swing in the trees next to the lake. Birds like darters, cormorants and kingfishers are common. The Brahminy kite is the most frequently sighted bird of prey. In the treetops you can hear, and if you look carefully see, the hill mynah or grackle, a much more attractive bird when out of a cage.

GETTING THERE

The nearby town of Kumily is connected by bus with Munnar, Cochin, 200 kilometres (124 miles) away, Trivandrum, 270 kilometres (168 miles) away, and Madurai, 140 kilometres (87 miles) away. Kumily is only four kilometres (two and a half miles) from the park headquarters at Thekkady. Its main street is lined with spice shops selling locally produced cardamom, pepper and other spices at cheap rates.

The route from Cochin or Trivandrum leads over the High Ranges to the tea plantations around Pirmede at 1,006 metres (3,497 feet), named after a respected Muslim saint called Pir Muhammad who lived in the area. His tomb is at Kuttikanam nearby. Pirmede could develop into a hill station but is at present a small settlement with a Kerala government guesthouse and is generally seen as no more than a place for an overnight halt on the way to Thekkady.

The road from Madurai to Kumily runs for its last part through a valley green with paddy fields and between two great arms of mountains.

Once at Kumily there's no shortage of three-wheeler scooter-rickshaws to take you to Thekkady.

There are several places to stay here, see page 284.

Visiting the Park

The 'season' is November to June and weekends can be crowded. If you want the park to yourself then the tail end of the monsoon (September–October) is the best time to visit. Motor launches regularly leave the boat landing between 7 am and 2 pm for two hour trips round the lake. There is a small charge per head but if you would like to admire the scenery and watch the wildlife at your own pace and in peace and quiet you can also hire special boats from the Aranya Niwas Hotel. In season, book in advance. Every morning there are three-hour treks into the jungle from the boat landing and there are short elephant rides — for the thrill of sitting on an elephant rather than seeing wildlife. With the permission of the wildlife preservation officer you can hire a jeep and drive to the **Mangala Devi Temple**, which lies within the park, away from the lake.

Ponmudi

Ponmudi is another would-be hill station which certainly qualifies for its views of the ghats in southern Kerala. It is around 1,000 metres (3,281 feet) above sea level and only 65 kilometres (40 miles) from Trivandrum. A trip to Ponmudi gives you a chance to see the hills, without losing much time from a beach-orientated holiday. Kerala Tourism arranges day tours of Ponmudi on weekends and holidays, but if you don't enjoy a conducted tour, there are frequent buses from Trivandrum and you can stay overnight in Ponmudi at a cottage in the Ponmudi Tourist Complex (Reservation Authority: The Manager, tel. 89230).

Practical Information

Hotels

Hotel information for places not listed here appears in the description of the area in the main text. What follows is only a selection of what is available. Most hill stations have a relatively short season during which it is often difficult to find decent accommodation on arrival. It is advisable to book in advance. The 'season' for most stations are the hot months of mid-April through to mid-July which coincide with most local school holidays, the Dussehra holiday period in October and in a few places, Christmas and New Year. However, during the off-season discounts, often substantial, are available everywhere.

Unfortunately, almost all hotels feel it is necessary to have satellite TV available so travellers don't miss the next episode of their favourite soap-opera, the latest news from the BBC or the current test match.

JAMMU

Asia Jammu-Tawi, Nehru Market (tel. 435757) is the town's better hotel.

Hotel Jammu Ashok, opp Amar Mahal (tel. 847621).

Hotel Green Top, Patni Top (tel. 7519). A modern hotel with facilities including separate lawns for each ground floor room and separate family huts.

Hotel K C Residency, Residency Road (tel. 542773).

Hotel Jammu Premier Pvt. Ltd., Residency Road (tel. 543436).

Hari Niwas Palace Hotel, Jammu Tawi (tel. 543303).

SRINAGAR

Since 1990 many hotels have closed or have been requisitioned by the government. However, some continue to operate like:

The **Hotel Centaur Lake View** at Chashma Shahi, which opened in the early eighties, and is the one hotel that has remained open throughout the troubles. It is situated next to the Sher-i-Kashmir Conference Centre on the lake shore.

In addition there are many other hotels along the Boulevard bordering the lake, eg **Hotel Shahansha** and **Hotel Palace**. Some others with budget accommodation are nearer to Dalgate.

Traditionally, the place to stay in Kashmir is on one of Dal or Nagin Lakes's houseboats. These are divided into five categories — deluxe , A, B, C and D — all in theory available at fixed prices however, prices can be negotiated. The deluxe houseboats are, if anything, more luxurious than a hotel of similar standard. Most houseboats are family run and bookings can be made through the TRC. Some of the well established groups are the **Meena Bazar group of Houseboats, M S Baktoo Group of Houseboats**, Sadrafal, University Road and **Sabnam Group** on Dal Lake.

For current information it is advisable to contact **The Tourist Reception Centre (TRC)**, c/o Director General of Tourism (tel. 472779) which continues to be the best source of information. The Centre provides lists of hotels and houseboats and will help make bookings. It also has an attached hotel block.

Pahalgam

In addition to the insulated tourist huts run by J&K Tourism, there are the **Hotel Highland** and **Hotel Heaven**.

Gulmarg

Hill Top is a comparatively new hotel built just before the troubles while **Hotel Gulmarg** has an exceptionally good location.

Leh, Ladakh

Hotels are graded from A to D though none is luxurious.
Tsemo La, Karzoo (tel. 52726) has clean rooms and a garden.

Shamhala, Skara (tel. 52067). Previously an Oberoi managed property with large rooms.

At Stok, 15 kilometres (ten miles) south of Leh is the luxurious **Ladakh Sarai** (tel. 52777) where accommodation consists of yurts (Mongolian tents) set in a large orchard looking north across the Indus. Bookings in New Delhi through **Mountain Travel India** (tel. 7525357, 7525032; fax 011-7777483).

The **Yak Trail** (tel. 52118).

DALHOUSIE

Aroma-n-Claire, Court Road, The Mall (tel. 2199) is centrally located with some reasonable rooms.

Mountview, Near Bus Stand (tel. 2120). Well located and pleasantly run.

Hotel Geetanjali (tel. 21155). Run by Himachal Tourism.

Silverton, Above Circuit House, Moti Tibba. One of a few family homes with guest accommodation, personal service and charm. Set in over an acre of pine and oak wood.

Fair View Hotel, Malviya Road (tel. 2206).

Nahar's Hotel (tel. 2175).

CHAMBA

The best hotel is still the Himachal Tourism's **Hotel Iravati** (tel. 2671). Himachal Tourism also manages the cheaper **Hotel Champak** (tel. 2774). The **Akhand Chandi**, Dogra Bazaar (tel. 2371) is next to the palace of the same name.

At Khajjiar, Himachal Tourism's **Hotel Devdar** (tel. 8233) has an attractive setting and basic facilities.

DHARAMSALA

Himachal Tourism's **Hotel Dhauladhar**, Kotwali Bazaar (tel. 24926) is the better hotel in lower town while **Hotel Bhagsu** (tel. 23191) with a large garden and good views is Mcleodgunj's best property. Himachal Tourism has a third hotel at **Kashmir House** (tel. 3101).

Hotel Tibet behind the Mcleodgunj Bus Stand is one of the Dalai Lama's concerns and has an excellent restaurant specialising in Chinese and Tibetan food.

Other, cheaper hotels in Mcleodgunj include the **Koko Nor** and **Green's Guest House**. There is also paying guest accommodation more suited for those staying longer periods.

Two hours east of Dharamsala (75 minutes from Kangra) is the delightful **Taragarh Palace Hotel** (tel. Baijnath 3034). Set in a 15 acre forested estate surrounded by tea gardens the hotel has 12 double rooms. Book through Mountain Travel India, New Delhi (tel. 7525357, 7525032; fax 7777483).

MANDI

Himachal Tourism's **Hotel Mandav** (tel. 22123) has reasonable facilities. The **Raj Mahal** is converted from a former royal residence but does not live up to its name.

KULLU

Silvermoon, Dhalpur (tel. 2488) and **Hotel Sarvari** (tel. 2471) are both run by Himachal Tourism and are near the maidan at the southern end of town.

The **Apple Valley Resort**, Mohal (tel. 66266) is a few miles out of town.

Span Resorts, on the road to Manali (tel. Katrain 83138) is expensive and has all facilities with cottages next to the river. It also has an extremely well stocked bar. Himachal Tourism also has the small **Hotel Apple Blossom** at Katrain (tel. 83136).

MANALI

Every year more hotels are opened in and around Manali. Many are small, family managed properties while others are unattractive and poorly designed. However, the charm of the upper Kullu Valley makes even these bearable.

Log Huts (tel. 52407) beside the river are 12 fully equipped cottages.

Ashok Traveller's Lodge, Naggar Road (tel. 52331) is a spartan building.

Hotel Ambassador Resort, Chadiyari (tel. 52235; fax 01901–52173) is a new hotel north of the bazaar. Many rooms are centrally heated in winter.

John Bannon's Hotel, Manali Orchards (tel. 52335). One of the traditional bed and all board family hotels run by the descendants of Manali's first apple grower.

Mayflower Guest House (tel. 52104). The old building has splendid wooden flours and panelling. Still run by Mr Negi and his family.

Banon Resort, New Hope Orchards (tel. 52490; fax 01902–52378). Another family run hotel.

Manali Resorts (tel. 52274, 53174). One of Manali's newer and more expensive hotels.

Hotel Picadilly (tel. 52156). As with many of the newer hotels this one tries to be more upmarket than it is but it is centrally located and has a reasonable restaurant.

Himachal Tourism properties include the **Hotel Rohtang Manaslu** (tel. 52332), the **Hotel Beas** and the rather basic **Tourist Lodge**.

At Naggar, 18 kilometres (11 miles) south of Manali, Himachal Tourism manages the **Hotel Castle** (tel. 84816). Can be booked through HPTDC Manali office (tel. 52325).

LAHAUL & SPITI

Since Spiti opened to foreign tourists in 1992 small hotels have been opened in Kaza, Tabo and other villages in the area. Most are very simple and many visitors prefer to camp. There is a HPTDC **Tourist Bungalow** at Keylong.

SHIMLA

There are any number of hotels, suiting all pockets, in Shimla. Many advertise themselves as 'honeymoon' accommodation. The Himachal Tourism Office on the Mall (tel. 252561, 258302) will help find accommodation to suit your taste.

Chapslee, Lakar Bazaar (tel. 73242). Many people believe it is worth going to Shimla simply to stay at this hotel which is one of the oldest surviving houses in the town. It was originally called Secretary's Lodge and was used in the 1830s as offices for the viceroy's staff. The 'Simlah Manifesto' declaring war on Afghanistan in 1838 was issued here. General Peter Innes changed its name to Chapslee and the house eventually became the property and summer residence of the maharaja of Kapurthala, whose family now run it as a hotel. The interiors are more or less unchanged, with ancient weapons and hunting trophies on the walls. Rooms are offered with food, which is of a high standard.

Woodville Palace, Raj Bhavan Road (tel. 72763). Located in Chhota (or small) Shimla this hotel was the former palace of the Raja of Jubbal and has plenty of period charm.

Oberoi Clarkes, The Mall (tel. 212991; fax 0177–211321). Old fashioned hotel with good food and a friendly atmosphere.

The Cecil Shimla, The Mall (tel. 201725; fax 0177–211024).

Asia The Dawn, Tara Devi (tel. 231162; fax 0177-231007). A modern and well managed hotel.

Holiday Home, Cart Road (tel. 72375). Three huge neon H's on its roof make this hotel one of the station's landmarks. It is reasonably priced and has the pleasant mannered service which characterises Himachal Tourism. Another HPTDC property is the **Hotel Meghdoot** (tel. 78302). Sadly, Himachal Tourism's famous Wildflower Hall, once the residence of Lord Kitchener when he was commander-in-chief of the Indian Army, was destroyed by fire in early 1993. There are plans to rebuild it.

There are numerous mid range properties including the **Honeymoon Inn**, the Mall (tel. 4967), **Himland Hotel**, Circular Road (tel. 3595; fax 0177–213045) and a **YMCA** (tel. 3341).

Kufri Holiday Resort, Kufri (tel. 280300). Sixteen kilometres (ten miles) from Shimla this is a local ski resort in winter. Himachal Tourism also manages the **Hotel Peach Blossom** (tel. 8205) at Fagu, 22 kilometres (14 miles) from Shimla, **Hotel Hatu** (tel. 8430) at Narkanda, 64 kilometres (40 miles) from Shimla and the **Hotel Golf Glade** (tel. 287739) at Naldehra, 26 kilometres (16 miles) from Shimla.

Chail

The **Chail Palace Hotel** (tel. 48143) is run by Himachal Tourism. The larger rooms in the main building have wide fireplaces and bathrooms fit for a king. The little remaining royal furniture adds elegance to the interiors. The kitchens, may they never be modernised, still have the original cooking ranges and tables worn down by the knives of generations of cooks. Apart from the main building, there are cottages in the grounds and the nearby **Himneel Hotel**.

Kasauli

The **Alasia**, The Mall (tel. 72008) is the original hotel in this, the least spoilt of hill stations. Himachal Tourism manages **Hotel Ros-Common**, Lower Mall (tel. 72005) and a **Tourist Bungalow**.

Dehra Dun

Most of Dehra Dun's better hotels are on the Rajpur Road heading north from the town towards Mussoorie.

Hotel Madhuban (tel. 654094). The best of a variety of hotels that has recently upgraded itself with extensive renovations.

Other mid-range properties on Rajpur Road include **Hotel Meedo's Grand** (tel. 657088), **Ajanta Continental** (tel. 659595) and **Hotel Himshri** (tel. 652583).

MUSSOORIE

Savoy Hotel, at the Library end or the Mall (tel. 632510, 632601–3). With large grounds that includes three tennis courts. It is at its best in the snowy winter months, when there are log fires in the rooms.

Fortune Dunsvirk Court, Baroda Estate (tel. 631043). Slightly quieter than most hotels, two kilometres from Library Chowk.

Hakman's Grand Hotel, The Mall (tel. 632559). A historic, but no longer grand, hotel that is still lively during the season when it offers a band.

Carlton Palisance, LBS Road (tel. 632800).

Hotel Shiva Continental, The Mall (tel. 632174). One of the town's newer mid-range hotels.

Hotel Solitaire Plaza, Picture Palace-Kincraig Road (tel. 632164).

RISHIKESH

Hotel Natraj, Dehra Dun Road (tel. 31099). One of the newer hotels just outside the town.

Hotel Ganga Kinare (tel. 30566).

Hotel Indralok, Railway Road (tel. 30555) and **Hotel Mandakini International**, Haridwar Road (tel. 30781) are both cheaper hotels.

The **Rishilok Complex**, Badrinath Road, Muni-ki-Reti has relatively clean but spartan budget accommodation.

NAINITAL

Most of the better hotels are at the northern end of the lake, known as Mallital.

Hotel Arif Castles, Jahargirabad House, Mallital (tel. 35801–3).

Holiday Inn, Grasmere Estate (tel. 35531).

Vikram Vintage Inn, Mallital (tel. 36177, 36179).

Shervani Hilltop Inn, Mallital (tel. 3128). Although modern the hotel is designed in old-fashioned bungalow style.

The above are all new properties catering to the larger domestic tourist business during the school holidays. All have cable TV, functioning bathrooms, restaurants and room service.

Among the older hotels are the **Swiss Hotel**, Mallital (tel. 3013). A traditional family-run hotel but no longer Nainital's best. It is in a relatively quiet location below Cheena Peak and has a garden. It offers wood fires in the rooms during winter and has ample hot, running water at fixed times. The owners go out of their way to make guests feel like one of the family.

Grand Hotel, The Mall, Mallital. A fairly good hotel overlooking the lake.

Cheaper accommodation is provided by UP Tourism at their Tourist Reception Centre (tel. 35337).

BHIMTAL

Spring Meadows Hotel & Health Resort, Mehra Gaon. Can be booked in Delhi through Orphic Resorts (tel. 6873447, 6873862).

There is a small Tourist Reception Centre (tel. 25) with limited budget accommodation.

RANIKHET

Hotel Moon, Sadar Bazaar (tel. 2258, 2382). Centrally located in the bazaar but it can be noisy because of it. Its reasonably priced restaurant is the best in town.

West View Hotel, Upper Mall (tel. 2261). Has a fine location on a pine-forested hillside, standard accommodation in large rooms.

Kumaon Mandal Vikas Nigam **Tourist Cottages**, near West View Hotel (tel. 2297). Simple accommodation and food. The reception desk will help arrange local excursions and long-distance taxi and bus bookings.

ALMORA

Golu Deva Tourist Rest House (tel. 2250). Located at the quiet end of the Mall, it has fine views overlooking the Kosi Valley. The rooms are spartan.

Binsar Valley Resort, Basoli Village, Almora. For bookings, contact the Delhi office at 1592, Sector C, Pocket I, Vasant Kunj (tel. 6896520; fax 011–6136099; e-mail: manipur@nda.vsnl.net.in, URL or website: www.binsarvalley.com).

D ARJEELING
Windamere Hotel, Observatory Hill (tel. 55041, 55042; fax 0354-55043). An old-fashioned three-star hotel with terraces and lots of character is still about the best in town.

Hotel Sinclairs, Gandhi Road (tel. 3431).

New Elgin Hotel, H D Lama Road (tel. 3314, 2882). Family run hotel with friendly atmosrphere.

Darjeeling Club, Nehru Road. Previously the Planters Club. Welcomes temporary members into its old 'Raj' surroundings. Central Hotel, Robertson Road (tel. 2033, 2745).

Bellevue Hotel, Nehru Road (tel. 2120). Centrally located with superb views of Kanchenjunga.

Among the cheaper hotels are the **Tourist Lodge**, The Mall (tel. 2611) with good views and the **Lewis Jubilee Complex**, Dr S K Pal Road (tel. 2127). The Tiger Hill **Tourist Lodge** (tel. 2813) is out of town but conveniently located for watching the snows at sunrise and sunset.

K ALIMPONG
Silver Oaks, Main Road (tel. 296). Centrally located, family run and the best hotel in town.

Kalimpong Park Hotel, Ringking Pong Road (tel. 304).

Himalayan Hotel (tel. 248). An old hotel with friendly service.

Budget hotels include the Tourist Bungalows, the **Tashiding Tourist Lodge** (tel. 654), the **Singamari Tourist Lodge**, Durpin Hill (tel. 384).

G ANGTOK
Tashi Delek, Mahatma Gandhi Road (tel. 22991, fax 03592-22362). One of the towns best hotels.

Nor Khill, Paljor Stadium Road (tel. 23186). Another good hotel in an old building with character·

Hotel Green, Mahatma Gandhi Road (tel. 22554), **Hotel Mayur**, Paljor Stadium Road (tel. 22752, 22825), **Hotel Tibet**, Paljor Stadium Road (tel. 22523, 23468) and **Hotel Orchid**, National Highway (tel. 22381) are among the budget hotels.

SHILLONG

Hotel Polo Towers, Oakland Road, Polo Grounds (tel. 222341).
Hotel Pinewood Ashok, European Ward (tel. 223116). Old bungalows in extensive grounds make this the best hotel.
Hotel Alpine-Continental, Thana-Quinton Road (tel. 225361).
The **Shillong Club**, Mahatma Gandhi Road (tel. 225497). Next to Ward Lake, it has good rooms and cottages for temporary members.
Other hotels include **The Broadway**, G S Road (tel. 226996), the Meghalaya State Tourism **Hotel Orchid**, Polo Road (tel. 224993) and **Hotel Magnum**, Police Bazaar (tel. 227797).

PACHMARI

Accommodation is still limited in Pachmari. Madhya Pradesh Tourism maintains and manages several bungalows and the best hotel.
Satpura Retreat, Mahadeo Road (tel. 52097). This is well located and the best hotel.
Panchvati Cottages, near Tehsil (tel. 52096), **Holiday Homes** (tel. 52099)) and **Amalatas** (tel. 52098) are also run by MP Tourism.
The PWD hires out suites at the Old Hotel Block and very cheap rooms at the New Hotel Block. Cottages can also he hired from the Nandan Van (run by the Special Area Development Authority).

MOUNT ABU

Hilltone (tel. 3112; fax 02974–3115). An expensive hotel with a good restaurant.
Palace Hotel, Dilwara Road (tel. 3121). Converted summer residence of the maharaja of Bikaner, three kilometres from the town but with large garden and lake.
Connaught House, Rajendra Marg (tel. 3360). Was previously the maharaja of Jodhpur's summer residence.
Mount Hotel, Dilwara Road (tel. 3150). An inexpensive Parsi run hotel.
Hotel Hillock (tel. 3277). Centrally located and modern.
The Rajasthan Tourism **Shikkar Tourist Bungalow** (tel. 3129, 3169). Basic rooms and tourist information office.

MATHERAN

Most hotels are tree-shaded, old-fashioned tin or slate-roofed bungalows. There is something to suit most pockets but during the season many hotels include meals in their tariff.

Rugby Hotel, Vithalrao Kotwal Road (tel. 30291). The best of the old British hotels. The Parsi owner now caters to a mainly Hindu clientele.

The Byke, next to Municipal Office (tel. 30365; fax 02148-30316).

Brightlands Resorts, Maulana Azad Road (tel. 30244). This well-run bungalow-style hotel has seven acres of grounds, its own dairy, a tennis court and stables. Non-vegetarian.

Lords Central (tel. 30228, fax 02148-30595). The most famous non-vegetarian establishment. Run by the likable proprieter Jamshed S Lord.

Royal Hotel, Kasturba Road (tel. 30247).

Usha Ascot, M G Road (tel. 30213).

Hotel Alexander, Madhavji Road (tel. 30251).

Hotel Regal, Kasturba Road (tel. 30243).

Many hotels close during the monsoon, the exception being Brightlands.

LONAVALA, KHANDALA AND KARLA

All three are close together, so you can stay anywhere in the vicinity and still reach the nearby caves with ease. Most of the hotels cater for weekend business from Mumbai and are generally quieter during mid-week.

Fariyas Holiday Resort, Frichely Hill (tel. 73852). A five-star hotel complete with five-star facilities and prices.

Biji's Hill Retreat, New Tungarli Road (tel. 73025). One of many three- and four-star properties with aspirations to be better.

Biryas Hill Resort, Hill Top Colony (tel. 2631).

Hotel Vallerina, Mumbai-Pune Highway (tel. 74108).

The Dukes Retreat, Mumbai-Pune Highway (tel. 73826).

PUNE

A fast growing city with many good hotels and guest houses.

Hotel Blue Diamond, Koregaon Park (tel. 625555; fax 0212-627755). A five-star business hotel with a formal atmosphere.

Hotel Aurora Towers, Moledina Road (tel. 631826).

Among the cheaper hotels is the well located **Hotel Amir**, Connaught Road (tel. 621840).

PANCHGANI

There are hotels to suit all budgets at Panchgani — both 'veg' and 'non-veg'. Also check for out-of-season rates.

Hotel Five Hills. A non-vegetarian hotel with plenty of rooms.

Hotel Aman. A poor imitation of a five-star hotel but with pleasant staff.

Cheaper and more appealing are the smaller, family-run hotels, converted from bungalows.

Il-Palazzo Hotel. Away from the small bazaar, this old-fashioned bungalow must have looked like a palace to the villagers of Panchgani when it was constructed. Now it is run by a Parsi couple who take great pains to make you feel at home.

Lord Panchgani, Mahabaleshwar Road (tel. 40079).

MAHABALESHWAR

There are over 100 hotels spread out over Mahabaleshwar's extensive plateau. Many operate a strict bed-and-board basis in the peak season. Out of season prices are reduced by as much as half. Many of the smaller family-run hotels have now been joined by larger and fancier properties with better facilities but usually without any character.

Valley View Resort (tel. 60066, fax 02168-60070). Has a health club and indoor swimming pool.

Hotel Anarkali, Kasam Sajan Road (tel. 60336). Open throughout the year. Clean and modern.

Brightlands Holiday Village, Kate's Point Road, Nakinda Village (tel. 60700, fax 02168, 60707). Four kilometres from the main town.

Belmont Park Hill Resort, Satara Road (tel. 60414).

Hotel Pratap Heritage, Valley View Road (tel. 60071).

The Maharashtra Tourist Development Corporation (MTDC) has an excellent location at the site of the Old Government House. There are many cottages on hire but, as with most MTDC operations, more could he made of them.

AMBOLI

One of the few places to stay is the Maharashtra Tourism **Holiday Resort** which has adequate accommodation and helpful staff. There is also a Forest Resthouse and a PWD Bungalow.

MADIKERI (MERCARA)

East End Hotel. A small hotel. The food is very good especially on a Friday when many of the planters of the district gather after having done their official work with the government and their weekly shopping. Bells ring from private rooms and bearers scuttle off with pegs of gin and whiskey.

Hotel Mayura Valley View, Raja's Seat (tel. 26387). Some of rooms have fine views.

Hotel Cauvery (tel. 26292). A modern building in the centre of town. It offers reasonable accommodation.

OOTACAMUND

There are many hotels in the town and during the season the best should be booked in advance, especially when the races are on.

Savoy Hotel, Sylks Road (tel. 44147; fax 0423–43318). One of the best, it is managed by the Taj Group and can be booked through any other Taj hotel. It is a well-maintained, bungalow-style hotel with a delightful garden, pannelled dining room and billiard room. The prices of the rooms are lower than Taj hotels in the big cities but there is a catch — from April to June you have to take American plan which pushes prices up steeply.

Fernhill Palace (tel. 43910; fax 0423–43318). Recently taken over by the Taj Group, this was once the summer residence of the maharaja of Mysore. Its compound consists of 72 acres of land including an Italian garden.

Merit Inn Southern Star, Hawelok Road (tel. 43601–6). Also has American Plan during the April–June season. A concrete hotel in the hills with a marble interior.

Lake View Hotel, West Lake Road (tel. 43904). All simply furnished double cottages which offer more space than the average hotel room.

Hotel Tamil Nadu, Charring Cross (tel. 44370). The state government's hotel is a building of curious design in green concrete and has a well kept garden. The upper range of rooms and cottages are surpisingly smart for a government establishment and much in demand during the season. Has a tourist information office.

Hotel Dasaprakash (tel. 42434). One of the best Indian-style hotels. Founded in 1948, it overlooks the racecourse. Rooms come in three classes and the top class is fairly attractive though not cheap in season.

As Ooty was the summer capital of the Madras government, it also attracted princely patronage. The rulers of Mysore, Jodhpur and Hyderabad were some of the most distinguished princely visitors, each of whom built a palace.

Tamizhagam. Previously called Arranmore Palace, it belonged to the Maharaja of Jodhpur. Situated away from the town centre, near the village of Fingerpost, it requires some determination to stay here. The man at the gate is instructed not to let in individual tourists, so you have to phone reception to check if there are rooms and warn them of your arrival or be prepared to insist on speaking to the manager over the intercom at the gate. Charges are reasonable.

Palace Hotel. A company has taken over the Nizam of Hyderabad's residence, which was known as 'Cedars', and is converting it into a luxury hotel.

Coonoor

With Ooty becoming over developed, Coonoor has become a popular destination in its own right. Unlike Ooty it does not get cold during the winter and has a pleasant climate throughout the year.

Taj Garden Retreat, Church Road (tel. 20021). Previously called Hampton Manor, this hotel with its pleasant grounds and rooms is now part of the Taj Group.

The Ritz, Orange Grove Road (tel. 20084, 20484).

There are numerous guest houses and budget hotels, including a YMCA, in the town.

YERCAUD

Hotel Shevaroys, Hospital Road (tel. 22288). On the main road above the lake, it is undoubtedly the best hotel. It has an immaculate garden and a restaurant serving south Indian and north Indian versions of continental food.

Hotel Tamil Nadu (tel. 22273). The state government's hotel is located on the Salem-Yercaud Ghat road on the shore of the lake. Its rates are reasonable and Indian and continental food can be served on order. There is also a tourist information counter.

For budget travellers there is a **Youth Hostel** which can be booked through the TNTDC office in Madras (tel. 560294, 584356). **NGGO's Holiday Home** near the bus stand has occasional rooms for non members.

KODAIKANAL

Most of the hotels are in the centre of town, but as the hill station is compact, they are within easy walking distance of the best views of the Palnis. Most offer discounts during the off season (July to mid-October and mid-January to March).

Carlton Hotel, Lake Road (tel. 40056). With 91 rooms and cottages this is the largest and most upmarket of all the hotels in Kodaikanal. It has a health club with sauna, jacuzzi, steam and massage. Indoor games include billiards and roller skating. The food is good and the lunchtime buffet, where you can eat as much as you like, is excellent value.

Sournam Apartments, Fernhill Road (tel. 40731). Has seven apartments plus a neighbouring Youth Hostel.

Sterling Resorts, Gymkhana Road (tel. 41119). 50 cottages standard or deluxe facilities.

Hotel Tamil Nadu, Fernhill Road (tel. 41336). A government-run hotel, a little too far from the town centre to be very popular — a kilometre and a half (one mile) from the bus stand and lake. Rooms are reasonably priced but a bit tatty.

Garden Manor, Lake Road (tel. 40461). A small and inexpensive but attractive hotel with seven rooms on the edge of the lake. Its only drawback is the proximity of the noisy main road which runs across the dam end of the lake.

Hotel **Kodai International**, Lawsghat Road (tel. 40272). Rooms and cottages.

Kodai Resort Hotel, Coakers Walk (tel. 40632). The interiors are much more spacious than most hotel rooms. The friendly management adds to the appeal.

MUNNAR

Government Guest House. A charming bungalow with six rooms located above the town centre. It is run by the Kerala Tourism Development Corporation.

Hotel The Residency (tel. 30247). A modern hotel with adequate facilities but poor service, located in the heart of the town.

Raj Bhawan or **Devicolam Guest House**, Devicolam. Room rates are extremely cheap and food reasonable. Advance booking through a Kerala Tourism office is advised. It is about eight kilometres (five miles) from Munnar.

JN Lodge (tel. 30212) and Muir Cottage in the **KDH Club** (tel. 30252) have a few simple rooms on rent.

PERIYAR TIGER RESERVE, THEKKADY

Outside the park, one kilometre from the entrance, two new properties have recently opened. These will soon be joined by a new Taj Garden Retreat. At present the best place to stay is the imaginatively designed and well run **Spice Village** (tel. 22314). This sensitively designed resort can also be booked through the Casino Hotel in Cochin (tel. 340221; fax 0484-340001).

Three properties of varying standards are managed in the park by the Kerala Tourism Development Corporation through whom all bookings should be made. **Lake Palace Hotel** (tel. 22023). Located on the Edapalayam promitary jutting into the lake, you can watch game from your verandah. It has the most desirable rooms of all the properties in the park and earlier belonged to the maharaja of Travancore.

At Thekkady, just above the jetty within the reserve, is the **Aranya Nivas** (tel. 22023). It has comfortable and clean rooms many of which are airconditioned. The restaurant is mediocre and there is a bar. **Periyar House** (tel. 22026) has reasonable budget accommodation.

There are also a few secluded Forest Department resthouses within the reserve which can be booked by contacting the Wildlife Preservation Officer, Forest Information Office, Thekkady.

Restaurants

Restaurant information for places not listed here appears in the description of the area in the main text. The best place for food is often in the hotels (see pages 269-284).

SRINAGAR

Rice is the staple of the Kashmiri diet, and is eaten with mutton, chicken or fish. Typical vegetarian dishes are *dam alu* (roast potatoes in gravy) and *chaman* (fried paneer in a thick sauce). Meat dishes are the sign of hospitality, and at a *wazwan* or banquet only one vegetable dish is generally served. Meals are washed down with quantities of Kashmiri tea.

Real Kashmiri food is available in Kashmiri homes but **Ahdoos** on Shervani Road and **Wazwan** at the Tourist Reception Centre are popular places.

LEH

Ladakh's cuisine revolves around Tibetan *momos* (steamed dumplings) and *tumpka* (chow soup) washed down with butter tea. The local brew is the barley based beer — *chang*. Many of the local restaurants serve noodle based meals.

DALHOUSIE

There are no restaurants of note in Dalhousie, but you are likely to get nourishing fresh food in your hotel, where it is cooked to order.

There is **Kwality** at Gandhi Chowk, **Milan** which is recommended for its large portions, **Metro** and **Moti Mahal** in Subhash Chowk, offering Indian, continental and some Chinese food. For more authentic fare there is a small Tibetan restaurant, The **Snow Lion**, behind the Dalhousie cinema on the footpath which leads from the bus stand to the Mall.

DHARAMSALA

The Tibetan food in Mcleodganj is cheap and extremely good. It is both vegetarian and non vegetarian. Be sure not to miss breakfast at the **Sangey Passang** by the bus stand which serves fresh round Tibetan bread with butter, homemade cottage cheese or jam, as well as fresh-set yoghurt in glasses. There are also many restaurants serving reasonable continental food but while here it is best to try the range of Tibetan cuisine.

DEHRA DUN

Kwality's on Rajpur Road is a reasonable restaurant and popular with generations of children on weekend leave from nearby schools.

RISHIKESH

The **Chotiwala** restaurant at the Swargashram is open from 9am to 9pm and serves fairly good food.

LANDSDOWNE

There are *several dhabas*, small restaurants, in the Market Road area. The best are the **Punjab** and **Anupam** restaurants.

DARJEELING

As with many hill stations the local cuisine has a strong Tibetan and Chinese influence. Among the many reasonable restaurants are **Valentino**, Rockville Road, **Glenary's** on Nehru Road and **Druk** on Goenka Road. **Keventer's**, also on Nehru Road, is popular for breakfast and tea.

KODAIKANAL

Next to the church is the **Hill Top** restaurant, one of many cheap and mediocre eating places in the station. There are foods for all tastes. The small, family-run **Silver Inn** on Hospital road, has continental food. Nearby is the Tibetan Restaurant, the Kodai **Milk Bar** and **Kwality Ice Creams** near the Kodai International School. Opposite the bus stand is the **Pandyan Mess**, while for north Indians there is the **Apna Punjab** restaurant.

None can compare for solid wholesome food with the **Manna Bakery** and **Restaurant** at Keith Lodge next to the Clifton Hotel on the road to Bear Shola Falls. The proprieter, C Israel Bhoonji, is married to a girl from Sheffield in the north of England, and between them they make excellent wholewheat bread and various home puddings such as apple pie. The Manna restaurant is a mecca for trekkers and Israel can put you in touch with a reliable guide to the paths around Kodaikanal.

Useful Addresses

KASHMIR
Fishing
For information on licenses and equipment dealers contact the Director of Fisheries, Tourist Reception Centre, Srinagar. The Chief Wildlife Warden's office is also here and can give details on visiting Dachigam National Park and the wetlands. The TRC also has camping equipment on hire and booking offices for bus journeys, Indian Railways (from Jammu) and Indian Airlines.

HIMACHAL PRADESH
Trekking Agencies
Chandertal Tours can be contacted c/o Robert Newbury, 20 The Fridays, East Dean, East Bourne, Sussex, England (tel. 01323–422213) and through Himalayan Folkways, c/o Roop Katoch (tel. 01902–53026; fax 01902–52378).

Paddy's Treks and Tours Pvt. Ltd., 12/14 Sarvapriya Vihar, New Delhi - 110 016 (tel. 6510703, 6528386; fax 011–6179951). Manali tel. 52490; fax 01901–52378.

Mountain Travel India, 1/1 Rani Jhansi Road, New Delhi 110055 (tel. 7533483, 7525357; fax 011–7777483). Both Paddy's Treks and Mountain Travel India operate throughout India.

Other operators in Manali include **Himalayan Adventures,** Mayflower Guest House (tel. 52185) and **Trans Himalayan Expeditions** (tel. 52489).

RISHIKESH
River Rafting
Himalayan River Runners, F-5 Hauz Khas Enclave, New Delhi 110016 (tel. 6852602).

SIKKIM
Permits
Foreigner's Division, Ministry of Home Affairs, Government of India, Loknayak Bhavan, Khan Market, New Delhi.

INFORMATION
Sikkim Tourist Office, New Sikkim House, 14 Panchseel Marg, New Delhi 110021 (tel. 3015436).

SHILLONG
Permits
Foreigner's Division, Ministry of Home Affairs, Government of India, Loknayak Bhavan, Khan Market, New Delhi.

INFORMATION
State Tourist Office, Meghalaya House, 9 Aurangzeb Road, New Delhi 110013 (tel. 3014417).

Recommended Reading

Ahluwalia, Major H P S. *Eternal Himalaya* (Interprint, New Delhi, 1982).

Ali, Salim. *The Book of Indian Birds* (Bombay Natural History Society, Bombay, 1977).

Allen, Charles. *Plain Tales from the Raj* (Andre Deutsch and BBC, London, 1975).

Allen, Charles. *Kipling's Kingdom* (Michael Joseph, London Times Books International, New Delhi, 1987).

Baig, Amita and Henderson, William (written, complied and edited by). *Facets of a Hundred Years of Planting — A Centenary of Planting in the Kanan Devan Hills Concession 1878-1978* (Tata-Finlay Ltd).

Baikie, R [formerly Superientending Medical Officer of the Neligherries]. *The Neilgherries: including an account of their Topography, Climate, Soil and Productions* (Calcutta, 1857).

Barr, Pat and Desmond, Ray, *Simla* (Scholar Press, London, 1979).

Basham, A L. *The Wonder that was India* (Rupa, Delhi, 1967).

Bharucha, Perin. *Mahabaleshwar — The Club 1881-1981* (Major J H Wadia, Secretary, The Club, Mahabaleshwar).

Bowen, F O. *Handbook of Kodaikanal* (St. Joseph's Industrial School Press, Trichinopoly, 1932).

Buck, Edward J. *Simla, Past and Present* (Summit Publications, Delhi, 1979).

Carrington, Charles. *Rudyard Kipling, His Life and Work* (Penguin, London, 1970).

Chetwode, Penelope. *Kulu — The End of the Habitable World* (TBI, New Delhi, 1990).

Crowe, Sylvia and Haywood, Sheila. *The Gardens of Mughal India — A History and a Guide* (Vikas Publishing House Pvt Ltd, Delhi, 1973).

Davies, Philip. *Splendors of the Raj — British Architecture in India 1660–1947* (John Murray, London and Dass Media, Delhi, 1985).

Eden, Emily. *Up the Country — Letters written to her sister from the Upper Provinces of India* (Curzon Press, London and Dublin, 1978).

Gazetteer of India, The. Vol. I Country and People (Publications Division, Ministry of Information and Broadcasting, 1965).

Jervis, Lt H. *A Narrative of a Journey to the Falls of Cavery; with an Historical and Descriptive Account of the Neilgherry Hills* (Smith Elder and Co., London, 1834).

Kaul, H K. *Travellers' India* (Oxford University Press, Delhi, 1979).

Kincaid, Dennis. *The History of Shivaji — the Grand Rebel* (Karan Publications, Delhi, 1987).

King, Anthony D. *Colonial Urban Development — Culture, Social Power and Environment* (Routledge and Keegan Paul, London, 1976).

Mitchell, Nora. *The Indian Hill Station — Kodaikanal* (University of Chicago, Dept. of Geography Research Paper No. 141, Chicago, 1972).

Murray's Handbook of Madras 1879.

Noble, Christina. *Over the High Passes — A Year in the Himalayas* (Collins, London, 1987).

Oliver, K. *The Hill Station of Matheran* (The Times Company of India, Bombay, 1905).

Panter-Downes, Moolie. *Ooty Preserved — a Victorian Hill Station in India* (Hamish Hamilton, London, 1967).

Parks, Fanny. *Wanderings of a Pilgrim in Search of the Picturesque, 2 vols* (Pelham Richardson, London, 1850).

Price, Sir Frederick. *Ootacamund — A History compiled for the Government of Madras* (Superintendent Government Press, Madras, 1908).

Subbayya, K K. *Archaeology of Coorg* (Geetha Books House, Mysore, 1978).

Swift, Hugh. *Trekkers' Guide to the Himalaya and Karakoram* (Hodder and Stoughton, London, 1982).

Walker, Anthony R. *The Toda of South India — A New Look* (Hindustan Publishing Corporation, Delhi, 1986).

Ware, Gary. *Trekking in the Indian Himalaya* (Lonely Planet, London, 1986).

INDEX